APPROACHING EARTH

APPROACHING EARTH

A Search for the Mythic Significance of the Space Age

By

Daniel Noel

AMITY HOUSE
AMITY, NEW YORK

Published by Amity House, Inc.
106 Newport Bridge Road
Warwick, NY 10990

Cover design by Klaboe & Siwek Associates

ISBN: 0-916349-12-8
Library of Congress Number 86-073084

Portions of this book have appeared in earlier versions as essays. The author wishes to thank the following journals and editors for permission to use this material, in substantially revised form, in the present volume.

Portions of Chapters 1, 2, and 4 as "Re-Entry: Earth Images in Post-Apollo Culture," *Michigan Quarterly Review*, XVIII, 2 (Spring 1979), 155–76.

Portions of Chapter 3 as "Approaching Earth: Reminiscences on Megaliths and Method," *Corona*, 1 (1980), 57–66.

Portions of Chapter 5 as "The Many Guises of the Goddess," *Arche: Notes and Papers on Archaic Studies*, No. 6 (1981), 93–111.

Portions of Chapter 6 as "Auf dem Weg zum Irrationalen durch fiktive Zauberei und feministiche Spiritualität: postmoderne Möglichkeiten," in *Der Wissenschaftler und das Irrationale: Zweiter Band: Beiträge aus Philosophie und Psychologie*, hrsg. von Hans Peter Duerr (Frankfurt am Main: Syndikat, 1981), S. 425–46.

Portions of Chapter 7 as "Der sakrale Raum im Raumfahrtzeitalter beim Wort genommen: Der Fall Arthur C. Clarke und die 'Quellen des Paradieses,'" in *Die Mitte der Welt: Aufsätze zu Mircea Eliade*, hrsg. von Hans Peter Duerr (Frankfurt am Main: Suhrkamp, 1984), S. 280–95.

The author gratefully acknowledges the following for having granted permission to use quoted material: —— From *Diving Deep and Surfacing* by Carol Christ. Copyright © 1980 by Carol Christ. Reprinted by permission of Beacon Press. —— From *Changing of the Gods* by Naomi R. Goldenberg. Copyright © 1979 by Naomi R. Goldenberg. Reprinted by permission of Beacon Press. —— From *Flights of Discovery* by Leo Deuel. Copyright © 1969 by Leo Deuel. By permission of Leo Deuel. —— From *Flights of Discovery* by Georg Gerster. Copyright © 1978 by Georg Gerster. By permission of Georg Gerster. —— Excerpt from *The Fountain of Paradise*, copyright © 1978, 1979 by Arthur C. Clarke. Reprinted by permission of Harcourt Brace Jovanovich, Inc. —— Excerpt from

Continued on page 235

PREFACE

In a book which reads throughout like a Preface of the "How I Came to Write This Book" variety, what need is there for a Preface? First, to comment on *why* the book has been written to read that way. Second, to provide a brief overview — a quick satellite scan, if I can indulge in a more fitting image — of where the book will be heading beyond the horizon of its Preface.

The idea of presenting a *first-person* account of my inquiry into the deeper implications of our recent space odyssey seemed necessary from the start. The inquiry was a protracted one, pursued during the decade after the last astronaut left the moon with Apollo 17 in December 1972, and before I ever began writing down my discoveries I sought to share them in a series of slide shows. Moreover, the pedagogical aim of these presentations was always to share the *process* of discovery, not just the results.

When, in the late 1970s, I produced the first essays which led to the drafting of the book beginning in 1980, a first-person narrative again recommended itself as a means of allowing the reader to participate in my search. Over the years what had originated as a speculative intellectual inquiry about the cultural attitudes which could launch the rockets and land men on the moon had become an impressionistic personal quest as well. In other words, it had evolved into a search combining imaginative participation on my part along with academic objectivity. This was a combination eventually demanded by the elusive nature of my interpretive goal and subject matter: to understand the "mythic" dimensions of something called "the Age of Space."

v

But such a combined search, in all its narrated idiosyncracies and complexities, needed the subjective involvement of the *reader*, too — and even more than a straightforward analytic treatment would. Hence, the farther along I got in writing up the findings of my decade of work on the project, the stronger grew my initial conviction that the reader must be brought into the very act of finding with a first-person format.

My search for the mythic significance of the Space-Age began with a number of cultural clues suggesting, rather surprisingly, that our old earth, newly visible from above and beyond, is the most important discovery of our space efforts so far and the proper focus for interpretation. Furthermore, in adopting this line of sight we encounter terrestrial images which call for — and call forth — a way of seeing counter to the literalistic calculation required to lift us off the planet, a metaphoric awareness more than a problem-solving mentality. How I happened upon these very basic findings is set forth in an introductory section of two chapters.

The second section, comprising Chapters 3-5, then actually begins to practice this metaphorizing way of seeing as it recounts my exploration of various earth images for the messages they might harbor about any emerging Space-Age mythos. To me, the most fascinating and fruitful of the images — seen as "geometaphors"— was woman, the traditional earth goddess in all her guises. And this imagery, in turn, directed me to the fanciful speculations narrated in the single chapter of Part Three.

Here is the center of the book, where the attributes of the ancient Greek earth mother, Gaia, are taken to be a kind of *mythic* grounding for the metaphorizing I had already been engaged in in Part Two. Thus, the method necessitated in the Age of Space to interpret earth images for their mythic implications — taking NASA's lofty perspective, as it were, and deliteralizing it — turned out to be a method with its own mythic sources. With this complex discovery, prompted in part by a poet's re-visioning of the first whole earth photograph as a ghostly portrait of a dancing woman, I was gradually sensing the Space-Age mythos to be not primarily an emerging plot line but an emerging method. That is, my metaphoric approach had begun to seem a mythic (or neo-mythic) means of perception in its own right; I was finding my goal in the manner of my going.

Next, Part Four expands the method with an adjunct to metaphorizing, a similarly playful process of active awareness which I had encountered in the concept of serendipity. As with the exploration of geometaphors in Part Two, Chapters 7-9 entail *engaging in* the process as well as describing it. For instance, I use unsought conjunctions or surprising connections in Space-Age data as substantive components of the argument in favor of this "serendipping" approach, so that it is displayed while being defined. The contributions of Arthur C. Clarke figure here, as well as the dangers of his literalism, but so do some words of Horace Walpole and the legendary island of Ceylon—home of Clarke, home of the "three princes of Serendip" from whose tale Walpole coined the term serendipity, and center of the earth in that same epochal photograph I had discussed in Chapter 6.

After this intimate involvement in serendipping the two closing chapters step back to tell how I found a theoretical (though still image-laden) structure for the entire two-sided approach I had demonstrated in the rest of the book. Drawing on aerial archaeology and Earth Art as models, I attempt to articulate the overall "mythodology" I had inferred from all my explorations.

Along with this, Part Five reports perhaps the major result of my search to date: the value of the metaphorizing and serendipping method in effecting a much-needed terrestrial reconnection. I conclude that this mental reconnection with the earth is both the oportunity and the imperative offered to us by the Age of Space *if* its deeper implication for culture and consciousness are sensed. The latter task, however, is a matter of *continuing* to interpret visions of earth mythodologically— even while space technologists, proceeding literalistically, prepare to abandon our home planet for the stars or others prepare to abandon it *to* the nuclear warheads.

As a last set of images, shared in an Epilogue, taught me, the search must be ongoing beyond any beginnings I may have made.

And this means it cannot continue to be merely *my* search. At no point in the book do I try to conceal the private factors in what I present, even when I am dealing with the most public pieces of evidence. I want my personally-flavored approach to Space-Age meanings fully accessible to all readers so that they can adapt it to produce their *own* very different versions of reconnection with their very own earth.

For Joanna

And in the Memory of
My Parents:

L.T. Noel
(1905–1980)

Eleanor Daniel Noel
(1908–1982)

Acknowledgements

In the course of a search as lengthy as this has been, one accumulates more debts of gratitude than one can gracefully acknowledge in print. I should, however, like to thank the following persons, none of whom is to be held responsible for the way in which his or her help influenced the final product.

For reading and commenting editorially on the complete manuscript at one stage or another: William G. Doty, James Hillman, Christopher Noel, Stephen C. Rowe, Lynda Sexson, and Norma Jane Skjold.

For all sorts of other assistance: Salvatore and Elaine Alfano, Luis Alvarez, Patricia Cox, Kathryn Davis, Robert Detweiler, Christine Downing, C.A. Fowler, Bradford Graves, Richard Grossinger, Shirley Jeffries, Carole Klein, Rhoda Lerman, John Loudon, Louise Mahdi, Audrey Miller, David L. Miller, Tom Moore, Thersa A. Murphy, Joanna, Rebecca, Jennifer, and Susannah Noel, Richard J. Payne, M.C. Richards, Randolph Severson, David and Bette Thomas, John R. Turner, Mary Watkins, Tess Zimmerman, and my students and colleagues since 1972 at Bucknell University, Goddard College, Emory University, Syracuse University, and above all in the still-astounding Adult Degree Program at Vermont College of Norwich University.

CONTENTS

III

Grounding

IV

Serendipping Down to Earth

APPROACHING
EARTH

PROLOGUE

On July 20, 1969, Neil Armstrong became the first human being to step out onto the surface of the moon.

Earlier in 1957, there had been the launching of Sputnik, and earlier still the World War II beginnings of the Space Age with the German development of the V-2 rocket. More recently the 1970s saw an orbiting rendezvous with the Russians, Pioneer and Voyager probes deep into the solar system, and an unmanned Viking landing on Mars. As we entered the '80s satellites had become commonplace, the Soviet Union continued to send cosmonauts into orbit, and the reusable space shuttle made its long-delayed debut. One of these shuttles—Challenger in early 1986—focused the most attention on the U.S. space program in many years by exploding shortly after lift-off with the loss of seven astronauts.

It was the National Aeronautics and Space Administration's Project Apollo, however, capped by the Apollo 11 odyssey of Armstrong, Aldrin, and Collins, which best represented humankind's Space-Age efforts and captured the imagination of the public. Captured it and then, apparently, lost it. More than one commentator has noted the comparative indifference with which our post-Apollo 11 space exploits have been greeted. Certainly since the last Apollo lunar mission over a decade ago the American space program has lost much of its glamorous appeal—and not a little of its funding support.

But below any shifts in popular enthusiasm how are these stupendous human accomplishments affecting the collective psyche, the mind of the age? The editors of the *Michigan Quarterly Review*, in the Introduction to their special issue of spring 1979 on "The Moon Landing and its Aftermath," observed that "new perspectives on the planet earth, on the heavens, on human nature and destiny. . .occurred almost subliminally, as the public mind gradually absorbed the fact that American technology had succeeded in realizing one of mankind's most enduring fantasies." They also added that "we realize now how little attention we spared in those tumultuous years to events in space so full of cultural significance that a library of commentary would not exhaust them."[1]

Surely the impact of Apollo has *not* ended, and is being felt still in ways of which we are not aware—or do not realize are related to the leap into space—ways which transcend our boredom at too many media-packaged blast-offs or our impatience with their cost.

An utterly unprecedented event stands before us for interpretation: *We have never before left the planet*. Surely having done so now is bound to change human culture and consciousness at a very deep level, and permanently. Massive reorientations do not happen without their "mythic" corollaries, their corresponding realignments in the patterns of human self-understanding, however unconscious and slow to surface. We cannot finally say that our recent indifference tells the true story of Apollo's significance for us as fellow inhabitants of an earth from which the astronauts were able, fleetingly, to break free. Moreover, we cannot presume to have yet discerned the deeper implications of our post-Apollo slowdown in space. In either case, the larger meanings and imperatives of the Age of Space still await our exploration.

One of the few commentators to realize this, Joseph Campbell, the comparative mythologist, wrote in 1972 that the moon voyage "has transformed, deepened, and extended human consciousness to a degree and in a manner that amount to the opening of a new spiritual era".[2] At about the same time that Campbell made his comment I started my own search to understand the meaning of the new era, the sub-liminal impact or collective dream of the Space Age, which I believe we have yet to bring to waking awareness. With an academic back-ground in the two interdisciplinary fields of religion and literature studies and the psychology of religion, several years of musing on the lunar landings, and an openness to the surprises of the imagination, I proceeded to examine the public evidence of space-related happen-ings. These I took to be the components of a possible mythos, images in the collective dream.

In this fashion I encountered a series of clues to the cultural sig-nificance I was seeking. I also sensed, early on, that the method of that seeking, the process of the search, was at least as important as my particular findings.

I
SEARCHING FOR MYTHIC SIGNIFICANCE
AFTER APOLLO

CHAPTER ONE

A LINE OF SIGHT

FIRST CLUES—THE APPEARANCE OF EARTH
IN SPACE-AGE MEDIA

The first piece of public evidence I was struck by was the earth itself, photographed from afar. These photographs seemed to me the most evocative achievements of the space program.

I was hardly alone in this, of course. Joseph Campbell's 1972 essay, "The Moon Walk—the Outward Journey," exclaims that "that fabulous color photograph of our good earth rising as a glorious planet above a silent lunar landscape is something not to forget."[1] (True to his own advice, two years later Campbell included a whole earth photograph as the final illustration in his massive volume *The Mythic Image*.[2] Already in 1966 Stewart Brand had mounted an inventive campaign to provoke space agency officials into releasing pictures of the whole earth. "There we were," he recalls, "having seen a lot of the moon and a lot of hunks of the Earth, but never the complete mandala."[3] Subsequently Brand began publishing his highly successful *Whole Earth Catalog*, and by the fall of 1968 the public was able to see views of the full disc of earth on its covers.

Brand's endeavors also provided a valuable link between the Apollo program and the growing ecology movement which was stressed in the contents of his *Catalog* and later in *Co-Evolution Quarterly*, a second publication he helped to found. Certainly the new concern for ecology (ritualized in 1970 on Earth Day) did suggest an area in which to seek out the mythic significance of our space odyssey. But the idea of "mandala earth" seemed to me to be saying more than Brand's focus on ecological consciousness alone—his and others' sense of earth's boundaryless holism—was capable of conveying.

"Mandala" is Sanskrit for "circle", and Brand uses the term to refer to the full circle of earth visible from space. However, "mandala" is a word with associations which extend beyond a mere indication of shape. The term is used in Tibetan Buddhism to describe a *yantra*, a visual device for meditation and spiritual centering, and has been adapted by the psychologist C. G. Jung and his followers as an image of evolving wholeness in or out of Buddhist contexts, a kind of mirror for the meaning of our selves-in-becoming.[4]

And so what Stewart Brand's allusions to the whole earth photographs as mandalas did for my search was to strengthen my conviction that the deeper impact of Apollo and the Space Age upon our cultural psyche had to do with the totally new view of earth—of ourselves—which it made possible. Nevertheless, the *meaning* of the mandala image of earth was far from clear. The earth-mirror contained something more than ecological imperatives, however pressing: something that might include the holistic aims and practical political necessities of the ecology movement, but which required a Jungian sensitivity to the varied expressions of myth to understand more fully.

So, despite their general suggestiveness, I felt the photographs of earth needed to be seen in both a larger and a more personally meaningful context than Brand provided. They also needed to be supplemented by further clues to the significance of our journey into space.

And my next bit of cultural data just happened to fulfill these needs, adding a personal artistic vision to the impersonality of the whole earth pictures. It came in the somewhat unlikely form of a cartoon.*

I ran into it in *The New York Times* at the end of 1972. The cartoonist had depicted the moon in the night sky as a giant porthole through which a helmeted astronaut is staring down at the earthly landscape in the foreground. What the astronaut sees from above, and what we see looking out at us, are four monolithic heads, brooding stone images strongly suggestive of the ancient mysteries of Easter Island.

*p. 1

This striking newspaper illustration accompanied an excerpt from philosopher William Barrett's new book *Time of Need*, a study of "forms of imagination in the twentieth century", chiefly the modern novel but also sculpture, painting, and, as I learned, popular films.[5] It was dawning on me around then that if it was the mythic meaning of the space odyssey I was after, I would need to attend not just to the publicly "objective" data of space technology but also to the publicly "subjective" expressions of the various artists who may have dealt with Space-Age matters.

In the case of the analyses in Barrett's book, a final chapter discusses the films *Sky Above Mud Below* and *2001: A Space Odyssey*, which, through "a stroke of chance", the author saw on successive days. This lucky experience pointed up for Barrett the curious conjunction — reflected most graphically in the newspaper cartoon — between the spaceman and the primitive, between technology's highest accomplishment and the lowliest origins of human culture on the planet.

Sky Above Mud Below documents the life of a Stone-Age tribe in New Guinea, while the second film is the lavish science fiction fantasy of our technological destiny conjured up by Stanley Kubrick and Arthur C. Clarke. Barrett's reaction to the two films' juxtaposition was to be impressed by how, in contrast to the bland and banal image of future humanity projected by the astronauts of *2001*, the "savages" of New Guinea "have the consolations of art as an organic part of life and a religion solidly imbedded in their social rituals."[6]

It was no doubt correct for Barrett to suggest that archaically grounded art and religion would have little influence in the sort of future consciously envisioned cinematic expression of Kubrick and Clarke. On the other hand, as I followed this connection between the archaic and the futuristic offered by the *Times* cartoon and *Time of Need*, while reflecting back upon my own viewing of the film, I realized that even *2001* by itself evokes an entire category of artifacts from prehistoric human life on earth. Indeed, I soon became convinced that at the level of the popular media our most significant recent encounter with these primitive artifacts came in seeing the outer-space odyssey fantasized in *2001*.

I was thinking of the mysterious rectangular slab which appears so dramatically in the film and forcefully reminds us of the megaliths and other sacred stones of primitive peoples. We see the movie slab first on the earthly prehistoric landscape, then in a lunar excavation of our near future, next in orbit around the planet Jupiter, and finally in what seems to be the Regency-style bedroom of astronaut David Bowman's mind. Each of these dramatic intrusions of the black rectangle makes possible a breakthrough for humankind into a new evolutionary phase: Our ancestor apes achieve the "second world" of intelligence associated with weapon- and tool-use; the lunar explorers discover we are not alone in the universe; circling Jupiter, our astronaut culture-hero is thrown through a "star-corridor" into a realm "beyond the infinite"— but possibly within the potentialities of his own psyche. In this latter realm he sees himself age and die, only to be metamorphosed into a wide-eyed star babe, floating toward earth in an amniotic bubble.

Each of these epochal developments in *2001*'s version of human evolution is fostered by an appearance of the strange slab, and we movie-goers wondered as we watched: What is it? What does the image of the megalith tell us about our Space-Age destiny?

As I reminisced about this mysterious image, so out of keeping with the futuristic space technology which was otherwise the virtual "star" of the film, I was led of course to the megalithic circle of Stone-henge on the Salisbury Plain in southern England. This mental as-sociation was reinforced by the knowledge that solar-worship and astronomical calculation were likely elements of Stonehenge's origin and purpose, since each of the manifestations of *2001*'s slab similarly involved conjunctions with the rising sun, planets, and moons. And in this respect the inclusion of the ancient image of the monolith in a film focused on the gadgetry and scientism of a presumed future turned out to have been at least half conscious and deliberate.

To recapitulate these first steps on my quest: In continuing my search for the mythic meanings of our Space-Age exploits I was led past the whole earth photographs to the cartoon and then into William Barrett's *Time of Need* with its discussion of *2001* as one of the "forms of imagination in the twentieth century". Since both the cartoonist and Barrett had stressed the strange juxtaposition between the spaceman, representing a technological future cut off from the earth, and the primitive or "savage", representing prehistoric art and religion very much connected to the earth, I was intrigued to find even more sur-prising evidence for this same correlation right in *2001* itself. Barrett says of the black stone slab only that "superior beings had planted [it] on the moon to serve as a warning device in case any civilization, like our own, should develop to a point where it was able to reach that satellite."[7] While his comment makes sense, he also refers to the slab as "the black megalith",[8] and it is this archaic image that deserves the special scrutiny he neglects to give it.

THE MEGALITH IN *2001* AND THE SACRED LIFE OF STONES

In a book called *The Making of Kubrick's 2001*, edited by Jerome Agel, I found evidence that the Stonehenge allusion of the cinematic slab was at least somewhat intentional. Agel quotes Kubrick's remark that "there was never any interest in relating the slab to Stonehenge" and Clarke's rather different comments: "I'm sure Stanley and I talked about Stonehenge, but I can't remember the specific details. I don't know if Stan has been to Stonehenge. I have many times." Then, four pages later, Kubrick admits to some connection between his black rectangle— which succeeded a tetrahedron design in the planning of the film because the latter "didn't look monumental or simple or fundamental", according to Special Effects Supervisor Con Pederson—and the Stonehenge monoliths: "The idea of a magical alignment of the sun, the Earth, and the moon, or of Jupiter and its moon was used throughout the film to represent something magical and important about to happen. I suppose the idea had something to do with the strange sensation one has when the alignment of the sun takes place at Stonehenge."[9]

With or without Kubrick's halting admission of intent, however, Stonehenge was only the most obvious connotation of *2001*'s evocative slab. There were the brooding stone statues of Easter Island, for instance, as in the *Times* cartoon, or the massive monolithic heads fashioned by the extinct Olmecs of Mesoamerica. The dictionary defines "monolith" as "a single piece or block of stone fashioned or placed by art, particularly one notable for its size," while the closely related term "megalith" simply means "large stone". The latter word is especially appropriate for designating the cromlechs, dolmens, and menhirs of Europe—that is, the chambers, table rocks, and single standing stones left by the prehistoric inhabitants of Ireland, Brittany or Malta. These megalithic sites were often related to burial of the dead, but in many cases seem to have involved the mysteries of fertility, birth, and perhaps rebirth.

The rune-stones of Scandinavia or the Pictish symbol-stones of Scotland, the black Ka'aba stone at the center of Muslim worship in Mecca, the medicine wheels of the American Indians, the rock paintings of Pyrenean caves and of the aboriginal Australian outback, the quartz crystals used in the sorcery of some shamanic practitioners — these are some of the other far-flung instances of the holy stones of earth. All along in the human history of the planet large stones have been held sacred, meteorites have been revered, and small stones have been carried as objects of paranormal power for healing, procreation, or ecstatic flight.

No doubt other sorts and examples could be cited, but even these few raised many questions for me, the most pressing of which were: Why should "sacred stones" have been so significant to terrestrial peoples just entering the world of culture after millions of years in the primary world of purely biological evolution?

And why — remembering the discussion of *2001* — do such stones appear in the popular imagination *now*, just as we inaugurate our Space-Age journey to the moon and beyond?

I knew that the fields of history of religions and Jungian psychology had proposed answers for the first of these questions. Mircea Eliade, the Rumanian-born scholar of the University of Chicago, has called the sacred stones an "hierophany", an appearance or manifestation of sacred power. In his *Patterns in Comparative Religion* he says that for primitive peoples "the hardness, ruggedness and permanence of matter"— epitomized by the megaliths —"was in itself a hierophany",[10] and he later comments that boulders and rocks "*strike* men's minds by their solidity, steadfastness and majesty".[11] Eliade then elucidates the idea of the "striking" quality of stone as follows: "Above all, stone *is*. It always remains itself, and exists of itself; and, more important still, it *strikes*. Before he even takes it up to strike, man finds in it an obstacle — if not to his body, at least to his gaze — and ascertains its hardness, its roughness, its power. Rock," he concludes, "shows him something that transcends the precariousness of his humanity: an absolute mode of being."[12]

Aniela Jaffé, one of C. G. Jung's closest associates and the editor of his autobiography, has discussed the psychological significance of the stone as a "sacred symbol". She stresses that "the intertwined history of religion and art, reaching back to prehistoric times, is the record that our ancestors have left of the symbols that were meaningful and moving to them."[13] More specifically, she notes that "rough, natural stones were often believed to be dwelling places of spirits or gods, and were used in primitive cultures as tombstones, boundary stones, or objects of religious veneration." She goes on to claim that "their use may be regarded as a primeval form of sculpture — a first attempt to invest the stone with more expressive power than chance and nature could give it."[14]

While Jaffé refers to the primitive tendency to alter stone only very slightly so as to allow for its "self-expression", her own sense, as a Jungian psychologist, perceives that the symbolic power of stones comes from their use as vehicles of *human* expression. Her conclusion, apparently quite contrary to that of Eliade, the historian of religions, is that "the animation of the stone must be explained as the projection of a more or less distinct content of the unconscious into the stone."[15]

These answers to the question of why stones should have had such significance in the life of early humans were not entirely satisfying to me. Aniela Jaffé's emphasis on symbols as projections of human significance onto the stones seemed at odds with Eliade's interpretation of sacred stones as "hierophanies" whose transcendent power "struck" human observers from outside. It was clear to me that, while the history of religions and Jungian psychology offered suggestive possibilities for interpretation, I would need to do further thinking, in or out of the contexts of those two fields, if I hoped to fathom the most primal meanings of the megaliths to primitive earthlings.

And given the inconclusiveness of my thoughts about the first question, how could I possibly settle the second, the enigma of an ancient megalith appearing in a futuristic film about a "space odyssey"? The reason for seeking to understand the appearance of sacred stones in prehistoric terrestrial culture was, after all, to make sense of their *re*appearance in the inhospitable technological culture of the Space Age.

But this way of framing the matter may depend too much on the supposed impact of a single film, so let me move ahead to consider another case of outer-space cinema.

STAR WARS, CLOSE ENCOUNTERS, AND THE ELEVATED SANCTUARIES OF EARTH

With its appearance in 1977, *Star Wars* became the largest box-office success in the history of the American movie industry. Although its playful "Perils-of-Pauline" style is a far cry from the somber seriousness of *2001*, and its story is set "a long time ago in a galaxy far, far away," futuristic technological gadgetry is as much a part of *Star Wars* as it was of the earlier space epic. And just as *2001*, I had discovered, contained its own elements of "mud below"—the totally terrestrial "old ways" evoked by Kubrick and Clarke's mysterious slab—so also does *Star Wars* surprise us with some significant imagery from the archaic art and religion of earth.

I am referring not only to the role of the so-called Force in *Star Wars*, with which the good sorcery of Alec Guinness' Obi-won-Kenobi aligns itself. Certainly the Force does seem to be a pre-technological, implicitly earthly ingredient in the film. But beyond this there is the setting of the all-important "rebel base", the headquarters of those whose dedication to the Force makes them scheme against the technological totalitarianism of the Empire and its minions. It is this secret site that the demonic leaders of the Empire spend the entire film trying to find and destroy, and from which the rebels launch their triumphant assault upon the Empire's menacing artificial planet, the "death star".

My memory after seeing *Star Wars* was that this rebel base, the hidden home of the forces of the Force, was in a ruined Mayan temple. The formidable array of credits at the close of the movie includes a brief reference to Tikal, a complex of temple ruins in Guatemala where the exteriors for the rebel base scenes were in fact shot. Tikal is the largest and one of the oldest of the Mayan sites, and Temple IV, which was most likely the stucture used for the filming, is the tallest edifice in pre-Columbian America, a 212 foot-high pyramid towering above the surrounding jungle.[16] I was aware from the researches of archaeologists as well as historians of religion that Tikal and other pyramid-temples were seen by the Mayans as a link between the earth and the sky, a sacred precinct where priest-astronomers could study the stars, predict the future, and approach the gods—and where the gods could descend to the people during religious celebrations. Although their functions seem to have been in several ways different from similar edifices in the ancient Near East, surely the *image* of the Mayan temple ruins evokes the pyramids of Egypt and the ziggurats of the Sumerians as well as recalling, finally, all the many ancient temples and elevated sanctuaries of earth.

What, then, is the archaic terrestrial temple-complex of Tikal doing in the outer-space swashbucklings of *Star Wars*? Aside from whatever tactical considerations the film's producers may have had in mind, why is the rebel base of this *extra*terrestrial fantasy a Mayan ruin? Why should such an earthy site house the forces of the Force?

Nor was I left for long with *2001* and *Star Wars* as the only instances from popular cinema of futuristic technological space fictions reverting to images from the deep past of our home planet. A year after the release of *Star Wars*, a film about UFOs came along to challenge the latter's box-office record (and to elicit, upon its rerelease in a revised version in 1980, critic Vincent Canby's praise as "a classic"[17]). *Close Encounters of the Third Kind* uses Devil's Tower in the Bear Lodge Mountains of northeastern Wyoming as the setting for a climactic meeting with the extraterrestrials, and it is noteworthy that this mountain first enters the film as a *mental image* implanted in the hero's mind by the space visitors. Thereafter, until he makes his way to the actual Devil's Tower site (significantly, in promotions for the movie this approach is along a highway aligned like a straight track toward the Tower, which is in turn back-lit on the horizon like the Stonehenge "heel stone" on Midsummer morning), he is obsessed with this image. He takes to sculpting it with dirt, with his shaving cream, even with his mashed potatoes at dinner, and again the question is: Why?

Why should such a mountain — in this case a massive flat-topped monolith similar to those held sacred by several Native American groups — be the precise place of encounter between humans and the outer-space beings? Why choose a site with such primitive religious associations when all the awe of the film is presumably directed toward the unimaginable scientific mastery of the extraterrestrials?

Obviously some site for a landing had to be chosen, and factors within the *Close Encounters* story line do account in part for the use of Devil's Tower. Nevertheless, the sacred mountains of earth, the elevated sanctuaries *par excellence*, have traditionally been seen as a prime point of contact between heaven and humankind, and perhaps this image, like those of the sacred stones evoked by *2001* and the temple ruins of *Star Wars*, has been "implanted" in us a long time ago as we entered the world of cultural evolution. It is true that such primordially sacred images have suffered eclipse in recent centuries, at least in urbanized areas of the globe, as science and technology have ever more rapidly superseded primitive religious traditions. We have seemingly moved, in our modernity, from a sacred to a profane culture; indeed the term "pro-fane" means "outside the holy precincts of the temple".

And yet, at just this point of profane science's most dramatic success — a mission to the moon reflected in the immense popularity of films celebrating space technology and extraterrestrial intelligence — the archaic imagery of earth-bound religion and art returns. Moreover, since the release of *2001*, *Star Wars*, and *Close Encounters*, one could cite, from the turn of the decade, the Disney comedy *Unidenti-*

fied Flying Oddball about an astronaut who goes through a time warp and lands in King Arthur's England, the television mini-series of Ray Bradbury's *Martian Chronicles* with neolithic Maltese temples serving as ancient Martian ruins, the opening episodes of the TV series *Galactica 1980* with their stress on the Galacticans' return to earth (including an intervention in the development of German rocketry at Peenemünde in 1944), and *Star Trek: The Motion Picture* with its focus on a future encounter between the Starship Enterprise and a homeward-bound space probe launched from earth in the twentieth century. Indeed, *The Empire Strikes Back*, the much-touted sequel to *Star Wars*, contains important scenes concerning the young hero's further schooling in the beneficent expressions of the Force which take place on a swampy planet called Dagobah. It is not at all clear how this planet's name was consciously selected, but "dagoba" is a word designating the ancient bell-shaped temples of the Buddhists of Ceylon.[18]

These other instances—among others—of earth images in outer-space cinema and TV underscore how widespread and popular their appearances are. In any case a main issue had already been brought home to me by the three films treated above: evidently, archaic images planted deep within us may have been triggered anew by our success in breaking free of the planet.

ARCHAIC EARTH IMAGES AND SPACE-AGE MEANINGS

But the meaning of the images was far from obvious. The three instances from futuristic cinema did share a few elements which could contribute to a composite meaning: one was a point of contact between earth and sky, mortals and gods, if only through structures providing a sighting line to the stars on the distant horizon. Another was the idea of death and rebirth, the ancient burial chamber as a womb for entry into new life, or even—especially with the *2001* megalith—as a boundary marker to memorialize some portentous passage. Again, however, like the theories about sacred stones advanced by Eliade and Jaffé, although these initial thoughts were suggestive of what messages might be arriving in our Age of Space by way of such imagery, more reflection would be required before one could draw any firm conclusions about why it should resurface today.

Whether as a reality striking us from long ago and far away or a power projected by our current though unconscious yearnings, the language of the imagery invoked is seldom unambiguous. Moreover, the rush up and out from earth, the technological thrust beyond the moon to find life on Mars and colonize space, would hardly be halted despite criticisms of its expense or temporary slowdowns. And this Space-Age movement away from earth was assuredly not being turned back by the sort of "soft" data I was encountering, data which—whatever its precise meanings in a new mythos—hinted at priorities more deeply terrestrial than were dreamed of even by the ecological activists on that first Earth Day in 1970.

Speaking of ancient man, and perhaps the earth itself, as "that primitive being", William Barrett closes his *Time of Need* with words worth considering as a further clue to the meanings I was seeking. "We seem to be headed," Barrett writes, "toward a civilization that would be the first to break its ties with that primitive being. To accomplish this would be a step more audacious than the mere physical leap into space. It would probably be mankind's most daring adventure yet. Will it succeed? Art seems to say no."[19]

It is clear that for Barrett, as for Aniela Jaffé, art is intertwined with religion, or once was. Both were outgrowths from a unified mythic matrix: "The art of those civilizations sprang from the same primitive needs of adornment and ritual [as their religions did]." Underlying both art and religion as their common psycho-cultural seedbed was myth, and underlying myth was the earth itself, to whose meaning myth in turn gave human expression in art and religion: "Earlier civilizations still hugged, whether they knew it or not, that primitive forebear to their bosom and preserved his ways. Their knowledge did not depart too far from the world of the senses which he had first set in order. Their myths repeated the patterns of his."[20] Again, "that primitive forebear" refers to archaic humankind, but could also, despite the atypical masculine gender, be taken as an allusion to earth itself as a mythic being.

The last page of *Time of Need* seems to be saying that the "primitive needs" associated with ancient myth, whether aesthetically or religiously voiced, cannot coexist with the Space-Age urge embodied in the NASA Apollo program to pull up our planetary roots in an ever-mounting monomania of technological mastery. But Barrett's warning had to be balanced by the surprising recent sightings of mythic imagery from terrestrial art and religion in some of the most "spaced-out" popular media productions of our earth-denying culture.

And so what Barrett's book finally suggested to me, even beyond pointing toward the films which were public evidence of that strange conjunction of spaceman and primitive, was that *how* we tend the archaic earth imagery re-arising in our Age of Space would be all-important. The aesthetic and religious language of mythic imagery, I have said, is seldom unambiguous. While pursuing the mythic meaning of such images as the megaliths, the Mayan temples, and the sacred mountain for most of the 1970s in my search for the larger significance of our space odyssey, I realized the need for the right approach to the material I was encountering. And if, as I soon grew to believe, the earth was our primitive forebear, was the "mandala" meant for our meditating now that we have at last achieved an outer-space perspective on ourselves? No simple snapshot, simply viewed, would suffice. A method had to be found which remained sensitive to the ambiguity, the semantic richness—indeed the endless mystery—of the mythic imagery of earth.

CHAPTER TWO

A WAY OF SEEING

If the three films discussed above raised questions about the renewed appearance of ancient megaliths, Mayan ruins, and sacred mountains in the apparently alien setting of space exploration, there were those around, I discovered, who felt they had found ready answers.

To the readers of Erich von Däniken's best-selling books on "ancient astronauts", it is as though *2001* could be taken as a factual documentary. Today's surprising connection between the human astronaut and the primitive earthling is seen as a mere echo of an archaic encounter between "space gods" and early humankind in which technological powers (most of them subsequently lost to us) were transmitted from on high to our ancestors. The evidence, such as it is, for this prehistoric meeting of earthlings and extraterrestrials is comprised of von Däniken's dubious inferences from various archaeological sites and artifacts around the world which, he claims, display depictions of space travel or suggest other supposedly unaccountable marvels of engineering and calculation.[1]

Von Däniken tells his readers that these archaeological data argue for an incursion into human evolution of extraterrestrials able to perform technological feats we are only barely equaling at present. Thus is the problem of the curious conjunction solved: We encounter archaic earth images today because our civilization is on the threshold of achieving—or recovering, with von Däniken's help—the technological prowess whose outer-space origins is dimly recorded in many of these same images. *This* message, which ignores the ambiguous mythic meanings of ancient religion and art so as to seize upon a single-minded decoding of the imagery, is a splendid example of how very difficult it is for our technologically-oriented minds to deal with pre-technological data.

And this led me to the methodological dilemma I asked myself about increasingly throughout the '70s as I continued to follow substantive clues to the possibility of a Space-Age mythos. Was it not conceivable, or even likely, that the cognitive style required to take us to the moon had developed as part of a literalistic problem-solving mentality which could block the authentic message of the archaic imagery at the outset? The dictionary defined literalism as "close adherence to the exact word or sense, often to the point of unimaginativeness". Such close adherence was no doubt necessary to the exact calculations and procedures of the space scientists and astronauts who lifted us off the earth. But by the same token I suspected that a return to terrestrial roots, a renewed appreciation of earth's mythic images, would call for precisely the imaginativeness, the adeptness in figurative or metaphorical expression, which our culture's literal mindset had had to devalue. And I wondered whether, to the extent that our entire contemporary culture is implicated in this mindset, the aerospace scientists and the astronauts who performed the procedures they devised would not be simply extreme examples of an attitude we all share (despite the primitive earthling who may yet, as the testimony of the arts suggests, lurk within each of us below the level of consciousness).

HOW TO APPROACH EARTH IMAGES AFTER APOLLO

I realized in the midst of my research that the choice of Apollo as the primary patron of our leap to the moon was an apt one considering this quite paradoxical situation: the featured role given to Apollo, the bright remote god of masculine order and rationality, implied that at least one ingredient of any emergent mythos of the Space Age would no doubt be its accumulated *resistance* to modes of perceiving, thinking, and speaking — nonliteralistic modes, I began to call them — which characterize the ancient "language" of mythic images. Unfortunately for the complications it might add to my quest, Apollo and his attributes were surely part of the significance I was seeking.

In 1974 I published an essay in the Jungian journal *Spring* and found when the issue came out that one of the other contributions was a report on a major research study concerned with "the psychodynamics of modern science". Ian Mitroff, a professor specializing in information theory and the philosophy of science, had been inspired by the Apollo 11 mission to mount a three-and-a-half year investigation of the attitudes toward the moon of the NASA scientists who were involved in analyzing the rock samples brought back by the Apollo astronauts. Through extensive interviews with 42 of these moon scientists, Mitroff discovered among other things that 78% of them had "no feeling" for the sexual dimension of the moon, its masculine or feminine connotations.[2]

For Mitroff, this unemotional masculine approach was very much in line with the selection of the name Apollo for the program to put men on the moon. He cited classics scholars like W. F. Otto and Norman O. Brown on Apollo's distancing and detachment, quoting Brown's Freudian comment in *Life Against Death* that "he is also the god who sustains 'displacement from below upward,' who gave man a head sublime and told him to look at the stars."[3] Mitroff's essay is entitled "Science's Apollonic Moon", "Apollonic" being an adjective form favored by James Hillman, the editor of *Spring* and himself the author of a number of works which touch on the meanings of Apollo. In referring to "Apollonic consciousness" in his *The Myth of Analysis*, for instance, Hillman says "we have called this consciousness Apollonic, for like its namesake, it belongs to youth, it kills from a distance (its distance kills) and, keeping the scientific cut of objectivity, it never merges with or 'marries' its material."[4]

These descriptions of the Apollonic bring me back to the dilemma I have stated as a major preoccupation of my search during the 1970s: How to approach the mythic imagery of earth from the attitudes and altitudes of Apollo and his space program; how to find, from the zenith of the Space Age, fresh opportunities for discovering the deep significance of earth. I had to acknowledge that my topic and my cultural conditioning gave me a partly Apollonic starting point. I needed somehow to incorporate this "given" into the mythic meaning I was searching for without being captured like Mitroff's moon scientists or, in their own way, Erich van Däniken's disciples, by an exclusively objective and literalistic vision of the relevant data.

Surely the *data* presented by von Däniken—the imagery of lines on a Peruvian plateau or of inscriptions on a Mexican sarcophagus, to take two of his favorites — *are* relevant. To dismiss such imagery because of the improprieties of his Apollonic interpretation was inadequate; what was required, I felt, was to approach this imagery with an alternative sensibility.

It is not only that von Däniken's theories do not succeed as scientific claims. Ronald Story's *The Space-Gods Revealed* is an effective critique of this primary aspect of his works, but from the standpoint of my concern for mythic significance, even had von Däniken's hypotheses been validated on scientific grounds, they would still fail to understand the meanings of the ancient aesthetic and religious material involved. The Story critique points up this more subtle shortcoming by reproducing a poster illustration for the film *Chariots of the Gods* which shows a U.S. rocket lifting off from a mishmash of pyramids and Easter Island monoliths, leaving them behind in its fiery wake.[5] Unlike the newspaper cartoon with the astronaut sighting the Easter Island stone heads from his lunar vantage point, the attitude of the von Däniken based film goes along with that Apollonic push up and out from earth which would deal with "unsolved mysteries of the past" (the subtitle of *Chariots of the Gods*) by jettisoning their semantic richness. Again, it came to seem imperative to me to find a way of seeing the archaic images which takes seriously the genuine elements of mystery and ambiguity which these images embody rather than giving them mere lip service with a problem-solving approach *à la* von Däniken, a projection of NASA's necessary literalism back into the mythic mode of consciousness it was designed, so to speak, to escape.

A METHODOLOGICAL CLUE —
NORMAN MAILER'S MOON BOOK AND
THE NECESSITY TO METAPHORIZE

There is no question of the scientific validity of the work done by the NASA scientists who analyzed the rocks brought back from the moon. It is clear from Ian Mitroff's study, however, that their approach, successful in Apollonic terms, would nevertheless be unable to appreciate any mythic significance in the phenomena they were analyzing.

Not so novelist Norman Mailer, an excerpt from whose book on the Apollo 11 mission I had read in *Life* magazine even before beginning my project in 1972. Mailer's last paragraph in *Of a Fire on the Moon* (which I read in its entirely only after noting William Barrett's comparison of it with *2001* in *Time of Need*) concerns a pivotal confrontation between the author and one of the rock samples brought from the moon to containment behind several layers of thick glass in Houston. Mailer's analysis of this moon rock is about as far as can be from that of the scientists studied by Mitroff:

> . . . she was not two feet away from him, this rock to which he instinctively gave gender as she — and *she* was gray, gray as everyone had said, gray as a dark cinder and not three inches across nor two inches high nor two inches for width, just a gray rock with craters the size of a pin and craters the size of a pencil point, and even craters large as a ladybug and rays ran out from the craters, fine white lines, fine as the wrinkles in an old lady's face, and maybe it was the pain of all these months of a marriage ending and a world in suffocation and a society in collapse, maybe it was just the constant sore in his heart as the blood pumped through to be cleared of love, but he liked the moon rock, and thought — his vanity finally unquenchable — that she liked him. Yes. Was she very old, three billion years or more? Yet she was young, she had just been transported here, and there was something young about her, tender as the smell of the cleanest hay. . .[6]

I quote at length to demonstrate how very different is Mailer's approach — with its easy ascription of gender, its account of the little rock as a microcosmic version of the moon itself, its overall unabashed projection of subjective feelings — from that of the moon scientists. A few paragraphs before this closing passage Mailer had cited Aquinas' dictum, "Trust the authority of your senses," as a favorite saying, and through his sensory contact with the moon rock at the end of the summer of 1969 he is able to get a purchase on some concluding thoughts about Apollo 11: "Looking at it, answers came, answers strong enough to send him back to Provincetown for the fall and winter haul of his book, and a little of the spring."[7] Mailer's "answers" are actually spread throughout *Of a Fire on the Moon*, but a single characteristically extended sentence here in these last pages sums up his major conclusions:

> Yes, he had come to believe by the end of this long summer that probably we had to explore into outer space, for technology had penetrated the modern mind to such a depth that voyages in space might have become the last way to discover the metaphysical pits of that world of technique which choked the pores of modern consciousness — yes, we might have to go out into space until the mystery of new discovery would force us to regard the world once

again as poets, behold it as savages who knew that if the universe
was a lock, its key was metaphor rather than measure.[8]

While there was much that was unclear in this statement, the om-
nibus idea that "the mystery of new discovery" might promote an at
once "poetic" and "savage" perspective on the earth—one which would
entail a reliance on metaphor rather than measure—grew in importance as a methodological clue in response to my increasing need to
know how to approach the Space-Age images so as to sense their mythic
significance.

Several elements seemed important. The emphasis on new discovery (which could be my own as well as NASA's) as a "mystery" was
in accord with my conviction that authentic myth contained an irre-
ducibly mysterious quality—or at the very least would have to present
a mysterious face to our initially Apollonic gaze—which had to be
recognized and respected as we drew near. A major means for doing this
would be to view the mythic images surfacing in the Space Age metaphorically rather than to adhere closely to their exact denotative sense,
seeing them only as literal signs pointing at objects to be measured in
a distant analytic manner. That the "poets" we would become in so
doing were also "savages" agreed with a notion from Barrett's *Time of
Need* that "art is perhaps a product of the archaic part of our nature"
with deep roots into the earth itself below any Apollonic accultura-
tion.[9] I knew this to be an idea about art voiced not only by Romantics
a century and a half ago but by other more recent thinkers. For instance,
the art historian, Sir Herbert Read, in his *Icon and Idea*, writes of the
"vitalistic" aspect of art preceding and underlying the "beautiful",[10]
while literary critic Stanley Burnshaw's *The Seamless Web* defines
poetry in the largest sense as a "creature-knowledge" counter to culture
and grounded in the body.[11]

To find this primitive poet within, however—to awaken our imaginative awareness and thereby gain some fuller access to the messages
the planet seemed to be sending—would not, I feared, be a small challenge in an era whose surface preoccupations are so very unpoetic. At
the very least the *unreflectively* nonliteralistic seeing and saying of
archaic peoples, including any kind of *automatic* recourse to metaphor,
seems barred to us by our technologized starting point: Apollo's imposing presence in the Age of Space means that only a *conscious effort*
at metaphoric communication, deliberate acts of "metaphorizing," can
hope to connect us again with the mythic significance of the imagery
we confront.

THE "SYNECTIC" PROCESS AND SOURCES OF METAPHORIZING

The central importance of Mailer's methodological clue, therefore, concerned the suggestion about the necessity to metaphorize. From my prior work on this mental process—I had written two essays on the role of metaphor in religious language—I took it that a connecting of factual dissimilars beyond mere comparison, a process usually signalled in language by the word "as", was an essential ingredient. Philosophical aestheticians like Owen Barfield[12] and Philip Wheelwright[13] had influenced my thinking on metaphor during the '60s, but perhaps the most intriguing work on the topic for me had been a little book called *Synectics*, by William J. J. Gordon, which I discovered in its paperback form in 1968.

The title is a coined word from the Greek which means "the joining together of different and apparently irrelevant elements".[14] That is, it is a virtual synonym for the sense of metaphor I wished to stress. Gordon's book deals with the development of creativity, and what so intrigued me was that although his is very much a problem-solving approach, emphasizing "operational mechanisms" which can "reduce to practice" abstract aesthetic notions of the creative process, thereby leading to an objectively evaluatable end product—all quite at odds with the individual experience of the artist and the subjective value of the art work—he is constantly obliged to acknowledge certain slippery realities about the psychological states he seeks to exploit.

Gordon never mentions the word "myth" and actually inveighs against theories of creativity which probe no further than the attestation of a "personal mystery" at the heart of the artistic process. But he nonetheless states that "the major effective components of creative process are subconscious; so that creative solutions to problems traditionally contain a high 'accident' quotient."[15] Moreover, when he comes to discuss the role of metaphor, distinguishing between "generative" metaphors which provoke discovery and "descriptive" metaphors which reflect a previous discovery after the fact, he not only returns to the subconscious element in creativity but grudgingly assents to the presence of mystery as well:

> Generative metaphors seem to take their inception in essentially subliminal process—a process of which we are not thoroughly conscious at the moment of its occurrence. Thus we tend to slide past the moment of inception, to regard it as mysterious and sacrosanct, to call it inspiration, and to overlook the possible effects of training and discipline upon the metaphor-making potential. However, even a good descriptive metaphor has a quality of 'mystery' about it as it postulates similarities between apparently unlike things. . .This quality of mystery then is present in both descriptive and generative metaphors, though to different degrees.[16]

Gordon decides that "the impression of mystery may derive from the fact that a metaphorical sort of activity operates not only on conscious but also on preconscious levels," and he advises that "the conscious attempt to make metaphors has a stimulating effect upon subliminal abilities to metaphorize in contrast to the apparently depressive effect that 'utilitarian' and 'logical' preoccupations have upon those abilities."[17] These encouraging words about conscious attempts at metaphor-making or metaphorizing—in which I also included receptivity to others' metaphors—struck me as a hopeful sign for my overall search.

For Gordon the use of metaphor is also related to the elements of "play and irrelevance" in the creative process, since the latter partly depends on "making the familiar strange". Play with words, for instance, "re-establishes the wide range of metaphoric suggestiveness inherent not only in language as a whole but also in single words and phrases".[18] He gives an example employing the familiar word "open": "Only by devising a new way to ask the question: 'what does *open* mean?' can we re-project the metaphoric and speculative potential inherent in the universal (open) and in the particular (examples of *open* and *openness*) which interplay with that universal."[19] Like play, the toleration and use of apparent irrelevancies is an adult's return to the attitudes and abilities, the "art", of childhood which have been schooled out of us by years of regimented education. At the extremes of this training syllogistic reasoning and computer systems help us to be more narrowly efficient and secure by screening out "the rich ambiguous data of our surroundings". Gordon points out, however,

> neither logic as a system nor computer-oriented 'science' is capable of the reaches of metaphoric and analogic relevance which the creative imagination can develop in its search for forms. The achievement of these higher orders of relevancy, enriched and widely diverse patterns of association, requires a redefinition of that which is traditionally accepted as relevant.[20]

Even accidents, says Gordon, are potential sources of new discovery for the prepared mind, and like the child who spills the pail of water intended for a further destination, we must be "willing to accept the interruption, to focus on the chance effects and designs which have resulted".[21] It should be mentioned here that this openness to the meaningfulness of accidents or coincidences—the sort of chance occurrence from which William Barrett drew significance when he saw *Sky Above Mud Below* and *2001* on successive days—was a factor in my own research which eventually deserved separate attention. It became for me not only an *aspect* of metaphorizing but also an *adjunct* to metaphorizing, one with its own seemingly special relation to the images of earth.

Perhaps what intrigued me most about Gordon's largely Apollonic treatment of creativity—as I reconsidered his book in the light of Norman Mailer's methodological advice to regard the earth as a poet or a savage with a Space-Age perspective—were his ideas about the *source* of metaphors and metaphoric activity. Not only were the ideas themselves provocative but the verbal images he used to present them were in each case uncannily, albeit accidentally, pertinent. He first discussed the importance of "the commonplace":

> Until the early part of this century the commonplace for most human beings included the barnyard and a continuous contact with plants and animals, with everyday reminders of the biological substratum of our existence. Urban life has obviously displaced this with a man-made and mechanical commonplace. The commonplace of the past was organic and concrete; the commonplace of the present is synthetic and abstract . . . Yet the concrete organic data of the world constitute the basis for metaphor, and the best we can do with abstract mechanical data is to impart to them the qualities of the organic data.[22]

The commonplace as the seedbed of metaphor is thus, most fundamentally, what he has already called "the rich ambiguous data of our surroundings". And when Gordon stresses that "concrete evocative commonplace must be distinguished from abstract impotent commonplace" he is led to the pronouncement couched in the first image I found so arresting: "The platform of abstract commonplace floats safely above the earth's concreteness, but we must risk abandoning it in order to grasp a more coherent creative product."[23]

Gordon's other idea about the basis for metaphorizing derives from the theory which holds that language is inherently metaphorical owing to the processing of sense impressions by the nervous system. He speculates that "perhaps the body is metaphoric",[24] a notion developed, as I had discovered earlier, in the aesthetic explorations of Stanley Burnshaw's *The Seamless Web*. In Gordon's case, the metaphoric image which turns up so suggestively at this point in the argument comes in his statement that, with the theory of language in question, "language is asserted to have its roots in metaphor and through metaphor in the rich, symbol-making earth of the nervous system itself."[25]

It is not quite clear how these two ideas of the origins of metaphor are meant to fit together. But taking my cue from Gordon's own suggestions about the importance of chance effects in metaphorizing, I chose to find it significant that in each instance imagery is employed which evokes the relation between outer-space remoteness and rootedness in the rich, ambiguous concrete earth (our bodies can be taken as the nearest instances of the biosphere). Moreover, Gordon—all the more tellingly for his own Apollonic inclinations—metaphorizes metaphor as this latter rootedness, much as Barrett had implied that primitive myth-making followed the sensory patterns (or patterning) of the earth.

Thus William Gordon's *Synectics*, which I reread in search of specific information on a metaphoric method for approaching earth after encountering Mailer's *Of a Fire on the Moon*, suggested that by way of its involvement in the mystery of new discovery, in unconscious processes, in play, irrelevance, and accident, and in the "savage" ambiguities of body and biosphere, metaphorizing's connective maneuvers to "make the familiar strange" provided the best avenue back to the mythic significance of earth images arising in the Space Age.

METAPHORIZING AS A WAY OF SEEING THE MYTHIC SIGNIFICANCE OF EARTH

Gordon's book, however, was not the only resource on metaphorizing which I drew upon as I continued my research during the second half of the '70s: Observations by James Hillman were also extremely helpful. It was Hillman who published Ian Mitroff's report on the psychology of the moon scientists cited above and whose neo-Jungian writings were a major, if indirect, influence on all my thinking about the deeper meaning of the Space Age throughout the decade. By way of his books *The Myth of Analysis* (1972), *Re-Visioning Psychology* (1975), and *The Dream and the Underworld* (1979), his editorship since 1970 of *Spring: An Annual of Archetypal Psychology and Jungian Thought*, and his essays in that journal and elsewhere, Hillman aided me in reappropriating the work of Jung after a period of neglect during the late '60s and also stimulated me with his own stunningly original contributions to depth psychology. In particular he strengthened for me the sense of metaphor's relation to myth and the involvement of both in ambiguity or mystery.

In *Re-Visioning Psychology* writing about "Psychologizing: Moving Through the Literal to the Metaphorical," Hillman notes how "literalism prevents mystery by narrowing the multiple ambiguity of meanings into one definition," while "by treating the words we use as ambiguities, seeing them again as metaphors, we restore to them their original mystery."[26] Metaphors, however, "are more than ways of speaking: they are ways of perceiving, feeling, and existing".[27] Hillman condenses metaphor and myth by calling the former "a mini-myth"[28] and the latter "the comprehensive metaphor",[29] adding that "like metaphor itself, the power of which cannot satisfactorily be explained, a myth also speaks with two tongues at one time, amusing and terrifying, serious and ironic, sublimely imaginative and yet with the scattered detail of ridiculous fancy."[30]

Because of this metaphoric duplicity, Hillman stresses,

> the revelation of myth within events confirms ambiguity, it does not settle it. Myth moves into meaning merely by taking one out of the literal objectivities, and the place to which myth carries one is not even a central meaning, or the center of meaning where things are supposed to feel certain. Instead, we hover in puzzlement at the border where the true depths are. Rather than an increase of certainty there is a spread of mystery, which is both the precondition and the consequence of revelation.[31]

Indeed, Hillman continues, "myths do not tell us how. They simply give the invisible background which starts us imagining, questioning, going deeper."[32]

Finally, in *The Dream and the Underworld* he states that "mythical images are not firm evidence for anything positive. They cannot carry systematic structures on their backs. They don't stand still long enough, and they are too shady. . .The support they might contribute to any positive reality is its background in fantasy."[33]

During the years after the Apollo moon missions, prompted by Mailer's book and my background reading in the works of philosophers such as Philip Wheelwright and Owen Barfield, I drew on the writings of psychologists William J. J. Gordon and James Hillman in my attempt to determine how to handle the archaic earth images whose meanings I was seeking in my search for the mythic significance of the Space Age.

What I learned was that, although as Space-Age moderns we undeniably begin from an Apollonic perspective which lends its name to our most dramatic success in outer space, it is possible to reenter, through a sensitivity to the metaphoric rather than literalistic aspects of seeing and saying, the mysterious revelations of myth concerning the multiple meanings of earth. By metaphorizing the mythic images arising afresh in the Age of Space—exploring sensory and semantic connections which involve a high degree of ambiguity, play, irrelevance, or accident—it seemed that I could come closer to what I was looking for. I would have to involve myself as a *participant* in metaphorizing, devising from various angles a new way to ask the question "What does *earth* mean?", knowing that any answers I might discover would provide mythic meaning only by drawing me deeper into mystery.

When Mailer wrote that the Apollo space program could provide "the mystery of new discovery [which] would force us to regard the world once again as poets", he was hardly referring to the Apollonic analyses of the moon scientists themselves, let alone to the "ancient astronauts" hypothesis put forward so unpoetically by Eric von Däniken. For Mailer the mystery of new discovery is a complex one; his conclusions about it, as I have said, were provoked in part by communing with one of the little rocks brought back from the moon. These conclusions were also called forth by a surrealist painting on the wall at a Houston party just after the Apollo 11 launch.

RENÉ MAGRITTE'S METAPHORIZING VISION

The painting, which Mailer subsequently chose for *Of a Fire on the Moon*'s dust jacket, is *The Invisible World*, by the Belgian surrealist, René Magritte. It shows a big gray boulder about four feet tall sitting on the floor of a reddish-brown drawing room in front of open French doors through which can be seen a black balcony-railing and then an expanse of calm blue sea under menacing clouds. The stone itself is reminiscent of some awesome sacred object venerated by primitive peoples, but in the drawing room setting it also presents an image evocative of the final appearance of the strange megalith at the foot of the dying astronaut's bed in *2001*. Mailer records his own impressions upon first seeing the painting: "The silences of the canvas spoke of Apollo 11 still circling the moon . . . It was as if Magritte had listened to the ending of one world with its comfortable chairs in the parlor, and heard the intrusion of a new world, silent as the windowless stone which grew in the room, and knowing not quite what he had painted, had painted his warning nonetheless. Now the world of the future was a dead rock, and the rock was in the room."[34]

It is not obvious what this warning portends. Maybe to Mailer the stone signifies the moon itself as a dead rock which threatens our future with the temptation to live where there is no liveable habitat, at least not without our adapting ourselves *out* of our humanness. This may in turn be what our technological civilization as a whole is doing — even before we build space colonies or actually settle on the moon — as we forsake the messages of earth and pollute the environment.

Mailer's reading of the painting implies that the mystery of new discovery was not one sought by the Apollo project, since, as a "warning", Magritte's vision seems a negative commentary on the ambitions of the space scientists and astronauts themselves. In any case, it is more like ambiguous messages such as Magritte's than the public declarations of NASA which can prompt us to regard the world, with Mailer, as "savages" or "poets," to reenter, in imagination, the past and planet of our origins. René Magritte's works have been described as presenting "the mystery of the visible",[35] and along with the language of his titles — apparently designed to help perplex us out of habitual seeing — the *visual* language of his surrealism, I sensed, could be a valuable lesson in how to approach the archaic terrestrial imagery I had been meeting in Space-Age media.

The great gray boulder of Magritte's *The Invisible World*, to take an image from his visual language which played along with the initial clues offered by the newspaper cartoon and *2001*, reappears in several of his other paintings. Often it floats in space as weightlessly as a cloud, aligned with a tiny crescent moon, suggestive of Kubrick and Clarke's portentous astronomical conjunctions. After pondering enough of these works I began to see the boulder and the cloud as interchangeable, and indeed in *The Song of the Storm* a cloud rests on the ground with the rain falling into it. It is hard to dispute critic David Sylvester's estimate of Magritte: "The sight of his alternatives renders reality more mysterious."[36] This statement again indicates how well the painterly metaphors of such surrealism—drawn, no doubt, from the archaic earthling within the artist—can serve as an avenue back to the mythic.

My first actual attempt, then, to apply the method of metaphorizing to the earth images I was encountering happened with the help of the surrealistic vision described in *Of a Fire on the Moon*, a vision which I later followed up with my own modest research on Magritte. With surrealistic eyes, I felt, we could come to see the moon and the earth as boulders floating cloudlike in space, the former a dead rock as manhandled by Project Apollo (or perhaps, if we recall Mailer's rendezvous with the tiny lunar sample, as a vital, ever-virginal stone maiden), the latter—the earth—a massive monolith, a single colossal sacred stone.

I began to explore such metaphorizing possibilities for their intimations of any emerging Space-Age mythos, attending with ever-growing fascination to the contemporary cultural reappearance of ancient megaliths and other instances of what I came to call "geo-metaphors".

II
EXPLORING GEOMETAPHORS

CHAPTER THREE

MEGALITHS BEYOND MEASURE

"There are more legends associated with this group of standing stones than with any in the British Isles."

Paul Devereux, a stocky thirty-fivish Englishman who edits *The Ley Hunter*, a lively publication reporting the search for alignments ("ley lines") thought to connect various sites on his native landscape, sipped a beer, dragged on his dwindling cigarette, and gestured toward the slide on the screen next to him. His remarks and the image to which he was pointing on that evening in 1979 took me back some six-and-a-half years to January 1973. This was when I first heard a certain song playing in the tiny bookstore of Goddard College, in north central Vermont where I had gone to teach.

I had just begun my research on the Space-Age mythos after pondering the last Apollo lunar mission and concluding that although there were predictable paeans to our technological mastery and provacative but isolated insights from artists and cultural commentators, no comprehensive reading of the deeper implications of our leap beyond earth was forthcoming. There was no reason I should not make my own attempt, but I hardly expected it would have to take account of the melody in the Goddard bookstore.

I couldn't make out many of the words of what I supposed was a rock ballad, but I learned that its title was "Roll Right Stones" and that it was from an album called *Shoot Out at the Fantasy Factory* by the

British group, Traffic. Intimidated by my unfamiliarity with "the current music scene", I assumed the song's title must be a rock culture reference to another and more famous British band, The Rolling Stones, and that its lyrics were arcana beyond my deciphering. Even after buying and playing the Traffic album for myself I made no attempt to respond to the words of "Roll Right Stones" as anything other than sounds in a pattern of sounds which had become powerfully evocative for me.

It was not until a few months later in 1973, while reading to my nine-year-old daughter in preparation for a family summer trip to England, that I ran across an allusion to a town called Great Rollright and then a description of a megalithic complex (with its accompanying folktales) actually called the Rollright Stones. Needless to say, this sent me scurrying back to the Traffic ballad to listen more carefully. While the lyrics were not easy to follow they did indeed refer to the veritable megalithic Rollright complex, suggesting this site's abiding significance in the Space Age.

EARTH MYSTERIES IN OLD AND NEW ENGLAND

This discovery fit with eerie smoothness into my project on the post-Apollo mythos, which, under the impetus of "clues" like *The New York Times* cartoon, William Barrett's *Time of Need*, and the monolith in *2001*, I was increasingly trying to understand as a Space-Age reconnection to the earth and its mysteries. I put together a slide-lecture in order to share the earth images I had been finding, and at this point an audiotape of Traffic's "Roll Right Stones" became a part of my presentation.

Unfortunately, our trip to England that summer could not include a visit to the Rollright Stones themselves, but my first sight of Stonehenge and the huge stone circle at Avebury intensified my fascination with the megaliths. In the years after 1973 I read all I could about them, as images of sacred stones figured more and more importantly in my research. Then, in the fall of 1977, my frustration at not being able to get back to England to see the Rollright Stones at first hand was alleviated by the erruption of a relevant academic controversy close to home.

A conference on "Ancient Vermont" introduced me to the claim that in Vermont and neighboring states stone structures, previously ignored or thought to be colonial root cellars, were actually pre-

Columbian in origin: Celto-Iberian, perhaps, or Phoenician.[1] The main person making this claim was Barry Fell, a retired marine biologist who had taken up the study of epigraphy, ancient inscriptions, and whose book *America B.C.* had just appeared.[2]

While Fell and other adherents to his theory — amateur investigators of New England antiquities, academics from outside archaeology and a few mavericks from inside, assorted dowsers and New Age onlookers — presented tantalizing data at the conference, orthodox archaeologists were unconvinced[3] (*America B.C.*had already been scathingly reviewed by England's most prestigious professor of archaeology, Glyn Daniel of Cambridge.[4]) To me the adherents were much the more interesting group than their detractors, but I had to admit that the evidence they put forward was from far from conclusive. Indeed, upon reflection some of this evidence seemed to match Jung's characterization of flying saucer sightings as "a 99 percent psychic product": That is, these terrestrial sightings may have been in large part a projection of unconscious fears and longings onto the New England landscape. For my brand of research, of course, such projections might be the very stuff of a Space-Age mythos and therefore valuable as such, but on a conscious level the "Ancient Vermont" enthusiasts were unconcerned with these considerations. Despite their more flamboyant style they seemed to be in pursuit of the same sort of scientific validation which their opponents held up as a final standard of truth.

Neither side appeared to be aware that another approach to the data was possible, any more than Erich von Däniken and his critics were aware that ancient mysteries could speak a valid mythic language out of their very mysteriousness. All in all, it struck me that here in Vermont was a "shoot out at the fantasy factory" in which the adversaries were equally oblivious to the psychic factors involved: the projections and methodological passions animating what was finally a unified quest for accurate measurement, clinching factual evidence, proof positive.

The debate on the Vermont stone enigmas continued beyond the autumn of 1977 and I continued to follow it, while developing a metaphorizing approach to the data which would, I hoped, avoid a fixation on factual proof. By early 1979 I decided I could wait no longer to explore the Rollright Stones for myself, and so I engineered a financially questionable family holiday in England for the summer.

The stones lie in the Cotswold Hills on private land a few miles northwest of Chipping Norton, a market town which is itself northwest of Oxford. The complex is actually quite well known in England, but few Americans I have talked to about my work have heard of it. I detected no American accents on the August morning when my wife and I roamed around the site.

We parked our rented car at the edge of the road which occupies the Oxfordshire-Warwickshire border. The King Stone, by itself across this road from the main circle, was the first element of the complex to attract us. It is an odd-shaped eight-foot-high menhir of heavily pitted limestone resembling a hooded figure leaning backward under a heavy load clutched at its stomach, or else a rhinoceros-like animal staring up at the sky at an angle. The name of this solitary monolith refers to one of the many Rollright legends which I had read to my daughter six years earlier in preparation for our other English trip. A witch named Mother Shipton from Shipton-under-Wychwood, says the legend, turned to stone a would-be king of England, his five knights whispering among themselves about their leader's megalomania, and a force of over seventy foot soldiers.[5]

It is part of this legend that the power-mad commander was petrified in Warwickshire and all his men in Oxfordshire, and we had to cross the road, back past our car, to a plowed field outside the King's Men circle to see the Five Knights. These latter stones, probably a collapsed dolmen (the supports for an earthen barrow or burial chamber), do indeed whisper to one another as their pockmarked and lichen-colored surfaces huddle together, giving fleeting glimpses of human expression. Another Rollright legend tells that every midnight they and the King Stone return to life and go down the hill to drink at a small stream.[6]

The seventy-odd King's Men constitute the almost perfect circle of stones we entered last. The diameter of this circle is hardly more than 100 feet and few of the stones in it are taller than a man, but the seeming geometric precision of their placement couples with the craggy, meteoritic look of each individual stone — roughness poised in tension with the appearance of accuracy — to create an undeniable aura of something having been carefully planned here in the Bronze Age or earlier which our science fails to understand. For instance, a number of the stones have small holes in them which may have been bored to allow for sightings between the King's Men and the outlying soldiers, or between stones at various points on the circumference of the circle. But if this is the reason for the holes, we have no idea why such sightings should have held any interest.

Admittedly the recent science of archaeoastronomy has been investigating the possibility that many ancient megalithic complexes were oriented to provide sighting lines to the Midsummer sunrise, say, or to the appearance of some important star on the horizon. Unfortunately, however, no such alignments have been verified for the holes in the Rollright Stones, and as modern investigators in search of facts we have little more than the legends to tell us why these stones were set up here. For instance, an additional tale holds that the King's Men assume their living forms and dance in a ring every night.⨳

MEASURING MYSTERIES VS. METAPHORIZING

High on their windswept hilltop in the Cotswolds, the stones were an "earth mystery" mysterious enough, I felt, to require an alternative interpretation, one more in keeping with the folk legends themselves, one perhaps even closer in spirit to the haunting sound of Traffic's music about them. This thought also occurred to me as part of my attempt to apply Norman Mailer's idea that the mystery of new discovery in our space exploits would cause us to see the world once more as "savages" or "poets", reliant on "metaphor rather than measure". The earth images I was exploring could be taken as manifestations of the mystery Mailer had in mind. Remembering as well the philosopher Gabriel Marcel's wise distinction between *problems*, which one can "solve", and genuine *mysteries*, which one cannot, I knew that the methodological imperative for my kind of research was to handle the imagery so that the mystery behind it is not reduced to a problem for solving, to respond to the archaic terrestrial images in such a way that their mysterious background would be nurtured *as* mystery, allowing it to flower and yield on its own ambiguous terms the mythic significance I was seeking. Hence my recourse to a metaphorizing approach to the images, which brought me back to the Rollright Stones and the need to treat them as a "geometaphor" rather than force them into a factual explanation to satisfy either the old line archaeologists or those New Age geomancers who unwittingly shared the same aims.

It was clear in the case of the "Ancient Vermont" argument that neither side had the slightest interest in nurturing mystery or (recalling also James Hillman's words on myth) hovering in puzzlement at the edge of true depths. However valuable their investigations might prove scientifically, I saw that the approach finally shared by both factions could give me no direct help in finding the deeper meanings of our space odyssey. Although the combatants in the Vermont shoot out could add new megalithic imagery to my growing data pool, *their* conscious intention, again, was precisely to measure and factually to prove—"to *solve* these mysteries", as President Kennedy had put it in launching the manned space program.

Although I was well along toward these methodological conclusions by then, it was not until hearing Paul Devereux talk about ley lines and related phenomena upon my return from England in the fall of 1979 that I fully realized the older debate across the Atlantic, between orthodox archaeologists and their opponents, displayed similar features to the Vermont controversy and harbored similar implications for my work. Devereux had come from London to see the supposed pre-Columbian sites in New England and was speaking and showing slides at the home of an acquaintance of mine, Sigfrid Lonegren, a man who at that time edited a journal for the American Society of Dowsers in nearby Danville, Vermont.

The gathering that early October night stood staunchly in the camp of archaeological heterodoxy as regarded the Vermont stones, and was happy to hear from Devereux that the establishment in British archaeology was not going unopposed. After setting forth his definition of what kinds of landmarks line up so as to indicate a "ley" and giving some of the history of "ley-hunting", starting with the publication of Alfred Watkins' *The Old Straight Track* in 1925[8] and revived in 1969 by the appearance of John Michell's *The View Over Atlantis*,[9] he moved into the presentation of his most recent material. This latter was a departure from ley-hunting *per se* but no less dubious in the eyes of orthodox researchers overseas.

He began to speak of the year-old "Dragon Project", an attempt to monitor a given megalithic complex with a broad spectrum of "instruments" from ultrasound devices and geiger counters to the intuitions of psychics and the divining rods of dowsers (which many in his Vermont audience were convinced could detect occult energy fields as well as underground water or metal). The composite results of this monitoring would then be assessed for whatever patterns and anomalies might be evident. The site chosen for this effort was the Rollright Stones.[10]

It was hypnotic to see on the screen the same gnarled monoliths I had touched only two months earlier. Devereux, beer and cigarette in hand, was nearing the end of his talk. Ultrasonic monitoring of the type used to study bat behavior had been tried at the Rollright site from the beginning of the Dragon Project, he said, and some very provocative findings had emerged.

On a scale of one to ten the normal ultrasound background level is a one, but every morning from a half hour before dawn to a few hours after dawn there were readings of six or seven, with no bats in the neighborhood. The highest of these early morning readings yet recorded came on February 24, 1979—two days before the total solar eclipse visible in northwestern United States and Canada.

Devereux concluded his presentation by inferring that perhaps with environmental sensitivities beyond our own the people who set the Rollright Stones in place did so in response to the ultrasonic effects of certain configurations of stones, choosing the pattern which brought about the effects most useful to them. Evidently the almost perfect version of what we call a circle, together with the outlying King Stone and Five Knights, formed the configuration they had arrived at to meet their needs, needs which may have included a distant early warning system for eclipses.

This was all quite fascinating. Devereux's slides were alluring and his speculations not without plausibility. From the alternative perspective I had in mind, however, the most valuable part of his revelations about the Rollright complex was a further inference he neglected to draw. When I suggested it to him he hardly objected, but it clearly held little interest for his line of investigation.

What I inferred was that measure—at any rate quantitative measure—might finally be an epiphenomenon at megalithic sites like the Rollright Stones; geometrical considerations could have been and therefore still would be a mere reverberation of some more basic factor. Even the "sacred" geometry often cited by investigators such as Keith Critchlow[11] and Anthony Roberts[12] as being embodied in megalithic structures and those Christian sanctuaries (such as Chartres Cathedral) which displaced them, a geometry sacred because it reflected symbolically certain timeless essences of mysticism or metaphysics, would not necessarily be primary in these earth mysteries.

There is an additional legend that the stones in the main Rollright circle cannot be counted,[13] and for us today, I thought, with our tendency to overvalue literalistically certain knowledge (even in metaphysics, where a univocal symbolism can function as literalism once removed), measure, the "metry" in "geometry", might itself need to be taken figuratively. In other words, an unaccustomed metaphoric sensitivity might have to become the primary yardstick of our understanding of the stones, certainly of their mythic significance as images of irreducible mystery.

HELP FROM PASCAL AND HERACLITUS

These notions about the subsidiary importance of a measuring approach to megalithic enigmas were, I believed, newly relevant in the Age of Space. They bespoke an alternative emphasis which was hardly original with me, however, and which I recalled from my reading as having been voiced prominently by at least two major figures in the earlier history of Western thought.

Some 300 years ago, at what is generally considered the start of modern philosophy, Blaise Pascal, himself a mathematical genius, made a plea for *l'esprit de finesse* (the intuitive mind) in contrast to *l'esprit de geometrie* (the mathematical mind) represented by the approach of his contemporary René Descartes with its emphasis on "clear and distinct ideas". A few years ago, while reviewing an admirable book by Brian Wicker called *The Story-Shaped World*, I was most interested to encounter Pascal's plea lined up with the specific words of advice from Norman Mailer which were so central to my reflections on method. Wicker was making the point (in a discussion of theology) that for Mailer or Pascal on the one side, just as for Descartes on the other, modes of thinking, styles of language, and even entire world views cannot finally be separated:

> When poets and story-tellers talked of God in the language of Mailer's 'savages,' by way of metaphor, they were also choosing its accompanying metaphysic. Whereas, when the philosophers. . . spoke of Him they did so (if at all) in the sophisticated abstract language of geometrically-defined objects and value-free physical laws.[14]

This statement reminded me of James Hillman's insistence that "metaphors are more than ways of speaking: they are ways of perceiving, feeling, and existing." Moreover, as I considered the implications of the sacred stones geometaphor, it was striking how well the description of the theological language of "the philosophers"—e.g., Descartes—whom Wicker sets over against Pascal and Mailer applied to the investigators who were arguing over megalithic phenomena in England and

America. Like Descartes speaking of God, the "Ancient Vermont" and "ley lines" combatants, I had found, used "the sophisticated abstract language of geometrically-defined objects and value-free physical laws."

Another example of these issues being raised in an earlier historical context comes from Bruno Snell's *The Discovery of the Mind*, a study of the beginnings of European thinking in Greece. I had read this book first in the early 1960s and returned to it for help in clarifying the specifically mythic dimension of the Space Age. At a time closer to the fashioning of the Rollright Stones than to our own, pre-Socratic Greek thought, according to Snell, was moving from a mythic to a logical mode by way of differing uses of the comparison as a verbal form. Between the poetic similes of Homer and the analogies of science and philosophy came a shift in emphasis which Snell explains by contrasting the thought of Heraclitus with that of Empedocles.

Empedocles is clearly the more "sophisticated" thinker, whose logical use of comparisons is akin to the mathematical thought style of the Pythagoreans:

> . . . in the field of mathematics the 'is as' or 'equals' of these comparisons came to be taken quite literally. . . The technique of the mathematicians is somewhat like the procedure of Empedocles: he takes a comparison based on a verb metaphor and renders it scientifically unobjectionable by excluding from the event everything that is not motion. Similarly mathematics transforms the comparison based on an adjectival metaphor into a scientific method by operating only with those attributes which are quantitative in character.[15]

Obviously Empedocles' quasi-mathematical literalism would influence his attitude toward verbal images, and it was here that Snell highlighted the distance between him and the more mythic or "savage" Heraclitus:

> . . . the similes of Empedocles, as it were, strive to leave the language of imagery behind, since the process which manifests itself both in the explanatory figure and in the event explained is best defined through the device of an abstract physical law. . . But the truth which Heraclitus has set himself to unveil cannot be expressed in any other way except through an image. Heraclitus shows us the meaning of the 'necessary' metaphor. We realize that the reality which it expresses lies far below the level of human or animal activity, that it is one with the very roots of our existence.[16]

Reading this account of Heraclitus' stress on the necessity of concrete metaphoric imagery in contrast to the lofty abstract literalism of Pythagoras and Empedocles, I was brought back yet again in my thinking to Mailer's post-Apollo advice and, by implication, to my inference that geometry, even sacred geometry, may not have been the primary factor in the origins of the Rollright complex. In developing this perspective on megaliths as geometaphor I did need to acknowledge that, like the first stages of a rocket launching, the scientific-technological thrust of centuries, fueled by thinkers such as Pythagoras, Empedocles, and Descartes, with their quest for mathematical and logical certainty, was indispensible for our movement up and off the planet where we could experience the mystery of new discovery. (Robert Graves recounts that both Pythagoras and Empedocles were venerated as reincarnations of Apollo at Crotona in Ancient Greece.[17]) I also had to grant that in a similar fashion the two-sided scientific push to unravel the enigma of the megalithic remains in old and New England may have been crucial in presenting us with an equally mysterious new discovery, or recent rediscovery.

Nevertheless, I felt very strongly, after all, about the importance of realizing that both the orthodox and heterodox groups investigating the megaliths do so without the interpretive counterweight of a Heraclitus, a Pascal, or a Mailer. They thereby run the risk of mishandling the mystery, reducing it to a problem in their mania for the clear and distinct solution, and missing the mythic significance of the terrestrial sightings however valuable their findings may turn out to be for Apollonic science-as-usual.

While I could, of course, understand the straight archeologists' continuing to pursue the unambiguous goals of science, it was surprising to me to find that those among the English heterodoxy who claimed to be "metaphysical" or even "mythic" in orientation—that is, the devotees of sacred geometry and "geomancy" who saw the ancients as landscape engineers with occult motivations and messages—were no less enthralled by many of those scientific goals and no less impatient with the metaphoric and intuitive approach of a Heraclitus, a Pascal, or a Mailer. For this imaginative group of writers contesting the British archaeological establishment, "earth mysteries" such as those at the Rollright complex are to be meticulously, neatly *solved*. Despite their avowed opposition to orthodox science's materialism, its linear rather than cyclical view of history, and its disregard for hidden metaphysical meanings, these neo-Pythagoreans appeared to me to be as Apollonic as the mainline archaeologists in their need for an antimetaphoric certainty and an abstract geometric precision which would dissipate the mystery of genuine myth by allegorizing away its aesthetic-pictorial imagery.

KEITH CRITCHLOW AND "SACRED GEOMETRY"

Keith Critchlow, a scholar of architecture whose *Time Stands Still: New Light on Megalithic Science* is the most sophisticated example of this English school of nonestablishment research into the archaeological enigmas, initially struck me as coming tantalizingly close to an approach such as I was working on to see the stone structures as a geometaphor. Critchlow's book, with evocative color photographs of the megaliths by Rod Bull and the author's own geometrical diagrams, actually employs a concept of myth as an important means of throwing new light on megalithic science.

Unfortunately, the use of the term "science" in the subtitle is telltale. Intended, perhaps, as an honorific designation in contrast to establishment archaeology's view—frequently attacked by the geomancers —of the megalith-builders as brutish barbarians practicing benighted propitiatory rites, the idea of these ancients as astronomers and geometers with a modern scientific concern for precise measurement, strict logical inference, and univocal modes of expression could also be seen as a subtly patronizing disparagement in its own right. With its disrespect for the properly prescientific religio-mythic priorities and practices more likely to be found in megalithic culture, it was not, finally, so far from von Däniken's denigrations of the nontechnological aspects of his favorite phenomena. No doubt such unwitting patronization would be part of an unconscious projection onto the imperfectly understood mindset and motivations of these "primitive" peoples of twentieth-century fantasies of a "purified" science, a science which I would find insufficiently alternative—because insufficiently attuned to the archaic terrestrial rootedness, the sensuous mediation of mythic images—to the currently prevailing Apollonic paradigm.

But what of the presence of "myth" in the intellectual environment of *Time Stands Still*? What seemed to me to be happening in the book is that Critchlow, who refers fairly often to the myth scholar Mircea Eliade, is not himself engaged in the academic study of religion or mythology, and his notion of the nature of myth is a distortion based on his personal neo-Pythagorean commitments to the sacred geometry thesis. While these commitments are impressively buttressed by quotations from Critchlow's reading of mystical texts and esoteric philosophies East and West, they do not equip him, as an architect with undoubted geometrical expertise, to deal with the metaphoric language of mythic images.

On the first page of his Introduction he attests that "we uphold the traditional sense of the term myth, which is a relating *in time* matters which are essentially timeless; matters which are central and psychological and spiritually accurate, yet not by their very nature expressible in literal (a = a) terms, as they deal with the essential meaning of being human."[18] While the unexplained phrase "the traditional sense of" was troublesome — it probably refers to his "traditionalist" allegiance to metaphysical schools of thought such as René Guenon's or Frithjof Schuon's, but this is not made clear in the context of defining myth — the concept of myth enunciated here was superficially unobjectionable. The clues to the distortion at work lie rather, I realized, in Critchlow's recourse to the tandem assumption that essential timelessness (*vide* his book's main title) and timeless essences (as of human nature) are necessarily the truths being denoted by myth. These "matters", I came to be convinced, do not at last "matter" enough for myth. That is, they are too exclusively static, certain, and absolute to exhaust the rich semantic resources of myth, too confidently and quickly cut off from the rootage of mythic imagery in the stuff of earth. Admittedly the language of myth is nonliteral, but it is surely also sensuous rather than abstract after the fashion of Critchlow's geometrical and mathematical media. And while he was right to contrast mythic expression with a = a literalism, his own philosophical predilections, I noted, lead him to champion an allegorized a = b brand of "symbolism", an unvarying code scarcely respectful of the inexpressible aspects of reality, terrestrial or otherwise, which the concretely ambiguous imagery of myth means to express.

Time Stands Still is an ambitious and in many ways brilliant work. The philosophy which informs the book, although opting out too easily from late-modern presuppositions, such as relativity, which seem psychosocially obligatory for the present despite their own historical relativity, may finally tell the true story about our state of being in the cosmos, and while reading *Time Stands Still* I wished for a long chat with Critchlow concerning such possibilities. Regrettably, in any case, my search for the mythic significance of the Space Age was not successfully concluded by my discovery of Critchlow's writing (or his film

Reflections about these same geometric symbolisms). For me the megaliths constituted one composite geometaphor connoting something of the significance I was seeking; but they did not offer much help to my approach when treated, however brilliantly, as precise signs for painstaking measurement and allegorical decipherment.

ANTHONY ROBERTS AND "GEOMYTHICS"

While I was in England in the summer of 1979, visiting the Rollright Stones and other geometaphoric sites, I was fortunate to make contact with one of the other unconventional investigators of earth mysteries. Anthony Roberts and I were able to converse only by phone, having missed each other both in London and in Glastonbury (a town with multiple Arthurian and mystical associations which he had written about in *Glastonbury: Ancient Avalon, New Jerusalem*). However, because of our conversation Roberts was kind enough to send me a copy of his new book, *Sowers of Thunder: Giants in Myth and History*,[19] upon my return to Vermont.

I was immediately attracted to Roberts' work because of his use of the term "geomythics" to describe his way of handling the megaliths and related enigmas of the English landscape. My first assumption was that, like my neologism "geometaphor", Roberts' idea of geomythics was arrived at in deliberate contrast to the measuring mentality implied by "geo-metry". Although, as I learned, Roberts was still in the early stages of developing his methodological concept, this contrast was not, apparently, his primary motivation. He explains in his Introduction that "the intellectual exactitude involved in weaving together such subjects as myth, folklore, architecture, religion, anthropology and geophysics has made it necessary to coin a new word that attempts to sum them all up. The author has created the *portmanteau* word 'geomythics,' meaning earth-myths or myths in relation to earth's metaphysical situation — topographically, historically and in cosmic time and space."[20] This laudably holistic intention takes no note of any conflict between myth and measure. Indeed, in defining his use of another centrally important term, "geomancy", Roberts says: "At the roots of geomancy lies geometry, and the geometrical relationships between all phenomena make up the determining patterns that assert geomantic reality in an intellectually definable form."[21]

As for Roberts' use of myth *per se*, like Critchlow's *Time Stands Still*, there were encouraging allusions to Eliade and Jung in *Sowers of Thunder*. But as I pondered the overall drift of the book I found that the use of such resources was only a way of presenting the usual geomantic theories with an aura of support from myth scholarship. There was even the suggestion that Jung's and Eliade's ideas on myth as "racial memories" might confirm the von Däniken-like thesis of intervention into prehistory by extraterrestrials. This sort of literalism — it is a form of the "euhemerist" reduction of myths to disguised accounts of historical figures and events — was the farthest thing possible from the approaches of contemporary myth scholars, however they may differ among themselves on other points of interpretation.

And so, although I continued to hope for assistance in my search for future modifications of Roberts' "geomythics", and I certainly valued all the geometaphorically pertinent lore he was collecting, what I had read by the fall of 1979 represented, at bottom, a very different approach to the megalith mysteries than the one I had been trying to employ. As it happened, the assorted English geomancers *did* help clarify how my metaphorizing method could be applied, and what some of its larger implications might be, just by the contrast that became evident between their orientation and mine. When I heard Paul Devereux speak about ley lines and the Rollright Stones that October evening in Vermont I was enabled to focus some of these matters of differing method and motivation. It was clear, for instance, that we *did* share, as a base from which to diverge, an enduring fascination with the megaliths themselves, and as I have mentioned above I preferred the mavericks' lively style to the humorless (though no doubt scientifically more correct) pronouncements of most of the archaeologically orthodox. I was, moreover, pleased to find that Devereux, who arrived in Vermont about the same time that Anthony Roberts' gift of *Sowers of Thunder* appeared in my mailbox, had written the Foreword to the Roberts book. Here Devereux opens his remarks with a statement about the specific megaliths which had first struck me — in *The New York Times* cartoon of late 1972 — as a clue to the meanings of a possible Space-Age mythos. "On the shores of Easter Island far out in the Pacific," his Foreword begins, "there stand giant stone heads, or stone heads depicting giants, that disturb us with their ambient mystery."[22] And he adds another comment which seemed applicable, with due accounting for the differences between Blake's "dark Satanic mills" and the towers of Cape Canaveral, to my search as well: "It is only to be expected that the Earth Mysteries would take birth in Britain: this country was the first to experience the 'dark Satanic mills' of the Industrial Revolution and it will be the first to register the necessary spiritual counterbalance."[23]

THE ROLLRIGHT STONES—MEGALITHS AS GEOMETAPHOR

And what, after reviewing all these considerations, could be said about the meanings of the Rollright Stones? Treated as a geometaphor rather than as a strictly measurable or literalistically soluble problem for science—whether straight or occult science—the Rollright complex could be seen in several ways.

As a stone circle it suggested an illusion of perfection projected upon the invariably *im*perfect manifold of earthly phenomena, a fantasy which extended to achieving a fixed and final count of the stones in the circle (which one of the folk tales quite properly warns cannot be numbered). This wish for unambiguous measurement and mathematics, like the largely imaginary linearity read into the landscape by the ley lines enthusiasts—a quest for straight, unimpeded connections which included an alignment through the Rollright circle, according to Watkins' *The Old Straight Track*[24]—was both evoked and defeated by the stones. What this means is that the placement and number of the megaliths were regular enough to reward approaches preoccupied with measuring and enumerating, but also *ir*regular enough, as at Rollright, to suggest the subjectivity actually at work in ambitions and claims about their ultimate literal precision.

In this context, then, the megaliths could be seen as perfect and precise only metaphorically, since objectively their rough randomness was just as often triumphant. One possibility of the Rollright Stones geometaphor was thus a vision of earth as an ancient stone configuration the significance of which was at least in part a matter of the fantasies projected upon it, illusions of ideal order in space.

Another area of implication for this geometaphor as I encountered it by way of the Rollright Stones between 1973 and 1979 lay with the legends associated with them of witches, petrified men, giants, and even fairies—the last ones in England were reported to Sir Arthur Evans in 1895 as having disappeared down a hole near the Rollright King Stone.[25]

The connection of witches with megalithic circles was not limited to Rollright, and metaphorically this reinstated the importance of feminine powers and purposes in the meaning of such sites. Orthodox archaeology has, I learned, discarded the diffusionism which could claim that a presumed matriarchal culture from the ancient Near East and Mediterranean colonized northwestern Europe or otherwise promoted the erection of the megaliths. Radiocarbon dating techniques have shown that structures in Brittany and the British Isles were built at least as early as those in the areas to the south and east where matriarchies may have existed. Of course the possibility for an independently originated Great Mother cult at locations like the Rollright Stones is still a conceivable basis for the legends concerning Mother Shipton and her coreligionists, but little objective evidence survives to support such a claim scientifically.

Metaphorically, however, the association of Goddess-worship with the Rollright Stones by way of the folk tales about Mother Shipton was a more valid avenue for mythic conjecture. Mother Shipton herself does not become one of the stones in the tales of Rollright: rather she turns into an elder tree,[26] and when a flowering branch of an elder—which does in fact grow beside the King Stone—is cut on Midsummer Eve, the stone is supposedly seen to nod.[27] I was intrigued to realize that the Sir Arthur Evans who collected this and other accounts of the folklore of Rollright later went on to be the famous excavator of Minoan Crete, certainly as credible a center of the Great Mother cult as any we have.

Mother Shipton's role regarding the Rollright Stones, in any case, was to produce them, as it were, by petrifying men engaged on a patriarchal journey of ambition and conquest. (There was another Mother Shipton in Yorkshire, famous for her prophecies, whose origins are connected with a well, the waters of which turned to stone objects left in them.[28]) This, then, suggests that the stones can be seen as men whose warlike inclinations are held in check by feminine craft, and this scenario might be extended to seeing the stones as petrified giants, or heads of giants, as well. Here the earth would be a giant stone man presided over by an elder-branch witch, or perhaps by the "White Goddess", for in checking Robert Graves's book of that title I noted his association of the elder with the changing goddess of the moon's phases whom he saw as underlying much of Western myth and myth-oriented poetry.[29]

The connection of the Rollright Stones with fairies would offer yet another ambiguous geometaphor. In this context the King Stone and, by extension, the entire complex, marks the site of the disappearance of fairies into the underground, which is their usual abode in the folklore of the British Isles. Beyond this, however, there is something about pointing to a place of disappearance and subterranean concealment which seems to indicate the very nature of fairies themselves. Since megaliths are frequently related to burial and burial mounds, and fairies have often been considered spirits of the dead who owe their small size to dwelling in the cramped quarters of neolithic grave barrows, the megaliths become gravestones of the little people. In the folktales of Mother Shipton she challenged the would-be King of England—now the King Stone—to take seven strides and then be able to see the nearby village of Long Compton; but his line of sight was blocked by a long grave mound or tumulus. Furthermore, the spell Mother Shipton cast upon the wrong-headed warlord and his men can be likened to the "enchantment", or *faerie*, which lies at the roots of the English word "fairy" (from the French *Feés*, derived in turn from the Fata or Fates of Greek myth).

Finally, Katherine Briggs, whose *The Vanishing People: Fairy Lore and Legends* I read in 1978 to learn of these factors, chooses the title of her book as an appropriate one to describe fairies because they were traditionally only visible between one eye-blink and the next[30] and because, as at Rollright, they were supposed to have vanished from the British countryside long ago. This geometaphoric aspect of the megaliths would therefore allow us to view the earth as under the enchantment of its underground spirits, always just out of sight: a vast burial mound or megalithic chamber controlled invisibly from within by beings whose normal span on the surface has passed.

One more direction in which to take the megalith image occurred to me in my metaphorizing. It converged suggestively with the geometaphor that had come from René Magritte's surrealistic paintings of floating boulders. A central feature of the Rollright folk tales is the movement attributed to the stones: the King Stone nodding when the elder branch is cut, the midnight dances, the nocturnal trips down to the nearest brook. Somehow, as part of the enchantment—the petrifying—or perhaps as a release from the spell under certain conditions, the stones move, despite being the very emblem of motionlessness and gravity.

This is not, I discovered, an enigma exclusive to the Rollright Stones. Anthony Roberts claims the motif of dancing megaliths is repeated in all stone lore and points to one of the early names of Stonehenge: the *Chorea Gigantum* or Giant's Dance. The word "Stonehenge" itself is supposed to be Saxon for "place of the hanging stones", again suggesting levitation, lightness, and movement.[31] How this paradoxical quality came to be ascribed to the megaliths, on the other hand, I never learned. There are, to be sure, occult explanations having to do with lost powers of magical levitation as well as more psychological ones such as Mircea Eliade's thesis that stone "strikes," that it moves into the consciousness of the primitive perceiver because of its awesome nonhuman size, shape, and solidity. Perhaps, in any case, the proper participation of the human onlooker is crucial to the experience of the stones' movement. No doubt elaborate rituals were once performed among the stones — incantations, even sacrifices. Underlying any of these operations may have been a worshipful willingness to suspend disbelief, a reverent or indeed an intense pursuit of the possibilities of human projection, an attitude of receptivity to the subjective impressions made by and upon megaliths. Conceivably no other conscious attitude then competed with that one.

For us today this sort of imaginative involvement is difficult to come by. Our Apollonic tendency is to distance ourselves, measure, problem solve, enlighten all mysteries. Our projections only occur in spite of our deliberate intentions, and so they are unconscious and unpursued. My own sense after spending several years with the archaic imagery of the megaliths, freshly fascinating in the Age of Space, was that a conscious indulgence in the metaphorizing processes surrounding projection might most nearly replicate the mythic context required to see the stones nod, dance, float, or hang in space.

Bruno Snell speaks of the mythic mode of Heraclitus as entailing "receptivity".[32] In my efforts at approaching earth images I hoped to adopt this quality of mind, but I hesitated in realizing that receptivity, with its connotation of passiveness, is merely how an Apollonic culture, petrified in its characteristic attitudes toward the world, might see the psychology of a mode it can no longer fully experience. I persisted in believing what I learned over the years since 1972, that the mystery-nurturing perspective Norman Mailer recommends is appropriate to understanding a phenomenon like the Rollright Stones in a way that supplements, deepens, and if need be challenges the researches of the multifarious contemporary champions of l'esprit de geometrie. However, in following this course the need to correct for inherited biases — acknowledging that we do start from these biases and cannot simply wish them away — seemed to necessitate a receptivity which is far from passive, and therefore hard to grasp.

Monitoring the mythic imagery transmitted in a song or a slide show, or hidden in the references of even the most literal-minded

investigator, would call for this dynamic receptivity, the almost paradoxical maneuver underlying William J. J. Gordon's "conscious attempt
to make metaphors". This is the approach I intended in conjuring up
the megalith geometaphor: Can we today, with our Apollonic *vantage
point*, move beyond our exclusive reliance on Apollonic *attitudes* and
see our planet as an enchanted ring, a seeming circle, of sacred stones
enlivened and instructed by the dancing witches of the White Goddess,
or else, once more, as a holy monolith hovering in space—a massive
weightless petrified giant?

CHAPTER FOUR

MORE AND MORE GEOMETAPHORS

Continuing to take Mailer's *Of a Fire on the Moon* as a suggestive source of geometaphors, I quickly found several more such whole earth images which I began exploring in the middle of the decade. The first two—and they lead to a third—appear in his description of the earth view available to the returning Apollo 11 crew:

> Slowly the earth will grow in the window. Blue she will gleam and brown and gray and silver and rose and red. Her clouds will cover her like curls of white hair, her clouds will turn dark as smoky pearls and the lavender of orchid, her clouds will be brown and green like marsh grass wet by the sea, and the sea will appear beneath like pools of water in the marsh grass. The earth will look like a precious stone, blue as a sapphire, blue as a diamond, the earth will be an eye to look at them in curious welcome as they return.[1]

Although the gender here is feminine and mention is made of the earth as a stone, pointing back to the permutations of the megalith geometaphor, the emphasis is primarily on the image of a *precious* stone and then on the earth as "an eye to look at them."

JEWEL AND EYEBALL

The geometaphor of the precious stone is not restricted to Mailer's perception. I once heard Alan Watts, the author of works on Asian religion, remark that the photographs of the earth from outer space show it to be the most beautiful of all jewels. The etymology of the word "jewel" takes us to "joke" or "sport," so that Arthur C. Clarke's vision of the earth in the novelized version of *2001* as "a glittering toy no star child could resist"[2] also fits with the jewel image of the earth as whimsical yet precious, valuable in its very rarity and insubstantiality, and perhaps beautiful beyond any geometrical precision in its shaping. Astronaut William Anders of Apollo 8 called the whole earth *he* saw a fragile Christmas tree ornament in a darkened room,[3] and we can also include here images drawn from games and sports: the earth as a bowling ball, for instance, or a "big blue marble".

But what of the whole earth as an eye looking back at us while, with Mailer, we follow the astronauts home? *Of a Fire on the Moon* tells of Neil Armstrong having trouble sleeping during his first rest period after the moon walk because the eyepiece of the lunar lander's telescope was poised in front of his face. This caused the earth to stare in at him, as he put it, like a "big blue eyeball".[4] When, in 1950, C. G. Jung tried to carve into a block of stone the words and images representing the deep feelings he held for his retreat tower at Bollingen on Lake Zurich, he had the following experience (as I found in rereading his autobiography, *Memories, Dreams, Reflections*, in 1974): "I began to see on the front face, in the natural structure of the stone, a small circle, a sort of eye, which looked at me. I chiseled it into the stone, and in the center made a tiny homunculus. This corresponds to the 'little doll' *(pupilla)*—yourself—which you see in the pupil of another's eye. . ."[5]

Using Jung's statement as a way to extend and enrich Mailer's geometaphor of the eyeball—and taking note that in Jung's reminiscence we have an eyeball in a megalith—I wondered what little doll of ourselves we see staring back at us from the precious "earthstone" only now visible, after so many aeons, to our Space-Age viewing. Put in these terms, reacting to the earth as eye would also establish a connection to Jung's adaptation of the mandala of Tibetan Buddhism. As I had been aware earlier in considering Stewart Brand's term "mandala earth", Jungian psychology employs this visual device for psychic integration as a kind of mirror by which analysands may become more aware of the process of their inner development.

MANDALA EARTH

The image of the mandala itself has several aspects worth pondering for their geometaphoric possibilities. According to José and Miriam Argüelles, whose book *Mandala* I encountered in 1973, "the Mandala is fundamentally a visual construct which is easily grasped by the eye, for it corresponds to the primary visual experience as well as to the structure of the organ of sight. The pupil of the eye itself is a simple Mandala form. The eye receives light and projects its images outward through the form of the pupil, that is, through the center of an elementary circle."[6] The Argüelleses also refer to one of Ralph Metzner and Timothy Leary's essays on psychedelic experience, where it is attested that the "mechanism of the mandala can also be understood in terms of the neurophysiology of the eye" and "the center of the mandala corresponds to the foeval 'blind spot.' Since the 'blind spot' is the exit from the eye to the visual system of the brain, by going 'out' through the center, you are going *in* to the brain."[7]

However it may be with the literal neurophysiology of the eye, the metaphoric implications of "seeing" in relation to the circle and its center are manifold: writing on yoga, Mircea Eliade notes that not only does the word "mandala" mean "circle", it may also be translated either "center" or "what surrounds".[8] Moreover, these implications are applicable in that richness to the whole earth image. As with the approximately circular megalithic complexes of the British Isles and Europe, the issue of objectively established geometric precision versus random arrangements—upon which, out of deep subjective needs, a pattern of perfection like the circle is projected—seems present here. Certainly psychic factors are involved in the seeing of the centered mandala circle.

The latter can be called an idealized circle, and in exploring the mandala geometaphor it is necessary to realize that the disk of the whole earth is not in actuality a true circle. This simply underscores the appropriateness of a metaphorizing rather than literalistic approach to the symmetry which characterizes the mandala image.

Sometimes the idealized shape of the mandala extends to a "squaring" of the centered circle, so that circles contain squares—as in Tibetan paintings where an elaborate "palace" will have portals in the middle of each of its four sides (suggesting also a cross focused on the center of the square)—or squares contain circles. The mandala can also be three-dimensional, not only as the sphere of the eyeball but as what Giuseppe Tucci's *Theory and Practice of the Mandala*—cited several times in the Argüelles book—calls "maps of the cosmos" embodied in many of the temples of Asia.[9] Indeed, the Argüelleses maintain that "all sacred religious structures partake of the Mandala principle: the Egyptian and Mexican pyramids; the temples of India; Buddhist stupas; Islamic mosques; the pagodas of China and Japan; and the tipis and kivas of North America."[10] Here the mandala as an architectural microcosm of the world is almost already a geometaphor: the earth as a floating four-square temple or, extending the image even further, the perfect city, the New Jerusalem.

This connection allowed me to reenvision the Mayan temple ruins of *Star Wars* as a mandalic geometaphor and to consider under the same heading the fact that the *Star Wars* sequel, *The Empire Strikes Back*, gives the name "Dagobah" to the planet where the young hero is instructed in the white magic of the Force. (Dagobah is used on the island of Sri Lanka to designate Buddhist shrines or stupas.) In late 1979 Terry Gips, an artist and teaching colleague, showed me architect Olivier Marc's *Psychology of the House*, translated from the French two years earlier. Marc agrees with the Argüelleses that, as he puts it, "all religious buildings . . . are mandalas in three dimensions." He goes on to say, however, that "stupas may be considered the purest example of these . . . ,"[11] and he offers the following description of the Great Stupa of Sanchi in India:

> Cosmic in conception, it is a hemisphere resting on the ground, surmounted by a square enclosure, and bearing on its vertical axis three superimposed spheres. The whole is surrounded by a square balustrade with four doors facing each other. Looked at from above, it seems to be set inside a square, and is a circle surrounded by four doors in the shape of a cross. In the centre of the circle rests the square of the upper balustrade, and in its centre the projected circle of the three superimposed spheres. With its alternating concen-

tric squares and circles, whose common centre is accentuated by
the cruciform disposition of the doors, the Great Stupa is the exact
image in relief of the layout of a mandala.[12]

One other instance of the three-dimensional mandala— at least
as regards imagery of the center—which I found evocative is the world
mountain: Mount Meru in Hindu iconography, for instance. This led
me to recollect the sacred mountain, Devil's Tower, in *Close Encounters
of the Third Kind* and to take it, too, as a mandalic geometaphor. Of
course, a conical mountain hanging in space may be a bit awkward
(though no more so than the conical capsules of the early astronauts),
but the vision of mandala earth with some sort of paradisal summit
at its center seems acceptable, especially when the mountain is elon-
gated into a cosmic axis or pillar connecting the sky, the earth's surface,
and the underworld. This interconnection, after all, would be particularly pertinent to the mythic significance of the Space Age, when
our having achieved the cosmic heights of the sky allows, and may
demand, a new relationship to the earth.

The center, at any rate, is crucial to both the mandala and the
mountain, as well as to those concentric religious structures which
stand somewhere in between. Mircea Eliade comments that "the mountain, because it is the meeting place of heaven and earth, is situated
at the centre of the world, and is of course the highest point of the earth.
That is why so many sacred places —'holy places', temples, palaces, holy
towns — are likened to 'mountains' and are themselves made 'centres',
become in some magic way part of the summit of the cosmic hill."[13]
Later in his compendium on traditional mythic imagery, *Patterns in
Comparative Religion*, Eliade notes that "the temple of Borobudur," a
stupa-like Buddhist structure in Java, "was itself an image of the cosmos
and was built in the shape of a mountain."[14]

This brings us back around to Giuseppe Tucci's idea of the mandala as a map of the cosmos, almost a geometaphor by definition (and
scientific maps of the world, according to the history of cartography,
have been distorted by subjectivity and cultural bias to the point of
constituting mandalas themselves[15]). To which Tucci adds that

> . . . it is the whole universe in its essential plan, in its process of
> emanation and of reabsorption. The universe not only in its inert
> spatial expanse, but as temporal revolution and both as a vital
> process which develops from an essential principle and rotates
> round a central axis. . . the axis of the world on which the sky rests
> and which sinks its roots into the mysterious substratum.[16]

As I reviewed the many variations on traditional mandala imagery collected by the Argüelleses and others I realized that their significance in the Space Age was not necessarily a direct equivalent of their doctrinal meaning in this or that religion a thousand or more years ago. Applying aspects of the mandala to the earth as I was approaching it in the 1970s required a constant regard for indirect and nontraditional possibilities of meaning, possibilities plural and often imprecise, appropriate to the sort of metaphoric attitude which was needed, I believed, to move from our Apollonic altitudes down to the mysteries of a mythic earth. Even the Jungian use of mandala imagery in evoking the psychic development of modern persons, I suspected, could turn out to be insufficiently metaphoric; that is to say, it could — depending on how the imagery was dealt with — be employed as a too-pat formula transferring traditional mandala teachings unambiguously as the fixed significance of a Space-Age patient's dreams or artwork.

However, with such cautionary thoughts in mind I was prepared to see the whole earth as a mandala which, from our unparalleled contemporary perspective, not only hinted at *its* own meanings but also reflected back enigmatically *our* inner significance as products of the planet. Indeed, *each* of the geometaphors I was surveying might be a mirror for human self-exploration as well as a clue to the nature of our home (or the home of our nature). In either case we were given the opportunity to read "messages from earth" sent to our culture and consciousness to tell us the true story, the deep mythic implications, of our leap into space.

Here, then, were three mythic images of earth, or geometaphors, to consider: the whole earth as jewel or bauble, as eyeball, and as mandala (in all of its many ramifications from magic circle to concentric temple or city and cosmic mountain). From my work on the nature of metaphoric activity in relation to the earth-rooted and mystery-shrouded meanings of myth, I knew that the main point was not to seize *the* metaphor of earth, as though finding the one "correct" geometaphor could penetrate the ambiguity which surrounded the mythic significance I had sought, giving me a clear-cut solution to a problem. Even should such a strategy succeed, it would fail to yield the meaning of the mythos by losing touch with the very qualities which make myth myth.

GARDEN AND MACHINE

Therefore, following the far-out imagination of René Magritte in the continuing quest for a Space-Age mythos, I was propelled toward one of Mailer's American literary forebears and to more of my geometaphors.

One of Magritte's most enigmatic paintings—I saw three versions in my research during the '70s—is called *The Domain of Arnheim*. It presents a range of mountains looming in the background with the central peak in the shape of a bird's head. The foreground contains either a room with a broken window on the fragments of which is painted the identical background visible beyond it, or a balcony wall on which sits a bird's nest with three eggs. The title is, in Magritte's way, expectably and evocatively baffling as a direct denotation of the painting's message. (I wondered for a time whether it could refer to Arnhem Land in the outback of Australia, or even, somehow, to the work on artistic perception of the psychologist Rudolf Arnheim.) It turns out, however, that Magritte's title points quite clearly to a tale by Edgar Allan Poe, or rather to three interlocking tales: "The Domain of Arnheim," "Landor's Cottage," and "The Landscape Garden."

The basic plot of all three of Poe's stories involves the conception and fabrication, by a man of unlimited wealth, of a huge and unique landscape garden. The motivation for this project is explained as the improvement of the only aspect of "wild nature" which seems, to the artistic eye, to suffer from defects or excesses: namely, the *overall composition* of all her particular beauties. And when the narrator of one of the tales wonders why nature should have even *this* "susceptibility of improvement", he is told by Mr. Ellison, the wealthy protagonist, that it may be a matter of our limited perspective.

This leads to a fanciful but instructive speculation, as recounted by the narrator: "'It is easily understood,' says Mr. Ellison, 'that what might improve a closely scrutinized detail, might, at the same time injure a general and more distantly observed effect'. . .There *might be* a class of beings, human once, but now to humanity invisible, for whose refined appreciation of the beautiful, more especially than for our own, had been set in order by God the great landscape-garden of *the whole earth*."[17]

Here, some 125 years in advance of Steward Brand's *Catalog,* Poe has himself italicized the phrase "the whole earth" in a passage which suggests in a most direct manner another geometaphor, one which sparked multiple associations in my mind when I first discovered it in its rather obscure literary setting. The image of the garden actually overlapped with the mandala image to some extent, since square or rectangular walled gardens figure in Islamic iconography—and, through this, in Persian rug designs—as a mandalic vision of paradise; indeed the word "paradise" comes from the Persian where it means "walled garden". Joseph Campbell has pointed out that the returning Apollo 8 astronauts saw the earth as "the one oasis in all space, an extraordinary kind of sacred grove, as it were, set apart for the rituals of life. . ."[18] The focus on the center in the case of the garden mandala reveals, most often, a fountain whose waters, in *axis mundi* fashion, interconnect underworld, earth, and heaven. According to the Argüelleses, the Muslim mystic Ed-Din conceived of the spiritual universe as "the Garden of the Essence", the center of which is the Essence itself. This latter he compared in turn to "a fire in which all is burnt, and also to a fountain—the Fountain of Paradise—from which all pours forth".[19]

To the extent that the garden geometaphor focuses on the earth as an *organic* entity there also arises the related notion of the mandalic world center (where the world axis breaks the earth's surface, which sometimes means the summit of the world mountain) as an *omphalos* or navel. Eliade quotes Wensinck's account in *The Ideas of the Western Semites Concerning the Navel of the Earth* of a sacred text which said that "the Holy One created the world like an embryo. As the embryo proceeds from the navel onwards, so God began to create the world from its navel onwards, and from there it was spread out in different directions."[20] At the same time this world navel is seen as a sacred stone: the *bethel* (Beth-El is Hebrew for "House of God") where Jacob had his dream of the ladder of angels—certainly an *axis mundi*—or the definitive omphalos itself, the traditionally conical or pyramidal white stone at the shrine of Apollo in Delphi. Geometaphorically this indicates that not only may the earth be seen as a megalith in the blackness of space but that its center or navel can be visualized as another stone, one classically related to the presiding deity of the program and the mentality that landed men on the moon.

But if the garden image retrospectively deepened the geometaphors of mandala and megalith, its organic focus led me to new whole earth images and implications as well. Initially I was reminded of the garden's opposite, the machine, in the form of Buckminster Fuller's famous Spaceship Earth image. I had read Fuller's *Operating Manual for Spaceship Earth*, published the year of the Apollo 11 mission, and had found his assertion that "our spaceship is. . .a mechanical vehicle" highly dubious.[21]

I felt vaguely upon first reading Fuller what John Woodcock articulated clearly a decade later in the *Michigan Quarterly Review*'s 1979 issue on "The Moon Landing and Its Aftermath": ". . .whatever truth there is in Fuller's view, the Earth is not entirely mechanical, and we now possess knowledge of only the smallest pieces of it. Fuller's Spaceship Earth seems oversimplified in the way it subsumes the biological and political realms under the laws of mechanics."[22] Woodcock entitles his essay "The Garden in the Machine: Variations on Spaceship Earth", and the chief variation he addresses is the Princeton University physicist Gerard O'Neill's idea of orbiting space colonies as the solution to our current problems of overpopulation, energy, and ecology.

O'Neill, says Woodcock, envisions "total human control over nature", but actually neglects the organic aspects of his colonies, thinking it sufficient merely "to surround the garden with the machine". Woodcock is strongly critical of such an attitude:

> O'Neill assures us that all this can be done with current technology, but we see no awareness of the complexity and dynamism that distinguish the organic sphere from the mechanical sphere, no discussion of the real unknowns, which are the biological and social challenges of putting together, and keeping together, an almost completely artificial and self-sufficient biosphere for human habitation. O'Neill appears equally oblivious to the problematic realms of space colony psychology and politics. In this he reminds us very much of Fuller. His dream, his proposal, flowers beautifully in the mechanical realm, but one wonders: will anything else?[23]

That was also my worry when O'Neill's idea was first publicized in the mid '70s. I had seen the science fiction film *Silent Running* in 1973 and had been at first attracted to its vision of lovingly tended greenhouses floating through space, but even in the film the gardener-hero resorts to homicide in working out his relation to those who have authority over the spaceship which encompasses his garden. Moreover, O'Neill's space colonies struck me as miniatures of Fuller's view which pointed up in another way the shortcomings of the latter: the Spaceship Earth emphasis could indeed transform the planet we have known into a *colony* instead of a *home*, and give us a "canned" version of organic life on earth.

Because the college where I had taught since 1973 sponsored a program on "social ecology" every summer during the second half of the decade I was aware of the more promising work of John Todd, an annual guest lecturer in the program. Todd was the director of the New Alchemy Institute, begun on Cape Cod, Massachusetts, in that same epochal year when men first walked on the moon. Like O'Neill's space colonies, Todd's small "designed biosystems habitats"—such as the Ark, built by the New Alchemists on Prince Edward Island, Canada—are miniature worlds or, as he calls them, "terrestrial capsules".[24] But John Woodcock is quick to point out that "the two critical differences between the Ark and O'Neill's space colonies are, first, the care with which the organic side of things has been worked out for the Ark, and, second, the fact that the Ark's biological and climatic systems are linked, or coupled, with an essentially supportive exterior garden environment, which makes them inherently more stable than those whose exterior environment is outer space."[25]

I also knew that Todd's involvement with my college's social ecology program bespoke a significant concern for the psychology and especially the politics of his terrestrial capsules. Given my own concerns, however, I was additionally impressed that Todd had made central use of two terms with metaphoric connections to ancient religio-mythic themes: the Ark and alchemy.

As I came back to the geometaphor of the garden itself I thought of at least two other recent visions of the earth which stressed the organic over the mechanistic. One was Lewis Thomas's view of the earth as a fragile cell-like organism within which human beings are a kind of nervous system. This image from *The Lives of a Cell* in 1974 accorded intriguingly for me with William Gordon's idea that metaphoric activity is rooted in the "rich, symbol-making earth of the nervous system itself". Thomas's view thus suggested that metaphorizing was in a fundamental sense *the* human function within the earth organism. It is also worth noting in this context his declaration concerning language as the uniquely human mode of biological communication: "Ambiguity seems to be an essential, indispensable element for the transfer of information from one place to another by words, where matters of real importance are concerned."[26] All of this was powerful testimony from a biologist to the reality of the connection I was exploring between mythic images, treated as such by means of metaphorizing, and the planet of our origins.

The second variation on the image of an organic earth came from James Lovelock's "Gaia hypothesis", a notion of the earth as an autonomous being creating and adjusting the organic conditions, from the atmosphere to human life, necessary for its own continuance. Lovelock, an English scientist, got the name for his theory from a Wiltshire neighbor, the novelist William Golding—whose spell-binding account of prehistoric terrestrial culture I recalled reading years earlier in the novel *The Inheritors*.[27]

Gaia (sometimes spelled "Gaea") or Ge is the name of the ancient pre-Olympian Earth Goddess of Greece. As it happened, this same geometaphor came to me from yet another association with the garden image of earth. In probing the implications of the latter image I had had recourse to a brilliant historical study of "the esthetics of nature" called *Man in the Landscape* by Paul Shepard, whose caricature of Fuller's Spaceship Earth vision—Shepard described it, I believe, as "the great tool-and-die works in the sky"—I had also noted sympathetically in a newspaper review. The Shepard book contains a chapter on "The Image of the Garden" with the provocative claim that "men's best communication to one another about the nature of the world is made in garden art, and . . . the message is Mama."[28]

MOTHER EARTH

Once again by way of the garden I had encountered Gaia, Mother Earth, the furrowed field and fruitful harvest being related in the mythologies of many traditional cultures to the processes of fertility and birth, or death and rebirth. Along with the presence of witches and their rituals in the midst of a megalith geometaphor like the Rollright Stones, this implied to me that the move from the masculinized moon of the Apollo landings to the archaic imagery of earth is among other things an odyssey in search of woman's mysteries and a shift in our orientation towards psychological femaleness—what those attuned to emerging currents of feminist spirituality have termed "the return of the Goddess". This struck me as an image of earth authorized by its own deepest etymological foundations: given the etymology of the word "etymology" (which goes back to the Greek *etymos*, meaning true or genuine), Gaia was a "true naming" of earth, the identity of the "ge" in "geometry" and in my "geometaphor".

The geometaphor of woman was indeed deserving of whatever sensitivity a male researcher could muster in exploring its implications for a Space-Age mythos.

CHAPTER FIVE

THE MANY GUISES OF THE GODDESS

For the ten miles or so between St. Just and St. Ives the B3306 highway twists along above the Atlantic ramparts of Cornwall's West Penwith coast. Except for these two towns there are no other saints' names to be found on this granite shoreline of abandoned tin mines and pre-historic remains. The stony villages one drives through on this route — Morvah, Treen, Zennor — were to be sure swept into Methodism by John Wesley's stirring visits in the 1740s. But they are of even greater religious interest for certain non-Christian associations. This upland area of Cornwall's southwesternmost district was for centuries a center of witchcraft.

ALONG THE WITCHCRAFT COAST OF CORNWALL, SUMMER 1979

On the sunny first Sunday of August in 1979 my wife, our two youngest daughters, and I cruised north in our rented car up the B3306 toward St. Ives. We had just left a side road between Morvah and Madron from which we had walked to the Men-an-tol, a doughnut-shaped stone flanked by two perpendicular menhirs. These stones had been set up in neolithic times, perhaps as part of a burial chamber with the hole-stone providing a 15-inch circular entrance. In more recent ages, and as part of the local practice of witchcraft, babies were passed through the hole nine times "widdershins"— against the sun or counterclockwise —as a cure for scrofula or rickets. According to Eleanor Bertine's *Jung's Contribution to Our Time*, C. G. Jung, a large man, had squeezed through the opening 59 years before in a somewhat whimsical ritual of initiation and rebirth. This would have been while he was holding a small seminar at Sennen Cove, a village back down the coast beyond St. Just and a short cliffside walk from Land's End, the last jutting promontory of Cornwall and of mainland England.[1]

We had visited Sennen Cove early that morning and found the hotel at the end of Marias Lane, overlooking the village and Whitesand Bay, where Jung and his party had most likely stayed in 1920. Although slimmer than Jung I felt strangely reluctant, for reasons it took me months to understand fully, to reproduce his crawl through the Men-an-tol, even after my wife and daughters scrambled through in a cele-bratory mood: the next day would be Jennifer's eleventh birthday.

The Sunday we happened to visit the Men-an-tol was the day of the annual Morvah Fair, commemorating, so legend says, the marriage feast of Jack the Hammer and Genevra, the daughter of a giant named Tom and his wife Joan. I later read in William Bottrell's nineteenth-century *Traditions and Hearthside Stories of West Cornwall* the state-ment that "in Jack the Hammer and Genevra, or An Jinnifer as she came familiarly to be called, many of the ancient families of Morvah and the adjacent parishes had their rise."[2] Less than two miles from where we had stood at the Men-an-tol was Chun Castle, an Iron Age hill fort to which the folk tales assign the role of Jack and Genevra's dwelling place.[3]

The Men-an-tol holestone itself certainly qualified as one of my mandalic geometaphors, a magic circle which was a megalith as well. However, at the time of my visit I was more intent on the sexual sym-bolism of the Men-an-tol as a kind of birth canal, a visual metaphor heightened by the presence of the two phallic menhirs standing upright in front of and behind the holestone. On the ground nearby a discarded carton which had contained prophylactics was a blunt suggestion that powers of fertility were still presumed to linger on the moors and tors surrounding the Men-an-tol. On the horizon was the circle of stand-ing stones known as the Nine Maidens. Like the nineteen Merry Maid-ens at Boleigh some miles to the south these stones were imagined by the early Christians of the area to have been young women who were petrified for dancing on the Sabbath.

As we continued north along the coast, dodging an occasional tour bus on the narrow, hedge-flanked highway, we came to the village of Zennor, a name which Bottrell says is Cornish for "holy land".[4] We drove right through the village that day—to my eventual regret when I learned that this was the home of the "white witches", or "Charmers", of Zennor, usually old women skilled in herbal medicine and the casting of spells to counteract the "ill-wishing" of "black witches". One in particular, Margaret Daniel, attracted my attention since Daniel is my mother's maiden name, from whom I derive my own first name. In a booklet on *Cornish Customs and Superstitions* which seems to have been excerpted from Robert Hunt's 1865 *Popular Romances of the West of England* (many of these romances in turn taken from Bottrell's writings) I read that the Zennor Charmers were especially famous for being able to stop bleeding—the bleeding, for instance, of a stuck pig— just by *thinking* of a charm. An informant wrote as follows about visiting one of these white witches left in the Zennor area a century ago: "I found her to be a really clever, sensible woman. She was reading a learned treatise on ancient history."[5]

Another little pamphlet I acquired in Cornwall claimed that one could become a Cornish witch by climbing nine times onto the Giant's Rock by the roadside above Zennor, a rock which used to be a "logan", or rocking, stone almost impossible to balance upon. I was also informed that "all Cornish witches regarded the wild and lonely place called Trewa, near Zennor, as their home. . .The exact spot where they met was marked by a massive pile of granite blocks known as the Witches' Rock. This has now unfortunately been removed. Formerly, to touch it was a safeguard against bad luck."[6]

But I learned all this about Zennor and its Charmers, as I say, only later, so that after slowing down the car for a few S-curves between granite cottages we were quickly north of the village on the way toward St. Ives. I have supposed that my lack of information at the time is what caused me to neglect Zennor, but perhaps the same strange reluctance that had seized me at the Men-an-tol was to blame.

Another similar incident that August Sunday along that coast I cannot attribute to my being uninformed. In planning our trip to England I had bought an Ordnance Survey map of the West Penwith, or Land's End, district of Cornwall. These maps, as anyone knows who has rambled around England, are almost unbelievably detailed: the scale is one-and-a-quarter inches to the mile, and every prehistoric megalith and tumulus is marked, as are many individual houses and barns. It was while studying—I think I could justifiably say meditating over—this map of isolated Cornwall's farthest coast that I happened upon the name of a settlement just north of Zennor consisting, so it seemed, of just two farmhouses with their outbuildings.

The name of this less-than-hamlet, on a narrow lane down toward the ocean from the B3306, was Wicca. The map also showed a small stream flowing nearby which emptied into the Atlantic less than a mile below at an inlet called Wicca Pool.

WOMEN'S RELIGIOUS EXPERIENCE AND
THE EMERGENCE OF WICCA
(A MALE'S SURVEY OF FEMINIST SCHOLARSHIP)

As I pondered my map in the early summer of 1979 this five-letter word effectively summed up for me the entire issue of the nature of women's religious experience, an issue I had been trying to deal with since the beginning of the decade in my role as an academic humanist in the field of Religious Studies. The word *wicca* was one that etymology had discovered at the roots of our words "witch" and "witchcraft".

I had first encountered this term only in 1977, at the behest of the "Women and Religion" group at the annual meeting of my professional society, the American Academy of Religion or AAR. This same group, however, had been concerned with the issue of women's religious experience since its founding at the 1971 meeting, when Carol Christ, then a graduate student at Yale, convened the organization and gathered the votes to elect Professor Christine Downing of Douglass College to the Vice-Presidency of the AAR as a whole. This insured her automatic succession to the Presidency in 1974, the first time a woman had held that office. Chris Downing had been my graduate school colleague at Drew University in the early '60s—her paper on "Daydreams" followed mine on "Metaphor" at that 1971 meeting, and the next year she chaired the first Women and Religion session on the theme "Myth and Sexual Stereotype." Throughout the '70s I was privileged, as Chris Downing's friend, to receive copies of her careful essays on the concept of myth and her moving personal pieces on the contemporary religious relevance of the ancient Greek goddesses.

Since one of my academic specialties is the relation of literature to religion, I was particularly interested to witness Carol Christ's efforts to interpret women's literature as a reflection of women's religious experience. She developed this theme in papers on the novels of Doris Lessing and Margaret Atwood at the AAR meetings of 1973 and 1974. The latter conference also saw the emergence of another feminist scholar working in my second major area of interest, the psychology of religion. Naomi Goldenberg's paper on "Female Religious Experience in Jungian Psychoanalysis" in 1974 was the first of several in which she creatively criticized and adapted to feminist purposes the depth psychology of Freud and Jung. The 1974 AAR meeting afforded me personal contact with these two women—and with their colleague, the theologian Judith Plaskow— when I served with them as the only male on a panel of fifteen to discuss "Women's Experiences as a Basis for Theology".

During the next two annual meetings Christ, Goldenberg, and Plaskow continued to be active, as the Women and Religion group was elevated to the more permanent status of a "discipline section". In 1975 all three women made presentations from their respective areas of specialization to a session on "The Feminist Transformation of Religious Studies", while Naomi Goldenberg's 1976 paper, "Freud, Fathers, and the Jewish and Christian Religions", included the first invocation of the Goddess as a direct alternative to the patriarchal image of deity that I can recall at these annual American Academy of Religion conclaves (although the Goddess had also been invoked the previous April at a special conference on women's spirituality in Boston). The 1976 meeting also featured a panel discussion on polytheism in which I participated along with Chris Downing and James Hillman. Also on the panel was David Miller of Syracuse University, another friend from Drew Graduate School a decade before, whose 1974 book *The New Polytheism* had set forth theologically the case Hillman had made from the direction of Jungian psychology: that the Greek gods and goddesses are once again relevant to our inner lives.[7]

By the time the AAR members convened in San Francisco in 1977 these currents—literature, psychology, and theology's relations to the specific religious experience of women; the new interest in polytheistic mythology; the beginning of Goddess-worship as a desirable focus for feminist religion scholarship as well as feminist spirituality—all seemed to converge.

For one thing, Carol Christ and Naomi Goldenberg chaired a

workshop on "Wicca, Ancient and Modern: Phenomenology and Problems in Research". For another, Goldenberg introduced Zsuzsanna ("Z") Budapest, a practicing witch and feminist who, it turned out, had founded the Susan B. Anthony Coven #1 in Los Angeles a few weeks after Carol Christ had organized the Women and Religion group at the 1971 AAR meeting.

In San Francisco Z Budapest spoke and showed slides on "Wicce and the Return of the Goddess" (I found out afterward that the most frequently used term for modern witchcraft, "Wicca", is, curiously enough, a masculine noun, which may be why she used "Wicce", the feminine form). Budapest's slide presentation was not a scholarly one, but her personal presence was witty and powerful, and the predominantly female academic audience responded enthusiastically. As I took all this in at the 1977 meeting I reflected on how far the Women and Religion group had come in just six years, and how far I had come in following as closely as a male scholar could the challenges it was presenting to my field of study. Christ and Goldenberg summed up many of these challenges for me in issuing the following declaration regarding their workshop on Wicca:

> Wicca is an Old English word meaning wise woman. Wicca is also the name of a modern feminist religion with its own symbology, rituals, and practices. It inspires a world view which includes respect for nature and female powers, and for waxing and waning processes in the universe and in the individual. This development in twentieth century religion deserves the attention of scholars. But the study of the religion of Wicca raises problems of verifiability of historical claims; moreover, scholars must also dispel confusions with Satanism and prejudices against pagan religions.[8]

Pertinent developments in the period between my 1977 discovery that there was such a religion as Wicca—a religion the study of which pointed up with special sharpness the issues surrounding the nature of women's religious experience—and my discovery of a piece of earth actually named Wicca on my Ordnance Survey map early in the summer of 1979 can be summarized quickly.

I think it is fair to say that as far as the academic field of Religious Studies in America was concerned the transformations represented by the work of feminist scholars like Downing, Christ, Goldenberg, and Plaskow impinged on traditional scholarly approaches and assumptions even more insistently in the ensuing two years. Carol Christ lectured on "Why Women Need the Goddess" to a 1978 conference entitled "The Great Goddess Re-Emerging", and the next year she and Judith Plaskow edited *Womanspirit Rising: A Feminist Reader in Religion.*[9] This text included selections by Z Budapest and Starhawk, another witch whose own book, *The Spiral Dance: A Rebirth of the Ancient Religion of the Great Goddess,*[10] was also published in 1979. Finally, Naomi Goldenberg's *Changing of the Gods: Feminism and the End of Traditional Religions*[11] recapitulated her explorations of Freudian and Jungian psychologies of religion as well as featuring a chapter called "Feminist Witchcraft—the Goddess Is Alive!"

"FEMINIST WITCHCRAFT—THE GODDESS IS ALIVE!"

This and subsequent chapters of Goldenberg's new book provided a valuable focus for my thinking on the Goddess geometaphor as I headed for England that summer and underwent the experiences on the coast of Cornwall which came to feel centrally important to my search for a Space-Age mythos. Over the years at Goddard College between 1973 and 1978 I had supervised scores of individualized independent study projects by adult undergraduates, most of them women and many of these concerned with the meaning of women's religious experience. In the spring of 1979 one of these students, a woman who was later accepted into the graduate program at the University of Ottawa where Naomi Goldenberg teaches, lent me her copy of *Changing of the Gods.*

I was immediately struck by the discussion, in Goldenberg's witchcraft chapter, of the term which had increasingly fascinated me during the previous two years:

> Currently, most modern witches use the Old English word *wicca* to refer to a witch as a "wise woman." Etymologists quibble over this usage. About the only fact on which scholars and witches agree is that the first syllable, *wic,* has something to do with words that meant "to bend or twist." The word *wicker* and the Old English term for weave seem to be derived from *wic.* Since modern witches are very concerned with weaving in a metaphoric sense—with weaving spells and learning how to bend the world to their will, I see nothing inappropriate in referring to a witch as "wicca." We can consider the Old English term as having been reborn, so that it actually does mean "wise woman" in current usage.[12]

I was impressed with Goldenberg's sensitivity to the metaphoric possibilities of the etymology of *wicca* (I later learned that the root *wic* can also imply one who is flexible, compliant with the changing forces of the world). Another helpful contribution of Goldenberg's chapter was her summary of the guises of the triple Goddess: Witches, she writes, "teach that the feminine life force, i.e., the Goddess, appears in three forms—the maiden, the mother, and the crone."[13] The maiden, exemplified by Athena, Diana, or Kore, would be any young, unattached, or temporarily solitary woman who maintains her independence, her psychic virginity. The mother was a nurturing, life-giving presence such as Demeter, Hera, or Gaia. "Whenever a woman nurtures either a person or an enterprise," Goldenberg explains, "witches consider her a mother."[14] The crone, like Hecate of Greek myth, would be the older woman who finds and conveys wisdom or prophecy past menopause. Here in witchcraft's figure of the triple Goddess with its affirmation of woman's changing styles and stages of life was some of the flexibility implied by the term *wicca*.

This same flexible approach was suggested by the lunar imagery which witches associate with the Goddess: "The waxing moon is the maiden, the full moon is the mother, and the waning moon is the crone."[15] This, again, is Robert Graves's White Goddess, not only an emblem of witchcraft's acceptance of psychological transformation, but also, in the context of my own research on the Space-Age mythos, a much more cooperative, positive vision of the relation between the earth and the moon than the one promoted by Apollo's mission of conquest and analysis. Indeed, after his interviews with those he called "Apollonic moon scientists" Ian Mitroff had reported in his 1974 *Spring* essay that "it was *man*, not mankind, who in body, spirit, and soul took us to the moon, who landed on the moon, who took back some of that precious moon, and finally who analyzed that moonstuff. Nowhere in all of this was the feminine principle present."[16] The attitude with which the NASA project was carried out was all part of what Mitroff's editor James Hillman had already characterized, in his *Myth of Analysis*, as "the Apollonic fantasy, with its distance to materiality."[17] Certainly such a venture was very distant from the earth- and moon-reverencing priorities of witchcraft's worship of the triple Goddess.

But what, I wondered, of the *man* who finds himself in the midst of "witches"—in my case the feminist scholars of religion I had tried to stay in touch with during the '70s, or all the "wise women" whose work I had presumed to supervise over the years of my teaching at Goddard? Goldenberg had written that "because all forms of witchcraft give the

Goddess a male consort known as the Horned God all forms of witch-craft have the potential for including men in the mythology and rituals of the coven." Reading this was encouraging, but she went on to say that "in feminist witchcraft, the Goddess is valued more highly than the God, with the result that women have a higher position in the power structure." Moreover, in the "Dianic" branch of feminist witchcraft the separatist ways of the Goddess Diana are emulated and men are entirely excluded. Goldenberg closed out this discussion by quoting a male member of a non-Dianic coven: "'Men need to be humble in this time of history,' he said."[18]

THE INCIDENTAL MALE AND THE VIRGIN MOTHER GODDESS

Encountering all this in *Changing of the Gods* in the spring of 1979, I was far from certain whether I was humble enough to satisfy either feminist witches or the imperatives of contemporary cultural history, the history which would include what I had been interpreting as the Space Age. It did occur to me, however, that the sort of recep-tivity I was trying to cultivate in connection with my metaphorizing might require a dose of this very quality espoused by Goldenberg's male witch. In any event, when I found myself on the coast of Cornwall a few months later it is entirely possible that being humble — or being humbled — played a crucial part in my rather curious behavior.

I have already recounted my untoward reluctance to squeeze through the opening of the Men-an-tol holestone despite the willing acrobatics of my wife and daughters and the example of a burly Jung six decades earlier. I have also implied the coincidences between my daughter Jennifer's name and that of Jack the Hammer's wife Genevra, or An Jinnifer, but I should mention that there were several more: I have said that Genevra's mother was the giant's wife Joan — my wife's name is Joanna; I have referred to Jung's 1920 seminar at the Sennen Cove Hotel on Marias Lane — my daughter Jennifer's middle name is Marianne and my wife's maiden name is Lane; our other daughter ac-companying us that day in Cornwall was Susannah, not so far from Zsuzsana — as in Z Budapest — or even from the sound elements of "Susan B. Anthony," the name Z Budapest took for her feminist coven. These were, to be sure, far-fetched connections, but I have already em-phasized in discussing William Gordon's *Synectics* the importance of chance conjunctions to the metaphorizing process, and in any case, they suggested to me in their unscientific fashion that I may have been in the presence of the triple Goddess there on the coast of Cornwall — my daughter, my wife, and my mother expanding their identities, through these casual coincidences of nomenclature, into the maiden, the mother, and the crone.

Something, or someone, surely seemed to have humbled me, to have made me feel as incidental as the character Joe whom Margaret Atwood's heroine in the novel *Surfacing* selects to ritualistically impregnate her. Carol Christ had commented on this scene in her paper on Atwood, a paper I happened to figure in myself because after a reading at Goddard by Atwood and a discussion between me and Christ at the 1974 AAR meeting I became a somewhat incidental intermediary between female novelist and feminist critic during the revising of the paper for publication. I therefore had a special interest in seeing the final version printed in the journal *Signs* in 1976; I was particularly struck by her treatment of Joe's humble role in *Surfacing* and remembered it as I reflected on my Cornish experiences of 1979. Christ's comment on the ritual impregnation was that "as she conceives, the protagonist resembles the Virgin Mother Goddesses of old: at one with nature and her sexual power, in tune with the rhythms of the moon, complete in herself, the male being incidental."[19]

Another element of great interest to me was that at this point in her text Christ cites the chapter on "The Virgin Goddess" from M. Esther Harding's *Woman's Mysteries: Ancient and Modern.* Harding's book, a study focusing on the image of the moon from a Jungian perspective, had first been published in England in 1935, had gone out of print for over thirty years, and was re-issued by an American publisher in 1971, the year of her death. I had read the 1973 paperback edition, but I cannot have been very well attuned to its meanings at the time, for it took an essay on the book by Christine Downing somewhat later to bring home to me the importance of Esther Harding's idea of virginity.

"The Moon Goddess," says Harding, "belongs to a matriarchal, not to a patriarchal, system. She is not related to any god as wife or 'counterpart.' She is her own mistress, virgin, one-in-herself."[20] And, as Downing adds in her essay, "Harding suggests that in the same way we might call any woman, whether married or not, virgin if she, too, has her center in herself, does not do what she does to please or attract or win the approval of another, to gain his interest or love, is not dependent on what others think."[21]

For Chris Downing, recalling an encounter with Esther Harding at Drew University in the early '60s, it was this sense of virginity as an "in-one-self-ness" beyond physical chastity which was the most significant of the "woman's mysteries" explored by Harding's book. And if I remembered this same concept in Atwood's novel and in the non-fiction of Christ, Harding, and Downing it was not only because I was musing on my strong sense of being an incidental male at the Men-an-tol. In addition I was realizing that Esther Harding had also been on this Cornish coast in the 1920s; like Eleanor Bertine she had participated in the small seminars Jung had held here — Harding's notes are the most complete record we have of the 1923 seminar at Polzeath, some forty miles up the Atlantic coast from the Land's End area which included Sennen Cove, the Men-an-tol, and Wicca.[22] I also knew that John Layard, a Jungian psychologist and anthropologist who spent the last years of his life in Cornwall, had written an essay in 1944 in which he discussed "the virgin archetype", drawing on Harding's *Woman's Mysteries* and supplementing her mythological data with his own clinical evidence.[23]

ENCOUNTER AT WICCA, CORNWALL

With all these associations in mind, geographical as well as bibliographical, it is perhaps not so surprising that I was seized with a certain humility, conceivably at the pleasure of the Goddess, on that coast of witchcraft and antiquities. As we rounded a sweeping curve at the bottom of an incline a few miles north of Zennor, Joanna, following the course of the B3306 on the Ordnance Survey map, cautioned me to slow down. A tiny lane turned off sharply down to the left as the highway curved right. Driving on the left, I needed only to pull off into the top of the lane. I stopped the car, double-checked the map, and got out.

Below me green pastures hedged with stones stretched down to cliffs above the Atlantic. The lane led down to several houses almost hidden by tall trees. This was Wicca.

As I contemplated driving on down to the houses my attention was for some reason drawn to the ground at my feet. There lay a black feather, which I picked up. I then looked idly over to my near left, where several cows were grazing on the hillside. I suddenly did a doubletake

as I saw one cow, some sixty yards from me, facing the Atlantic, standing somehow horizontally on the downward-sloping diagonal of the
pasture. I squinted in the glare of that sunny Sunday until I could make
out a large recumbent granite stone under the cow's front legs, which
she was standing on as if it were a balcony overlooking the rootops of
Wicca. Without shifting her uncanny stance she turned her head and
looked at me.

I fingered the black feather for a moment, snapped a picture of the
still-staring cow, and climbed back behind the wheel of our little Cortina. I started the engine and moved back onto the B3306, heading
north. I caught a final glimpse of the cow in my rear view mirror; my
heart was pounding.

I had no idea what sort of omen the black feather might be, aside
from the usual negative connotations of blackness in white culture and
the connection of black crows with sorcery. But finding the feather at
my feet unnerved me in any case. And I hardly think I would have
noticed, let alone responded to, an ordinary collection of cows as part
of the foreground of my perspective above Wicca. The posture of the
cow perched on the stone, however, the cow who seemed to be standing on a nonexistent plane and who stared at me so unflinchingly, was
another matter. My reaction to her stance and scrutiny went beyond
being unnerved to physical symptoms of anxiety.

Once again, and even more so than at the Men-an-tol, I was being
humbled, and the signs struck me through a most visceral message that
this was not the time for a visit to Wicca. Since neither my wife nor
my daughters shared my curiosity about the settlement, and all three
wanted to get on with our trip, they scarcely questioned my hasty
resumption of the drive north.

THE HOLY COW'S HUMBLING PLAY

As a mythic image the cow made more sense to me than the black
feather. Several months earlier, at a conference in Montana in conjunction with the total solar eclipse visible there, I had met the novelist
Rhoda Lerman and discussed with her some of my speculations on the
mythic significance of the Space Age. I was already familiar with her
1973 novel *Call Me Ishtar*, an uproarious account — based in part on
The First Sex by the feminist author Elizabeth Gould Davis, whose

obituary Lerman had written for *Ms.*[24]—of the reincarnation of the
ancient Babylonian Virgin Mother Goddess as a suburban Jewish house-
wife in Syracuse, New York. The novel begins with a letter:

> To Whom It may Concern:
> What am I doing here? It is very simple. Your world is a mess.
> A Mess.
> Your laws are inhuman. Your religion is without love. Your love
> is without religion and both, undirected, are useless. Your pastrami
> is stringy, and I am bored by your degeneracy.
> But what's a mother to do? I'm here to bring it all back together
> again. I have always been the connection between heaven and earth,
> between man and woman, between thought and act, between
> everything. If your philosophers insist the world is a dichotomy,
> tell them that two plus two don't make four unless something
> brings them together. The connection has been lost.
> But I'm back. Cordially yours.
> I remain,
> Your Mother/Harlot/Maiden/Wife
> (The Queen of Heaven)
> P.S. Call me Ishtar[25]

Starting with the title pun on *Moby Dick*'s opening line—which I
especially appreciated as one who had written a doctoral dissertation
on Melville—*Call Me Ishtar* becomes more and more outrageous,
raunchy, and irreverent. With all this, however, it is genuinely intent
on affirming the prepatriarchal values represented by Ishtar, who was
no doubt as disrespectful of suburban-style gentilities as Rhoda Lerman. Late in the novel the reincarnated Ishtar's beleaguered husband
asks her in exasperation if she takes anything seriously. "'Oh, yes.' She
touched his sleeve. 'People who can't take jokes.'"[26]

In her chapter on Ishtar in *Woman's Mysteries*, Esther Harding had
noted that Ishtar not only dispensed fertility but also the prerequisite
sexual desire,[27] confirming the claim of Rhoda Lerman's Ishtar to be
the supplier of all connections. Harding went on to comment on some
of the specific images, or guises, under which Ishtar was venerated:
"From the inscriptions and invocations which have been preserved on
monuments, coins, and the like, we can gather something of the ancients' conception of her qualities and power. She is represented as All-
Goddess, Queen of Heaven, the Honored One, The Heavenly Cow."[28]
Harding further pointed out that as Hathor, the Horned Crescent, the
cow was also an image of Ishtar's Egyptian counterpart Isis.[29]

At the conference in Montana, an event organized around the

phenomenon of the moon's completely covering the face of the sun, Rhoda Lerman had spoken on the nursery rhyme which contains the line "and the cow jumped over the moon". She was working on her fourth novel, a story about a young girl on the holy Scottish isle of Iona in the fifth century who has been transformed into a cow.[30]

I cannot say how many of these details I recalled upon encountering the cow in the pasture above Wicca. I know I was reminded of Rhoda Lerman's "holy cows" in a general way because I had arranged for her to give a reading at Goddard College on that same August weekend of our tour around southwestern Cornwall. The black feather and the staring cow—a magically horizontal Ishtar or Hathor—had, as I have indicated, frightened me away, humbled me. The realization that Rhoda Lerman was reading from her "cow-manuscript" across the Atlantic at Goddard while I was having these Cornish encounters with the Goddess gradually introduced another emotion into my consciousness as I drove north.

To come right out with it, I began to seem faintly ludicrous to myself. My humbling, as I thought of the wildly light-hearted Goddess-worship manifested in *Call Me Ishtar*, felt more and more humorous as well. And if the Virgin Mother had been playing a joke on a prideful male perhaps the lesson was to laugh along at my own timidity that day while gaining, in the bargain, a bit more of that elusive receptivity I knew was required for an appropriately metaphorical approach to the mysteries of a mythic earth.

At some point in this process I also remembered that Naomi Goldenberg concludes her chapter on "Feminist Witchcraft—The Goddess Is Alive!" with a list of twelve key factors in "the phenomenology of modern witchcraft". The last of these factors is play: "Play is omnipresent in witchcraft. Rituals always have fun and jokes that are encouraged and truly spontaneous."[31]

BROUGHT DOWN TO EARTH BY HER FLEXIBLE CRAFT

As I began to reckon with the humor as well as the humbling of that August day, the coincidences continued to mount. Our next stop an hour or so north of Wicca on the Cornish Atlantic coast was an abandoned Royal Air Force airfield at St. Eval. Here the church of that name at the end of the runway had over the centuries been a beacon for ships trying to avoid the jagged Bedruthan Steps along the nearby shoreline — so much so that Bristol shipowners had paid to have a new tower for the St. Eval Church constructed a hundred years ago. During the Second World War the St. Eval tower had become another sort of beacon, providing a glide path for RAF planes coming in to land on that frequently foggy coast. An RAF flag hanging in the sanctuary, plaques on the wall, and airmen's graves in the churchyard were all silent evidence of the activity that had occurred at this now-deserted spot some thirty-five years earlier. We had stopped at St. Eval on our way back toward London because of my interest in the life and writings of Arthur C. Clarke, a figure of possible significance to my imaginings on the Space-Age who had been stationed here in 1944. I had not been prepared to find an RAF gravestone with the surname "Noel" on it from those war years, nor the name "Sampson Noel" listed as the church's vicar in the thirteenth century. Another conjunction in nomenclature was even more telling.

Several days earlier, browsing in a bookstore, I had looked up "St. Eval" in Christopher Bice's *Names for the Cornish: Three Hundred Cornish Christian Names.* I had found that the word "eval" may stem from the Latin *humilis,* from which in turn is derived the Cornish *huvel,* or "humble".[32] But the Latin *humilis,* I already knew, comes from *humus:* "ground or earth". This strongly suggested that St. Eval may have meant "St. Humble", and that both "eval" and "humble" implied, in effect, "down to earth".

I also knew that through a more dubious but no less satisfying etymology the word "humorous" had likewise been traced back to the Latin *humus,* so that it, too, contained the deep sense of being down to earth, or being brought down to earth, as in a pratfall after stepping on a banana peel. I had not yet, of course, articulated to myself these relations between terms I would later see as strikingly germane to my experience that day — humbling and humorous — and the name of the church at which two of my namesakes were memorialized. Even at the time, however, I somehow knew that one way or another I had been brought down to earth by the flexible craft of the feminine; my encounters with the Goddess on the far coast of Wicca had given me a geometaphoric vision more personal and thus more powerful than any of the other images of earth I had explored in the '70s.

III
GROUNDING

CHAPTER SIX

EARTH AS THE MOTHER OF METAPHORIZING

In my exploration of the geometaphor of woman I found that Naomi Goldenberg's *Changing of the Gods* pointed me to several interconnected issues pertaining to the perception of the earth—or the earthy: physical nature, flesh, matter—as feminine.[1] This relationship between the interpretation of earth images, on the one hand, and some of feminist spirituality's insights into nature as female and earth as mother or goddess, on the other, required careful reflection, since it led me beyond the notion that earth merely supplies the images for interpretation to the possibility that, in a certain sense, the planet itself also endorses the appropriate method for doing so.

"HOW WE KNOW"—
FEMINIST AFFIRMATIONS OF BODY, NATURE, MATTER

The chapter called "The Mirror and Mysticism" in Goldenberg's book begins by describing the focus of feminist theologians on human experience, an emphasis generally avoided in traditional theology. In particular, of course, this focus was on *women's* experiences and, since reference was made to Valerie Saiving and Judith Plaskow,[2] I was reminded of their symposium "Our Bodies/Our Selves?", at the 1976 American Academy of Religion meetings, which dealt with an especially problematic area of those experiences. As its title question implies, this symposium raised the issue of female bodily processes (menstruation, pregnancy, childbirth, lactation, menopause) which seemed to place women closer to "nature" than to "culture", together with the experience of being stereotyped and denigrated for this supposed connection by a patriarchy which felt itself closer to "culture" and deeply suspicious of a "nature" fit only for domination. Simone de Beauvoir had brought up this controversy in *The Second Sex* some three decades earlier[3] and, following her, anthropologist Sherry Ortner had continued the discussion with her 1974 essay "Is Female to Nature as Male Is to Culture?"[4]

Among other implications of this vexed question was one which impinged sharply on any thinking about the spirituality of women's experience. Carol Christ, whose feminist writings on the relation of religion to literature Goldenberg treats in her "Mirror and Mysticism" chapter, addresses this specific problem in the book which recapitulates those writings. *Diving Deep and Surfacing* starts out by citing both de Beauvoir's judgment that the identification of women with nature is to be opposed by feminists and poet Susan Griffin's more affirmative sense of that connection.[5] Griffin's *Woman and Nature: The Roaring Inside Her* had been, in 1978, an impassioned history of misogynist attitudes and practices over the centuries together with an intuitive exploration of how women might begin to express a new, non-patriarchal vision of their relation to nature. It closes with a series of short, lyrical chapters on "Our Nature", "This Earth", "Forest", "Wind", and "Matter".[6]

This last chapter is subtitled "How We Know" and, after my experience at Wicca on the coast of Cornwall in August of 1979, I was intrigued when I caught up with *Woman and Nature* the next winter to ponder Griffin's use of a blackbird as the image of the freedom or transcendence which she senses is possible in a re-visioned identification of women and nature:

> And she wrote, when I let this bird fly to her own purpose, when this bird flies in the path of his own will, the light from this bird enters my body, and when I see the beautiful arc of her flight, I love this bird, when I see, the arc of her flight, I fly with her, enter her with my mind, leave myself, die for an instant, live in the body of this bird whom I cannot live without, as part of the body of the

bird will enter my daughter's body, because I know I am made from this earth, as my mother's hands were made from this earth, as her dreams came from this earth and all that I know, I know in this earth, the body of the bird, this pen, this paper, these hands, this tongue speaking, all that I know speaks to me through this earth and I long to tell you, you who are earth too, and listen *as we speak to each other of what we know: the light is in us.*[7]

This is the single long sentence with which the book ends and, although Carol Christ acknowledges the depth of the "woman and nature" dilemma as analyzed by de Beauvoir and Ortner, she finally sides with Susan Griffin. Christ declares that women must counter the pernicious culture/nature, or spirit/matter, dualism by finding ways to own their connection, through bodily experience if not through the traditional roles assigned them in the patriarchy, to nature and matter, to the earth. In discussing Margaret Atwood's novel *Surfacing,* for instance, she says: "It seems to me that women must positively name the power that resides in their bodies and their sense of closeness to nature and use this new naming to transform the pervasive cultural and religious devaluation of nature and the body. Atwood's novel suggests that the opposition of spirit and body, nature and person, which is epidemic in Western culture, is neither necessary nor salutary; that spiritual insight surfaces through attention to the body; and that the achievement of authentic selfhood and power depends on understanding one's grounding in nature and natural energies."[8]

Diving Deep and Surfacing concludes with reiterated support for what the author calls "the new naming of women's bodies and connections to nature that emerges as part of the drive toward wholeness in women's spiritual quest".[9] Noting the distrust of this position by some feminists, Christ nevertheless decides that

> though the danger of simply reversing the old dualisms will remain as long as women simply react (and those in power force them to react) against their historic subordination and its rooting in the classic dualisms, I like to think that women's celebration of the body, nature, feeling, and intuition as [sic] the first stage in an attempt—which surely cannot be fully successful on the first try—to move toward a more whole way of thinking. . . I like to think about spiritual insights arising from connection to the body and nature, to imagine forms of understanding in which the body plays a part, and to begin to conceptualize a view of human freedom in which limitation by nature, death, and finitude is accepted.[10]

I later learned that Carol Christ's position here is one shared by those who mounted a Feminism and Ecology Program within Goddard College's summer institute on social ecology for 1980, suggesting that not only religion scholars or feminists intent on women's spiritual quest but also some more politically-oriented feminists, engaged in what Christ calls women's *social* quest, are able to affirm the connection of women with nature. As far as my own inquiry into the mythic meanings of the Space Age was concerned, I was particularly drawn, during my labyrinthine progress through the literature of feminist spirituality, to Christ's mention of "forms of understanding in which the body plays a part". Like Griffin's vision of identification with the blackbird as "how we know", it seemed to me that here was a clue to a relation between the feminine geometaphor—the image of earth as woman—and the mode or method of metaphorizing itself, since metaphorizing might be at the heart of this "feminine" way of knowing and spring from the same source. But further clues awaited me back in Naomi Goldenberg's *Changing of the Gods*.

METAPHORIC IMAGES MUST BE GROUNDED IN MATTER

Goldenberg's fruitful chapter on "The Mirror and Mysticism" also included a discussion of the psychology of James Hillman. In my previous reading I had found Hillman's work to be a creative departure from the Jungian thought which originally inspired it, and as I have indicated above, his writing on metaphoric images and Apollonic consciousness, among a number of topics, contributed significantly to the speculations I was engaged in throughout the second half of the '70s. For her part, Goldenberg's interest in Hillman was one component of her general project to adapt Freudian and Jungian ideas to the purposes of her feminist psychology of religion. In addition to an initial endorsement of the Hillmanian stress on the changing, ambiguous, polyvalent character of metaphoric images, she goes on to raise a difficulty she has with his "archetypal psychology"—and in so doing moves nearer to the subtle interrelationship I was beginning to discover between several important considerations: women's religious experience in affirming the body and nature, the feminine or Goddess geometaphor, and the metaphorizing approach itself.

Goldenberg's worry about archetypal psychology has to do with

Hillman's tendency, in opposing a literalistic handling of images, to use the term "imaginal" to refer to what she is afraid is exclusvely "the non-material world and . . . inaction or contemplation." She fears that Hillman's psychology will "become a hollow game of intellectualizing, removed from significant dealings with human life" if he separates the realm of images from the flesh and blood realities of life in order to avoid literalism.[11] She states that "the richest symbolic systems of Western culture have acknowledged the identity of image and matter," and while she agrees with Hillman's reminder that literalism "fails to recognize that 'concrete flesh is a magnificent citadel of metaphors,'" she replies that it is just as imperative for us to know that "metaphors are also flesh, that they are continuous with our bodily selves."[12] Finally, she attests that "the intimate tie between image and life is something which feminist theorists can teach psychologists of religion," adding the provocative comment that "witches know that their physical lives are changed by their images of the Goddess."[13]

When I first read Goldenberg's carefully nuanced critique of Hillman in 1979 I felt she was right to insist upon the tie of image to matter or to concrete flesh and blood life. I also came to see the weight she placed on this linkage as cohering with Griffin and Christ's acceptance of the woman-nature connection and their quest for a mode of understanding based upon it. On the other hand, my own metaphorizing approach had developed, under the influence of Hillman among others, as an alternative to any literalistic treatment of the earth imagery I was encountering. I therefore could not go as far as Goldenberg appeared to be going toward espousing just such a literalism. A middle ground, or middle grounding, would have to be found, one which allowed me to follow her feminist lead about the continuity of images and matter without at the same time falling into a literalistic reduction of imagery to "mere", inert matter—which is to say, falling prey to a narrow materialism of images.

In thinking through this issue I first reviewed Hillman's work and decided that, as Goldenberg had implied, he seems somewhat inconsistent. There is his running denunciation of the "peak-experiences" or spiritual "highs" of self-transcendence in favor of Keat's "vale of soul-making", the concrete context of everyday life with its characteristic supply of depressions and lowdown realities.[14] As the imagery here suggests, this was very much in line with my mythic focus on a Space-Age descent to terrestrial reconnection. However, there is an equally persistent penchant in Hillman's writing for claiming the essential independence of images from sense perception and the importance of an "underworld" of images which is finally just as divorced from the materiality of earth's surface as are the transcendent peaks and highs he had condemned.[15]

I therefore felt that I was facing an impossible choice of positions. Unlike Hillman, whose implied championing of what Susan Griffin had expressed as "how we know" is weakened by his ambivalent approach to earth and substance — an inadequate grounding for images — Goldenberg's stance would certainly affirm imagery's concrete materiality. However, the cost of her affirmation was a tendency toward literalism which would lead to a no less inadequate grounding — a kind of imprisonment in dead matter — and which scarcely jibed with my commitment to metaphorizing.

As it happened, Hillman's 1979 volume *The Dream and the Underworld* pointed the way for me beyond his own difficulties as well as Goldenberg's. There he acknowledges that the imagery he treats separately as earthly vale or maternal under*ground*, on the one hand, and the discarnate transcendent void of the chthonic under*world*, on the other, can *both* be seen as contained in the pre-Olympian figure of the Earth Mother Goddess of Greek mythology. "Against my distinctions," he says, "is the fact that one can as well view the entire complex of the underworld from the perspective of Ge, as does Patricia Berry. She then is able to see much of the chthonic spirit that I meet in Hades to be Ge, and that Gaia (Ge) is both material, maternal earth, and chthonic void with its own spirit. The question here," he concludes, "partly turns on how one regards earth."[16]

Needless to say, given my methodological preoccupations this last sentence caught my attention. I was attracted to any way of regarding earth which avoided the differentiation he was making between underground and underworld; remembering Goldenberg's criticisms I hardly wished to posit a realm such as Hillman's Hades in which image could be entirely separated from matter. Despite the hedge against literalism which such a disembodied world offered, it pulled away from change, life, and flesh.

GAIA—THE MATTER FOR METAPHORIZING

Accordingly I was anxious to pursue the more integrated treatment given the topic by Patricia Berry. Berry is herself an archetypal psychologist to whom James Hillman happens to be married. The piece to which he has referred is her 1978 lecture entitled "What's the Matter with Mother?" This was not an easy publication to locate, and I was lucky that David Miller, a temporary colleague while I was a visiting faculty member at Syracuse University in the spring of 1980, could loan me his copy.

Berry's essay starts the discussion of Gaia, the Great Earth Mother, by defining matter, "for", as she explains, "mother, this mothering ground of our lives, is connected with the word 'matter.' Mother and matter (*mater*) are cognates". She points out that there are two levels of matter: As a "universal substrate" matter is an abstraction which, in itself, is "unknowable, invisible, and incorporeal." On this first level, then, matter is a deprivation, lack, or void. The second level of matter, by contrast, is what she calls "the most concrete, tangible, visible, bodily," Augustine's "earth as we know it".[17]

This means that the idea of matter is itself pardoxical: "Matter (and by extension, mother earth) is both the most something *and* the most nothing, the most necessary (in order that something can happen) and at the same time the most lacking."[18] Berry grants that "there is something about the nature of earth that makes us take it more literally than we take the other elements,"[19] but the reason for our propensity to literalize earth and lose its metaphoric meanings, she speculates, is our resistance to the incomplete or void aspects of mother/matter, which makes us overcompensate by playing a venerable mythic role: "As a solar hero, one fights for the death of the mother's ambiguity. . . one casts aside less heroic modes that would allow the incompleteness of mothering ground to connect with the muses of metaphor, for whom lacking ground is fertile ground indeed. Metaphor depends on this sense of lack, this sense of the 'is not' with every 'is.'"[20] And here she adds importantly that "the hero's mother complex is characterized by his struggles to be up and out, and above her."[21]

All of this, once more, is entailed by the double nature of matter which Gaia embodies, for, as Berry phrases it, "Gaia's original realm included both the upper realm of growth, nurturance, and life and the underworld realm of death, limitation, and ending."[22] At a certain point in the development of Greek culture these two sides were split apart — an early symptom, no doubt, of our heroic mishandling of the earthly environment — and "the upperworld became a Demeter realm of concrete, daily life, devoid of the spiritual values, the sense of essence and the dark (and beneath the dark) carried by her underworld daughter,

Persephone."[23] According to Berry, this situation implies certain imperatives for the kind of grounding our imaginal lives require:

> In our efforts to establish a solid 'real' world and make the mother carry our concreteness, we have lost an aspect of her grounding — a grounding that has not so much to do with growth in any of the more concrete senses, our upperworld development (an over-growth that has now become cancerous). But much more to do with our mother in the underworld: the Persephone who rules over our souls in their essential, limiting and immaterial patterns; and, that original mother of all — Gaia — she who is Earth; and yet without contradiction, that deeper ground of support beneath earth's physical appearance, the non-being beneath and within being. Our fruitfulness, our fecundity, our sense of what 'matters,' has its roots in our very unsureness, in our sense of lack.[24]

The weight Berry places on what might be termed the insubstantiality of matter recalls the problem I had had with Hillman's formulation. Unlike him, however, she never neglects the other side of Gaia. Her observation that "Gaia made things stick" and was "mother as the settler, the stabilizer, the binder"[25] provides the mythic background for a frequently-cited epithet in archetypal psychology: Rafael Lopez-Pedraza's saying "Stick to the image!"[26] This is a plea to remain within the imaginal language of dreams, fantasies, and myths rather than complying with a translation into some presumed symbolic equivalent or abstract archetype which would forfeit the concrete, if ambiguous, immediacy of the image.

The sense of Berry's evocation of Gaia, then, is that here we have the content of imagery, the matter of metaphorizing (the matter which *makes for* metaphorizing, with its "is not" and its "is"), as the most concrete — answering Naomi Goldenberg's call for the continuity of image with flesh-and-blood life — *and* the most insubstantial — answering James Hillman's stress on the psychic and nonliteral. Gaia grounds metaphorizing by integrating both halves of materiality, hinting as well at the epistemological agendas Susan Griffin and Carol Christ find emerging from women's experience of their bodily relation to the natural earth.

Certainly Berry's work seemed an appropriate "mythic ratification"— an endorsement from the Goddess, perhaps — for my conviction that metaphorizing is the requisite method for our Space-Age reconnection to earth. Even her notion of how the solar hero fights the mother's ambiguity as he "struggles to be up and out, and above her" was germane to my efforts at reconnection. The solar hero *par excel-*

lence, after all, would be Apollo, patriarch of our manned space program, a program which has assuredly wanted to be up, out, and above the earth, and one which has traded upon literalistic calculation and the elimination of ambiguity in realizing its desire.

I noted as well that Christine Downing also deals with some of these issues in her book, *The Goddess*. I had seen her chapter on Gaia in an earlier version about the time I was pondering the Patricia Berry essay, and although she does not cite "What's the Matter with Mother?" she concurs that the original Earth Mother Goddess was "earth made invisible, earth become metaphor, earth as the realm of soul".[27] Moreover, Downing reminds us that it was Gaia who was the original sponsor of the grotto at Delphi (with its omphalos or world-navel) and who was eventually supplanted there by Apollo. "Aeschylus suggests," she writes, "that the transition from Gaia to Apollo was a peaceful evolution (via Themis and Phoebe). Hesiod and the Homeric Hymn to Pythian Apollo present a more violent struggle. Python, a female dragon created by Gaia as the guardian of the shrine, was slain by Apollo to make possible his usurpation of the oracle. Gaia responded by sending dreams to all those who might otherwise have come to consult Apollo's wisdom, until Zeus was persuaded by Apollo to order her to desist. So goes the story. I am not sure," Downing concludes, "she ever really did what Zeus commanded."[28]

Thus the Apollo we find so pervasively in control of modern consciousness is the power who replaced the Goddess. But if a *new* consciousness of earth is to come into prominence on the far side of Apollo's Space-Age ascendancy, Gaia will need to return with her dragon energies, her dreams, and beneath all, her ambiguous grounding for a metaphorizing form of understanding.

THE WAY OF WICCA—
GODDESS-WORSHIP AS IMAGINAL GROUNDING

And what was particularly fascinating to me as a sympathetic onlooker in the late '70s was to see that this return might indeed be beginning by means of feminist spirituality's current concern for the Goddess in all her guises. Moreover, one expression of this spirituality suggested it was actually possible to live out the imaginal grounding Gaia gives for the mode of knowing required to counterbalance Apollo today.

I have already described how my intellectual introduction to contemporary witchcraft culminated in quite visceral experiences on the coast of Cornwall in the summer of 1979. But it was in the fall of that year that I first heard about a new and comprehensive survey of neo-paganism in America, *Drawing Down the Moon*, by Margot Adler.[29] The well-chosen publication date was October 31, and although I could not acquire a copy on that day my interest in Wicca was nevertheless reinvigorated by the Halloween appearance at Goddard of Adrienne Rich.

Rich, of course, was a powerful poet whose book *Of Woman Born* had already sounded three years earlier the note Carol Christ and Susan Griffin were to echo by urging women to "think through the body".[30] In addition to reading her poems that night she spoke passionately of witchcraft as both a social protest and an alternative mode of spirituality, exhorting the women in her audience to reclaim the vilified name of "witch" together with the feast of Halloween itself. In the process of her talk she appeared to be making factual historical claims about the way witchcraft had functioned in past centuries, a topic I had found confusing to that point in my reading because of the distorted accounts of witches' activities left to us by their persecutors. I looked forward to Margot Adler's treatment to clarify and augment the information Rich was offering, but for various reasons I did not see a copy of her book until the following spring.

It was Rhoda Lerman, the author of *Call Me Ishtar*, who lent it to me while I was teaching at Syracuse, and what I found when I was finally able to read *Drawing Down the Moon* was a journalistic investigation by the granddaughter of the psychoanalytical pioneer Alfred Adler. Margot Adler's discussion of the philosophical questions raised by "Witches, Druids, Goddess-Worshippers, and other Pagans in America Today"—her subtitle—is often very sophisticated. A more recent reviewer's judgment that "as a serious study it deserves serious attention"[31] was certainly my own reaction upon working through the book in 1980.

More specifically, I discovered that Adler strongly implies contemporary witchcraft is grounded in the very metaphorizing imperative of the Earth Mother Goddess enunciated by Patricia Berry and Christine Downing rather than in literalistic beliefs about historical connections to ancient Goddess cults. She cites neither Berry nor Downing, but her chapter on "The Wiccan Revival" contains an account of what she calls "the myth of Wicca" in which she emphasizes that the notion of modern Wicca being rooted in a universal organized pagan religion dating back in an unbroken tradition to neolithic times cannot be maintained in fact. Such an historical picture, built on research by figures such as Margaret Murray, Robert Graves, Sir James Frazer, Charles Leland, and Gerald Gardner—research which has not survived the criticisms of later scholarship, or was as much mythopoetic as factual to begin with—can only be taken as a metaphoric model used to evoke appropriate attitudes in the present. And, according to Adler, since the early '70s this imaginal grounding has even been welcomed by Wiccans who had earlier held to the literal rootage of their tradition. Her further comment that this epistemological adjustment "in itself is a lesson in the flexibility of the revival"[32] forcefully reminded me of Naomi Goldenberg's speculations on the meaning of the "wic" in the word "wicca", not to mention the latter's remark that "although witches do often speak of the times of the matriarchies, most are more concerned with that concept as a psychological and poetic force than as an historical verity."[33] It was not until I had had access to the detailed discussion in *Drawing Down the Moon*, however, that I saw just how thoroughly metaphorizing had become the way of Wicca.

Adler's principal sources for what she terms "a revisionist history of the Craft"[34] are Isaac Bonewits and Aidan Kelly, two American witches with whose work I was unfamiliar but who had each written significantly about this issue. What she infers from their theories is that it is "creativity" which is "the primary Craft tradition".[35] Bonewits, for example, as early as 1971 in a book called *Real Magic*, and later in an article appropriately entitled "Witchcult: Fact or Fancy?", decided that "the 'Unitarian Old Religion of White Witches' existed in fancy, not in fact."[36] Kelly's revisionist account turns attention to the role of Gerald Gardner, a retired British civil servant whose publications during the '40s and '50s claimed to be presenting traditional witchcraft which had survived for centuries without adulteration in families and secret covens. Kelly, on the contrary, sees Gardner as having instituted a creative reform of his own which gave contemporary Wicca its central focus:

> The essence of Gardner's reform is that he made the Goddess the major deity of this new movement, and it is the Goddess who captures the imaginations. . .of those who enter into this movement. It is as if western civilization were ready to deal again (or finally) with the concept of Deity as Female. Whatever the reasons may be why this readiness exists, it is this readiness which justifies and sustains the Gardnerian movement, not a pseudohistory traceable to the Stone Age.[37]

He then adds another provocative point: "Everything in the Craft, no matter how useful, no matter how pleasing, even the Great Metaphor of the Goddess, is still only a metaphor."[38]

Kelly's insights felt like clinching data, after the reading I had done on feminist spirituality and witchcraft, for the supposition that if the Goddess were only a metaphor (or a geometaphor in her guise of Earth Mother) she had also somehow given birth to the very possibility of seeing her that way.

EARTH SHOWS HOW SHE SEES HERSELF

In considering all these clues I was reminded more than once of the far-from-feminist observations of Norman Mailer. It was Mailer, after all, who had come out with the only book directly on the space program which to any extent took into account its mythic or mysterious aspects. Moreover, as I have discussed earlier, Mailer's statement in *Of a Fire on the Moon* was the one which had led me to apply the notions of metaphor I had learned in the '60s to my search for a Space-Age mythos throughout the ensuing decade. "We might have to go out into space," he had said, "until the mystery of new discovery would force us to regard the world once again as poets, behold it as savages who knew that if the universe was a lock, its key was metaphor rather than measure."

At about the same time that I read Mailer's book in the early '70s I also ran across a collection of poems influenced by ideas of space travel called *Inside Outer Space*. One of its contributions acted as an unintended but amazingly affirmative response to Mailer's methodological advice. In May Swenson's poem, "Orbiter 5 Shows How Earth Looks From the Moon," the world was surely being regarded once again as a "poet" or a "savage" would behold it, by way of metaphor rather than measure. But when I had become acquainted later with the works I have drawn upon in this chapter I also began to realize that the role of the earth—the Gaia or Ge in "geo-metaphor" and "geo-metry"—was hardly a passive one. Earth was not only to be the waiting object of our metaphorizing regard; in the mythic attributes of Gaia and the Goddess-worship of Wicca she was as well suggesting *how she saw herself through us.*

This realization resonated powerfully for me with Susan Griffin's words: ". . . I know I am made from this earth. . ." Likewise, and perhaps even more pointedly, in the Swenson poem it is as though the Apollonic technology needed to produce a satellite photograph such as Orbiter 5's in 1967 were developed by the Goddess as a kind of triumphantly devious Delphic dream in order that Swenson (and those, male and female, who can follow her metaphorizing vision) might participate in the preferred method of earth's self-perception.

Swenson's title, "Orbiter 5 Shows How Earth Looks From the Moon," plays a wicked, or Wiccan, joke on the literalism of the satellite sighting, since the poem itself—a scrying of coastlines, continents, and clouds which gives us the figure of a woman—goes on to rescue the earth from that very literalism and returns us to the imaginal grounding we require in this Age of Space:

> There's a woman in the earth,*
> sitting on her heels.
> You see her from the back,
> in three-quarter profile.
> She has a flowing pigtail.
> She's holding something
>
> in her right hand—
> some holy jug.
> Her left arm is thinner,
> in a gesture like a dancer.
> She's the Indian Ocean.
> Asia is light
>
> swirling up out of her vessel.
> Her pigtail points to Europe,
> and her dancer's arm
> is the Suez Canal.
> She is a woman
> in a square kimono,
> bare feet tucked
> beneath the tip of Africa.
> Her tail of long hair
> is the Arabian Peninsula.
> A woman in the earth,
> a man in the moon.[39]

*p. 85

IV
SERENDIPPING DOWN TO EARTH

CHAPTER SEVEN

FROM OUTER SPACE TO SERENDIP: THE ARTHUR C. CLARKE CONNECTIONS

St. Eval is about 35 miles northeast of the settlement called Wicca on the Cornish Atlantic coast, and like Wicca it is too tiny to appear on any but the most meticulous maps. The parish church at the end of the runway was empty the day my wife, two daughters, and I visited. We were undisturbed as I pondered the Royal Air Force flag hanging inside, the name Sampson Noel on a list of former vicars, and the other Noel on an RAF gravestone outside.

We had stopped at this obscure site because I wanted to get "the lay of the land" at St. Eval airfield. But in less vague terms than that I cannot say I knew what I expected to find, the sort of evidence I would want to discover. The field had long been abandoned—or "disused," as the British say—but during World War II it was one of two Cornish bases where the RAF instituted a crucial new use of radar. In late 1943 and throughout 1944 a special group of RAF personnel was assigned to work with a team of American scientists from MIT to develop what was called a Ground Controlled Approach system. This system's important purpose was to use radar along with radio to "talk down" pilots for a safe landing in the often foggy weather of St. Eval or Davidstow Moor, the other base a few miles farther up the coast.

Neither of these abandoned airfields offered anything in the way of attractions for the average American traveler, and Joanna and the girls had to exercise more good-natured tolerance than I had a right to expect when I roamed around each site, taking pictures and making notes, with no clear sense of quite what would be relevant.

SPEAKING FOR THE SPACE AGE

It has been touched on earlier that the reason I was interested in St. Eval in the first place was that Arthur C. Clarke, the science fiction writer, had served there during the war. He had also served at Davidstow, for he was the RAF officer in charge of the new GCA "talk down" radar program.

My concern with Clarke's work as pertinent to exploring the mythic dimension of the Space Age had begun with *2001: A Space Odyssey*. He was the coauthor of the screenplay and had completed the novel version more or less simultaneously back around 1968, just before the Apollo 11 moon landing. The image of the film's enigmatic megalith had had such archaic terrestrial associations for an otherwise futuristic space-opera that it had been one of my earliest "clues".

I certainly did not have much prior acquaintance with literary science fiction when I began, and was by no means a scholar of the genre. But I tried to catch up a bit by reading some of the criticism and anthologies put out by Leslie Fiedler, Robert Scholes, Eric Rabkin, and Pamela Sargent.[1] I also read several of the highly acclaimed works by Ursula LeGuin[2] and, of course, some of Clarke's own prodigious production.[3] This was not, to be sure, a very broad or deep sampling, but it gave me at least the suggestion of a context within which to view individual works of Clarke.

Compared to the impressive artistry of LeGuin and some of the more venturesome writers included in the anthologies, his fiction came off as formally and linguistically uninventive, with thinly developed characters exemplifying the safe and apolitical lifestyle of a mid-twentieth century middle-brow engineer—however much projected into future heroics. And yet, in his conventional way Clarke was a careful craftsman, enjoyable to read and able to touch some deep mythic chords in his audience, especially with his favorite theme: the initial encounter between humans and extraterrestrials. In *Childhood's End* and *Rendezvous With Rama*, for instance, this encounter is handled with great skill. These were the two Clarke novels I read first in my review of his work, and I could readily see why, along with his fellow writers from science fiction's Golden Age in the 1940s and '50s —A.E. van Vogt, Robert Heinlein, and Isaac Asimov—he was considered a "founding father" of the genre.

But for me Clarke's importance went far beyond his skills or short-comings as a literary artist. As I worked through his fiction and learned about his life and other writings, I became more and more captivated. He increasingly seemed to me a representative figure of the Space Age, one who connected several of its most intriguing elements, both positive and negative, in his career and concerns.

This was not only because of his science fiction but also due to his science journalism and, indeed, his actual scientific work. For me the wider view of Clarke came particularly from my acquaintance with three books: *The Promise of Space*, which came out in 1968, the year of *2001*, but which I caught up with seven or eight years later; *The View from Serendip*, a 1977 collection of largely autobiographical essays; and then the first anthology of critical pieces on his work edited by Joseph Olander and Martin Harry Greenberg.[4]

From these last two volumes I found out that Clarke was born in 1917 in Minehead, a Somerset resort town on the Bristol Channel, the northern boundary of England's so-called "West Country" (usually defined as the four southwesternmost counties: Somerset, Dorset, Devon, and Cornwall). It was in 1930 that Clarke discovered Olav Stapledon's science fiction classic *First and Last Men* in the Minehead Public Library and the magazine *Astounding Stories* in the local Woolworth's. At age 13, then, he had begun to read and write in the genre, and he continued to do so when he went away to high school in the nearby town of Taunton and subsequently launched a career as an auditor in London from 1936 to 1941. By this time he was active in the British Interplanetary Society and was publishing his first stories under the pseudonym E.G. O'Brien—for which he received the nickname "Ego".

Between 1941 and 1946 he was in the RAF, rising from radio mechanic to Flight Lieutenant and, as noted above, participating in the development of radar technology and techniques. It was the nature of this RAF work combined with his science fiction writer's imagination which led him to the notion he wrote up for a 1945 issue of the journal *Wireless World*: the theory—conceived almost two decades before it was confirmed operationally—that a satellite placed in orbit 22,300 miles above the equator would be "geosynchronous", or stationary in relation to the rotating earth below.[5] This pioneering idea, the basis for an effective worldwide comumunications relay, impressed me as containing one of the most powerful images of our Space-Age culture, almost equalling the moon landings if not the whole earth photographs. Clarke's vision of the communications satellite hovering in its "magic orbit", as familiar now as the nightly television weather report, was the contribution which, more than any other, convinced me of his importance as a spokesman for the Space Age.

After his RAF service Clarke went through King's College of London Unviersity, from which he received his Bachelor of Science degree with First Class Honors in physics and mathematics. That was in 1948. He then took a position as a scientific editor, was married and rather quickly divorced, and in 1950 published *Interplanetary Flight*,[6] the first of approximately 25 nonfiction books. The following year his science fiction works — totalling at least another 25 — began to appear with the publication of *Prelude to Space* and *The Sands of Mars*.[7] His story "The Sentinel", the seed from which *2001* later grew, came out during this same period at the beginning of the '50s.[8]

By this time a fascination with the "space walks" available in the undersea world had led Clarke into skin diving. It was in mid-December of 1954, heading for the Great Barrier Reef of Australia on a diving expedition, that his ship stopped for half a day at Colombo, Ceylon. One of the people he met there invited him back to explore the seas around the island. He accepted the invitation and was so enthralled that he began living there more and more from 1956 on. As he says in *The View From Serendip*: "Now, more than twenty years after I first set foot on the island, I have at last been able to arrange my life so that I no longer have to leave."[9] The connection between Clarke's association with Ceylon (now the republic of Sri Lanka) and his writing activities turned out to be another surprisingly central factor in my finding him an exemplary figure.

To sum up Clarke's career: He is the author of some 500 articles or stories and 50 books, with total sales in the millions, and the recipient of numerous awards both as a writer and as a propagandist for space exploration. His exploits also include having been a television commentator for one of the Apollo missions — he wrote the Epilogue to the Apollo 11 astronauts' *First on the Moon*[10] — and testifying before the U.S. Congress Committee on Space Science. He himself reminisced about these sorts of experiences as early as *The Promise of Space*:

> Many events have combined, or conspired, to focus my main interests once more upon space travel. Perhaps foremost was three years' hard labor with Stanley Kubrick on *2001: A Space Odyssey*, which made me start thinking seriously again about probable

developments during the rest of this century. Another was a conducted tour of Cape Kennedy, with NASA administrator James Webb as a guide; yet another was being present at Comsat Headquarters the night Early Bird was launched. I could also mention the cumulative impact of seeing the first live television picture from the moon—meeting Yuri Gagarin and John Glenn—watching Echo slide through the equatorial skies—walking thoughtfully around the sacked and ruined birthplace of the god Apollo with . . . Wernher von Braun.[11]

AVATAR OF APOLLO

This last comment especially caught my eye. The presence of Apollonic perceptions and perspectives in space technology—signalled, of course, by NASA's use of Apollo's name—had made me attentive to Gaia's ancient adversary. If there were avatars of Apollo in Space-Age culture, certainly Wernher von Braun, the father of the German V-2 rocket program and of U.S. space efforts after the war, would be one.

But Arthur C. Clarke would be another, and given his widespread readership he may be the more influential of the two. And while a handful of other science fiction novelists may rival his standing in that realm, it is his involvement with fact as well as fiction which argues for his preeminence as *the* Space-Age incarnation of Apollo. Moreover, as my own investigation of him proceeded I came to see how a representative *failing* of Apollonic consciousness also characterized Clarke's sensibility, lying hidden in the relation *between* fact and fiction in his writing.

For many commentators viewing only his fiction, Clarke is seen as an optimistically rational champion of space exploration who is nevertheless—and perhaps only half-consciously—a kind of atheistic mystic or modern myth-maker. This reading of Clarke, which seemed initially very promising to the quest for mythic significance, is evident in the Olander and Greenberg collection of critical essays I encountered in the late '70s.

An impressive example, within this volume, of the prevalent view of Clarke's work is the contribution by Betsy Harfst, "Of Myths and Polyominoes: Mythological Content in Clarke's Fiction." Using the device of complex geometrical design (the "polyominoes"), Harfst presents an elaborate mythic interpretation of four Clarke novels based on concepts about myth put forward by C. G. Jung, Joseph Campbell, and, most importantly for my purposes, the historian of religions Mircea Eliade.

Harfst's essay is a generally deft application of the myth theories, but her use of Eliade contains an early indication that perhaps Clarke's ability to provide a Space-Age mythos is problematic. In describing the typical Clarkean hero she says that "unlike some of his more piously submissive Judeo-Christian ancestors . . . he will be *equal* to God in his autonomy."[12] Harfst then seeks to support her case with a passage from Eliade's *Cosmos and History* concerning "creative freedom". But it is clear that Eliade is not there discussing a figure such as Clarke's rational modern unbeliever, as she implies, but is rather referring to Judeo-Christian *faith*. It is only this faith, says Eliade, which can supply modern persons with the freedom they require, a freedom, in short, "which has its source and finds its guarantee and support in God".[13]

This God-grounded freedom is a far cry from the unbridled auton-omy—*equality* with God—which Harfst sees, quite rightly, in Clarke's hero. The misuse of Eliade here is noteworthy because it indicates that there might be a level of what Eliade would call "profanized" conscious-ness underlying and undercutting the mythological content which Harfst is able to display.

Another example of Clarke's distance from the religio-mythic perspective represented by Eliade is a comment he makes in his Epi-logue to *First on the Moon*. In contrast to Eliade's observation that "it was the great merit of Christianity to revolt against astrological fatal-ism, so powerful in late antiquity—and thus to restore man's confidence in himself and in the possibilities of his freedom,"[14] there is, again, Clarke's totally secular notion of human autonomy. His final remark at the end of the Epilogue states his position starkly: ". . . it may be that the old astrologers had the truth exactly reversed, when they believed that the stars controlled the destinies of men. The time may come when men control the destinies of the stars."[15]

These two small but telling instances suggested to me that like his typical hero Clarke foresees a scientifically-engineered autonomy far different from that envisioned in the Judeo-Christian belief-system to which Eliade refers. It would, moreover, be even farther away from what this system supplanted, according to Eliade: the sort of para-doxical freedom archaic religious peoples found in one or another sacred cosmos of cyclically-repeating patterns.

Indeed, Clarke's writings are replete with exclamations of a con-fidently profane modernity, including not a few breezy rationalist denunciations of ancient myth for its superstitiousness. His most positive appraisals allow only that it offers vague premonitory visions which it is the business of science and technology to "realize." For all his supposed sensitivity to the mythic dimension, Clarke seems to share none of Eliade's stress on traditional societies discovering reality precisely in the sacred fantasies their nonfactual myths narrated.

In this respect Clarke echoes the rhetoric of other Space-Age spokesmen—such as U.S. President Carter at a Congressional Space Medals award ceremony—who say of our missions to the moon that "we have taken the stuff of fantasy and dreams and we have turned it into accomplishment and reality."[16] It is this same focus on technological realization among mainstream science fiction writers that leads Leslie Fiedler, in the Introduction to his anthology *In Dreams Awake*, to offer a wry observation:

> . . . a basic appeal of the genre surely lies in its creation of technologically oriented mythologies to replace the older ones made obsolete by science. In order to survive, however, such mythologies had to be presented as if they were rooted not in 'wonder' and dreams but in 'extrapolation' from scientific 'fact.' Science fiction may be a literature of dreams, but its dreams are those of men dreaming they are awake.[17]

Fiedler's assessment struck me as entirely relevant to a man whose science fictional *nom de plume* had been "Ego". But a slightly different diagnosis of Clarke's problematic relationship to the domain of myth came to seem even more apt. Once again it necessitated a comparison between Clarke's outlook as a Space-Age exemplar and Mircea Eliade's perspective on traditional myth. In particular it entailed carefully juxtaposing what Eliade had defined as "sacred space" within a premodern world-view and what Clarke does with his geosynchronous comsat and his adopted home in the novel he produced in 1978, *The Fountains of Paradise*.

A SCIENCE FICTION OF PARADISE

The title of the novel, as Clarke points out in a brief Preface, is drawn from a saying ascribed to a papal legate, Friar Marignolli, in 1335: "From Paradise to Taprobane is forty leagues; there may be heard the sound of the Fountains of Paradise."[18] Taprobane was the Latin name for the island of Ceylon and is also the name of the fictionalized island in Clarke's novel. The "fountains" are an element of the plot by way of King Kalidasa's reign in 2nd-century Taprobane. It was at the base of his fortress atop the giant outcropping called Yakkagala, or Demon Rock, that a system of moats, fountains, and gardens, enclosed by a rampart, had been constructed.

From within this setting Kalidasa ruled with increasing unease, gazing nervously southward to Sri Kanda, the Sacred Mountain. On the summit of this cone-shaped peak was the temple of the Mahanayake Thero, Taprobane's High Priest, who disapproved of Kalidasa's bloody seizure of the throne and patiently awaited his downfall. This story of King Kalidasa, who had murdered his father and was eventually overcome in a final battle with his half brother, forms only the opening scene of *The Fountains of Paradise*. It serves to introduce the theme of the heaven-aspiring builder as well as the setting of the main narrative, which takes place in the Taprobane of our future two thousand years later.

Vannevar Morgan, the novel's chief protagonist, is a 22nd century engineer who has already created the world's largest bridge across the Straits of Gibraltar. He journeys to Taprobane to enlist the aid of a retired diplomat—Rajasinghe, who lives in the shadow of Kalidasa's Demon Rock—on a new and even more ambitious project.

During his stay with Rajasinghe Morgan becomes fascinated by the legend of King Kalidasa, and early one morning climbs up to see the remains of the latter's fortress-palace. Looking down from Yakkagala on the pools of the pleasure-garden, Morgan recalls the statement attributed to Friar Marignolli: "He savored the phrase in his mind: the Fountains of Paradise. Was Kalidasa trying to create, here on earth, a garden fit for the gods, in order to establish his claim to divinity? If so, it was no wonder that the priests had accused him of blasphemy, and placed a curse on all his work" (p. 35). Like Kalidasa two millennia before him, Morgan stares south toward the Sacred Mountain, Sri Kanda. It obviously figures prominently in his project, although the nature of this new feat of engineering is not immediately divulged. Morgan muses that "to Kalidasa, Sri Kanda represented both the power of the priesthood and the power of the gods, conspiring together against him. Now the gods were gone; but the priests remained. They represented something that Morgan did not understand, and would therefore treat with wary respect" (p. 38).

Morgan is thus portrayed as a thoroughly secular man, an engineer with an engineer's mind who admires Kalidasa's reign as a heaven-usurping prototype of his own ambitions. His Taprobane project is finally revealed as being the construction of a "Space Elevator" or "Orbital Tower" connecting earth with a geosynchronous satellite hovering above the equator. This structure, it is explained, was first conceived some two hundred years earlier by the Russian engineer Artsutanov but could not be built for lack of proper materials until the 22nd century. Successfully completing the project would provide an access to outer space much less costly than fuel-consuming rockets. But this Orbital Tower, Morgan had learned, could only be situated at a single place on earth. Not only must it be on the equator but, as Morgan's friend Maxine Duval says, "it turns out that Africa and South America are *not* suitable for the Space Elevator. It's something to do with unstable points in the earth's gravitational field. Only Taprobane will do. Worse still, only one spot in Taprobane" (p. 52).

The required location for the earth terminal of the Orbital Tower, then, is the summit of Sri Kanda, still occupied by the successors to Kalidasa's antagonist, the High Priest Mahanayake Thero. With this likely obstacle to Morgan's plans in mind, the meditative diplomat Rajasinghe ascends to Demon Rock to converse with the frescoes of goddesses on its face and observes that "our land may become the center of the world. . .of many worlds. The great mountain you have watched so long, there in the south, may be the key to the universe." And then he adds, addressing his favorite goddess-figure on the rock wall: "What could you possibly know of the *real* worlds beyond the sky, or of men's need to reach them? Even though you were once a goddess, Kalidasa's heaven was only an illusion" (p. 57).

The implication of Rajasinghe's soliloquy is that Vannevar Morgan's heaven is a real one—which is to say, a literal one, a matter of space technology fit for a hardheaded engineer in a future age even more removed than our own from traditional religious perceptions. Most of the rest of the novel concerns political maneuverings to get the project approved and the actual building of the Space Elevator, including a crisis which Morgan gives his life to overcome. During the former negotiations Morgan travels to the top of Sri Kanda to speak with the current Mahanayake Thero, making the trip by cable car rather than climbing "the longest stairway in the world" (p. 67) to the shrine of the Holy Footprint—Adam's, Siva's, or Buddha's, depending on which religious tradition one consulted—at the summit near the High Priest's temple.

The only other noteworthy theme of the book—and it is, as indicated earlier, a favorite of Clarke's — is the arrival of an alien spaceship from a distant galaxy. Starglider, as it is called, passes through the solar system for one hundred days, collecting information on the earth's cultures and technology and, according to the novel, giving a final death blow to human religions. The assumption is that these are crucially dependent on a geocentric anthropomorphism. To put it in the significantly excessive language of Clarke's text: "[Starglider] had put an end to the billions of words of pious gibberish with which apparently intelligent men had addled their minds for centuries" (p. 83).

At the close of *The Fountains of Paradise* it is fifteen hundred years after Vannevar Morgan's death and the completion of the Orbital Tower. A creature from the planet which had sent the Starglider probe is sitting atop Demon Rock with a group of earth children, looking south at the Sacred Mountain with Morgan's structure still rising from its summit. The creature — to which Clarke refers as "It" — says that It knows the latter was built two millennia after Kalidasa's fortress among the ruins on which It is seated. It therefore fails to understand why Morgan's creation has become known as Kalidasa's Tower.

PROFANING PARADISE — SACRED SPACE LITERALIZED

What I discovered in this recent work was the theme of heaven-storming *hubris* treated in an almost entirely non- or anti-religious context, one which went even beyond Clarke's sentiments of humanistic autonomy cited earlier. The novel therefore seemed an especially unpromising text in which to find images of traditional sacredness. But despite the steadfastly secular ideology pervading *The Fountains of Paradise* there are major motifs in it to which the history of religions has accorded great significance. There is, as a prime example, the paradisal imagery of the novel's tropical island setting.

In Eliade's essay on "Nostalgia for Paradise in the Primitive Traditions," as elsewhere in his work, he points out that numerous myths express the paradisal situation as involving both the closeness of earth to heaven — the latter's being "easily accessible, either by climbing a tree or a tropical creeper or a ladder, or by scaling a mountain"[19] — and the location of paradise itself "at the center of the cosmos" on the top of the highest peak.[20] These were motifs I had already considered in connection with the mandala geometaphor, but Eliade also describes how paradisal imagery informed the great voyages of discovery which, beyond their economic purposes, were quests for the Islands of the Blessed or some other version of an Earthly Paradise.[21] When geography became scientific, Eliade adds, literature took up this quest, and had continued "exalting the paradisiac islands of the Pacific Ocean, havens of all happiness, although the reality was very different. . ."[22]

Most of these paradise motifs are echoed in Clarke's Taprobane: King Kalidasa's pleasure-garden and fortress-palace at Demon Rock are obvious instances, as is Sri Kanda, the Sacred Mountain, with its Holy Footprint and stairway to the summit. Moreover, there is the Orbital Tower itself, a world-axis or Jacob's Ladder to heaven situated so as to make Taprobane, in Rajasinghe's phrase, "the center of the world. . . of many worlds".

The Tower particularly seemed to qualify as a symbol of sacred space in the inhospitable context of the novel's post-religious 22nd century. According to Larry Shiner's summary in a 1972 essay, the five principal characteristics of Eliade's symbology of sacred space are that it

1.   marks a *break* in the homogeneity of hitherto undifferentiated space;
2.   these breaks provide a spatial *orientation* especially when they bear the symbolism of the Center as almost all major breaks do;
3.   the Center is also an *axis mundi*, a break in plane which creates an *opening* between cosmic levels;
4.   by consecrating both a horizontal point of reference and a vertical axis of communication a *world* is founded;
5.   this foundation is seen as a *repetition* of the primordial act of creation by the gods.[23]

To varying degrees the Space Elevator as well as the paradisal imagery of Clarke's novel did seem to fulfill these qualifications. Thus, in the case of *The Fountains of Paradise* I was confronted by a popular document which at one level manifests the sort of confident irreligion one associates with a technological approach to the world, but which on a second level suggests Mircea Eliade's concepts of sacred space as reflected in the myths and rites of traditional cultures.

However, what eventually came through to me was that at yet *another* level a literalistic attitude toward the images and motifs in Clarke's work is the determinative one, undermining in a decisive and edifying way their value as positive elements of a Space-Age mythos. Instead of being treated as symbols in Eliade's fashion—or metaphorized, in mine—these once-sacred elements are seen as literal facts (sometimes as prospective facts) in a subtle process of profanization.

Finding out how Clarke came to write *The Fountains of Paradise* gave me my initial evidence of this profane literalism. In the collection of his essays mentioned above, *The View from Serendip*, he indicates that he began to conceive of the novel in 1966, which is also when he first learned about the possibility of an actual Orbital Tower.[24] In addition, he recounts that just after completing another novel, *Imperial Earth*, in 1975, he noticed that a Russian volume of paintings related to space exploration depicted a Space Elevator as "poised . . . immediately above Sri Lanka, though presumably the cable ends in Africa, since an equatorial site is mandatory and we're seven degrees north".[25]

What I inferred from this information was that Clarke had first been prompted to plan a novel dealing with the Orbital Tower in 1966 when he learned of the feasibility of such a project and actually began the manuscript a decade later upon seeing the Russian painting's suggestive inclusion of Sri Lanka—the island where he had been living since 1956. As I have emphasized, it was Clarke's own 1945 article which predicted the possibility of satellites hovering above the equator, so he naturally would have been intrigued with a device which made such dramatic use of one of them.

Of course, if such information and inferences begin to show that there is a factual basis, even a factual autobiographical basis, underlying Clarke's writing of *The Fountains of Paradise*, surely this is to be expected of any novelist. It is perhaps above all to be expected of a novelist who employs the classic science fiction technique of "extrapolation" from established data and procedures. However, the matter goes beyond standard science fiction extrapolation—or implies the inherent literalism of that technique—when it is realized that Clarke wishes the themes and images of his novel to be confirmed as factually true and technologically achievable. This is signalled first by his Preface, in which he feels called upon to explain that "the country I have called Taprobane does not quite exist, but is about ninety percent congruent with the island of Ceylon (now Sri Lanka)" (p. xiii). But a sense of the pervasive literalism in the novel is even more strongly reinforced by reading Clarke's section of Sources and Acknowledgments following his concluding chapters.

In this section he starts by saying:

> the writer of historical fiction has a peculiar responsibility to his
> readers, especially when he is dealing with unfamiliar times and
> places. He should not distort facts or events when they are known;
> and when he invents them as he is often compelled to do, it is his
> duty to indicate the dividing line between imagination and reality.
> The writer of science fiction has the same responsibility, squared
> (p. 256).

There follows Clarke's attestation that in the novel he has moved Sri
Lanka southward so that it straddles the equator, thus becoming a
scientifically acceptable earth terminal for the Orbital Tower. He also
carefully states that he has "doubled the height of the Sacred Mountain,
and moved it closer to 'Yakkagala.' For both places exist, very much as
I have described them" (p.256). Next Clarke emphasizes, at several
paragraphs' length, that the Sacred Mountain (Sri Kanda) and Yakkagala
(Demon Rock) in the novel are versions of Adam's Peak and Sigiriya
(Lion Rock) in Sri Lanka, respectively—he is anxious to call these
"trifling changes in the geography of Ceylon" (p. 256)—and that King
Kalidasa is based upon 5th century Ceylon's actual King Kasyapa.[26]

  Three full pages of these Sources and Acknowledgments are then
given over to the novel's paramount image: the Space Elevator. We learn
that the Russian engineer Artsutanov, referred to in Clarke's narrative
as the first man to conceive of the idea, is the actual name of the person
who did indeed propose a "heavenly funicular" (p. 258) in 1960. Even
the detail of the gravitational field's dictating Taprobane as the only
equatorial site for the Tower has to be provided with its factual justifica-
tion when Clarke avows that a beach on the southern coast of Sri Lanka
where he owns a house "is at *precisely* the closest spot on any large body
of land to the point of maximum geosynchronous stability" (p.261).

  These statements, I concluded, could be put together with others
inside the main text of the novel itself—e.g., Rajasinghe's questions to
the goddess-fresco: "What could you possibly know of *real* worlds
beyond the sky?"—to support the case that a desire for literalistic "realization" of sacred spatial imagery dominates Clarke's vision in *The
Fountains of Paradise*. Whereas for Eliade the paradisal islands of the
Pacific have been exalted as surviving mythic images in modern literature "although the reality was very different", for Clarke's purposes
the reality is not *allowed* to be very different; the intent is to show that
Sri Lanka and its Sacred Mountain *are* actually at the center of the
world, *are* paradise, and that an *axis mundi* can *in fact* be built, here

alone, connecting earth with heaven. Thus is the paradise of sacred symbology profaned.

RESCUING CLARKE'S CEYLON CONNECTION

When I finally saw that Arthur C. Clarke's literalism had colored his contribution as a Space-Age mythmaker, it occurred to me that here was a corroboration of the Apollonic presence I had felt in this representative figure. For if at one stage of Apollo's development he was the God of poetry, the attributes reiterated by James Hillman nevertheless predominate: distant and calculating discernment, the pseudo-poetic extrapolations of a scientific patriarch dreaming he is awake, seeing far but only from the ego's standpoint.

On the other hand, this hardly ended my fascination with Clarke. In addition to the sheer entertainment his writing had given me and the evidently affable persona he projected, I suspected he still had a helpful role to play in my own search. There were elements in his life and work which could lead toward an understanding of the mythic significance of the Space Age as long as they could be extricated from his well-intentioned literalism. Indeed, the subtlety of that literalism was itself a valuable lesson, if only in what to avoid. The positive side of Clarke's contribution, however, lay in the earth imagery he had highlighted. Like Erich von Däniken on a less sophisticated level, Clarke's mishandling of the images he had turned up in the course of a long writing career could not entirely extinguish their mythic resonance. They could yet be rescued.

Just as Apollonic space technology had unwittingly provided May Swenson an opportunity to metaphorize with its Orbiter 5 photograph, so had Clarke's Apollonic literalism supplied additional chances for metaphorizing with its focus on a hovering satellite's tie to the exotic island of Ceylon. Moreover, there was a provocative link between that first significant whole earth photograph and Clarke's involvements.

Early in my research I had seen the Orbiter 5 picture reproduced in Clarke's own 1968 volume *The Promise of Space*, where he had supplied the following suggestively-worded caption: "India and Ceylon are visible through light clouds near the center. . ."[27] The fact that he helped convey to the public a whole earth image with the specific mention of its being focused on Ceylon surely played a part in bringing to birth *The Fountains of Paradise*, which Clarke had begun to conceive of only a year or two earlier. This timetable for his novel's gestation, as I have said above, is suggested in Clarke's collection of autobiogaphical essays *The View From Serendip*.

I went back to this book after my examination of the novel because it offered additional data on the Clarkean connection between Ceylon and the geostationary satellite. If Ceylon were, indeed, the center of worlds in Clarke's fiction (a piece of fiction built around the notion of a magically orbiting satellite he had himself dreamed up decades earlier), as well as the first land to show up in the middle of an earth photographed by a satellite and popularized by his own *Promise of Space*—if Ceylon were central in these evocative ways, it certainly merited closer consideration, starting with Clarke's relationship to it.

"Serendip" is yet another name—besides Sri Lanka, Ceylon, and Taprobane—for the island Clarke happened upon in 1954. As he points out early in the book, this name is derived from "Sarandib", the Muslim traders' designation for what was an important landfall on their voyages. This importance is reflected in their tales of Sinbad, who encountered its Valley of Gems and elephant-carrying Roc birds. Clarke says that why he arranged his life so that he no longer needed to leave Ceylon is one of *The View From Serendip's* main themes.[28]

Much of the appeal of the island, he writes, involved the nearness of enticing undersea habitats. He eventually published several accounts of his diving exploits off Ceylon's coasts, most notably at Great Basses Reef to the southeast, where in 1963 he participated in the discovery of a man-of-war which had sunk 261 years earlier with a cargo of silver. Reminiscing about this experience after the lapse of a decade, he introduces a theme which was to become another crucial one for my speculations: ". . . I was looking back on the greatest adventure of my life from the far side of Apollo, *2001*, and much else. . . Looking for treasure, I had found something more important."[29] Later in the book he explains what he means by this remark.

It has to do with the nature of Ceylon's attractiveness for him. Above all, as he ruminates, it is the southern coast of the island, looking out upon 8,000 miles of unbroken ocean to Antarctica, which is "the source of the magic".[30] He recalls for the reader that he was born in Minehead, Somerset, and played along its seashore as a boy on what he calls "the beach of a great curving bay in the west of England", facing north across the Bristol Channel toward Wales. Much later, after spending several years in Ceylon, he fell in love with "an exquisite arc of beach" on that south coast and bought a house there, but saw no connection between the two beaches.

The resonance of these sites was only revealed to him, he narrates, in the American midwest on the other side of the earth. He was asked by a lady at one of his lectures why he had settled in Ceylon, and the deepest reason finally hit him:

> I was about to switch on the sound track I had played a hundred times before, when suddenly I saw those two beaches, both so far away. Do not ask me why it happened then; but in that moment of double vision, I knew the truth.
>
> The drab, chill northern beach on which I had so often shivered through an English summer was merely the pale reflection of an ultimate and long-unsuspected beauty. Like the three princes of Serendip, I had found far more than I was seeking—in Serendip itself.
>
> Ten thousand kilometres from the place where I was born, I had come home.[31]

AT THE CENTER, SERENDIP AND THE SATELLITE

This, then, is the eventual answer Clarke gives for why he resettled so far from England. And his surprising homecoming, like his chance encounter with Ceylon in the first place, brings up the theme I was to speculate about far beyond Clarkean contexts. It was a motif with roots in Ceylon—but also in England.

The three princes to whom Clarke is referring in the passage just quoted are the principals in an Arabian Nights-type fairy tale, *The Three Princes of Serendip*, which lies at the source of the notion of serendipity. *The View From Serendip* also includes an essay called "Concerning Serendipity" in which Clarke attempts to supply some of the history of this overused but inadequately understood term. As he says at the outset,

> 'serendipity' does not even appear in the excellent 1936 Longmans, Green edition of Roget's Thesaurus which still serves me well; yet I have come across it recently in articles on engineering and astronomy by authors who would certainly not consider themselves

to be literary stylists. However, though the word is usually employed in its correct meaning—of something useful or valuable
discovered by a happy chance—I have found that very few people
know the actual origin.[32]

He then goes on to divulge the term's roots, drawing on the OED rather
than any primary sources:

> The word was invented, or at least put on paper, by the essayist
> Horace Walpole in 1754—exactly two hundred years before I myself
> set foot on Serendip. According to the *Oxford English Dictionary*,
> Walpole told one of his numerous correspondents that 'he formed
> it upon the title of the fairy-tale *The Three Princes of Serendip*, the
> heroes of which were always making discoveries, by accident and
> sagacity, of things they were not in quest of. . .'
>
> Whether *The Three Princes* is a genuine folk tale, or whether
> Walpole made it up, I do not know. But the exotically melodious
> word 'serendipity' obviously filled a gap in the English language,
> though it seems to have taken two centuries to get into general
> circulation.[33]

This is the extent of Clarke's dealings with the definition and history of serendipity. But just because his own personal relations, as a
Space-Age exemplar, to serendipity and to Serendip were such strong
ones I was prompted to look more deeply into the matter than he did.

The imagery and implications of Serendip or Ceylon were already
becoming obvious. Here was another geometaphor, overlapping in
many respects with the mandalas discussed in Chapter 4, where the
paradise motifs of access to heaven, *axis mundi*, sacred mountain, and
centeredness were all introduced. In the case of Ceylon as an image of
the whole earth the details provided by the life and work of Clarke
added further occasions for metaphorizing. To reiterate: His transmis-
sion of the Orbiter 5 picture actually placed Ceylon at the center of
an earth viewed for the first time as only the Space Age allowed it to
be viewed, after which May Swenson's Gaia-grounded vision could
show us the woman in its midst and mists—with Ceylon, again, as the
"holy jug" in her grasp, the earthen omphalos through which life ab-
originally streams. And his novel, *The Fountains of Paradise*, while
revealing the subtlety of the Apollonic literalism against which a
metaphorizing approach would want to react, also presented images
such as Sri Kanda, with its stairway and Holy Footprint, which imply
imaginal grounding the reverse of Clarke's efforts to "real-ize" sacred

space merely in factual terms. The Holy Footprint of Adam, or Siva, or Buddha, for instance, could be playfully contrasted with Neil Armstrong's "one small step for man", Apollo's footprint in the lunar dust. Indeed, with Ceylon as a Space-Age focal point for such fantasizing (or a paradisal island suggesting the earth's true purpose in the sea of space), the Sacred Mountain at its very middle seemed an even more sharply focused center, the place of primodial contact with the plane of heaven. Moreover, once having seen through his profane literalizing it was possible to recognize Clarke's Space Elevator, a structure which could only connect with the earth at the summit of Sri Kanda, as a supremely powerful image for the Space Age of that sacred axial interrelation between the interior of the earth, its surface, its skies, and beyond.

This fictional idea of the Orbital Tower was a product of the commingling in Clarke's experience of Ceylon and its Sacred Mountain with his earlier pioneering work on the theory of the geosynchronous communications satellite. Only a deeper probe into the roots of the latter, I could see, would open up the full ramifications of the Space Elevator and the realms it connected.

But meanwhile there was that other agenda contributed by Clarke's Ceylonese imagery: to find the meaning of serendipity and its possible relevance to a Space-Age mythos. The role of Ceylon as the point of mythic reconnection to earth included not only its own most immediate geometaphoric attributes and its indirect relation to the Space Age by way of Clarke's comsat but also its suggestion of a style of seeking, an openness to unsought but revelatory conjunctions. Meditating on Serendip, in other words, gave me the impression that serendipity might be a refinement of the metaphorizing method I had decided, early on, was required for the search. I needed to pursue Walpole's term beyond Clarke's modest explanation.

And so, after having completed almost all of my reading in Clarke's work I began my exploration of these two themes, the satellite and serendipity, by traveling to his homeland.

FROM SERENDIP TO ST. EVAL

It was in particular a determination to know more about the genesis of the geostationary satellite that led me to St. Eval and Davidstow Moor on the Cornish coast in 1979. Not only was a journey to the veritable Serendip out of the question, but I suspected that England's southwestern corner had its own Space-Age significance.

Toward the close of his *View From Serendip* Clarke reprints his address to a conference celebrating the centennial of Bell's invention of the telephone. The conference, held at MIT in 1976, focused, understandably enough, on communications technology. Clarke's presence was partly owing to his work on the communications satellite, and that was the topic he addressed as he began his remarks. "Back in 1943," he recounts, "as an extremely callow officer in the Royal Air Force, I was given a mysterious assignment to a fog-shrouded airfield at the southwestern tip of England."[34] He goes on to relate how he worked with the American team from MIT on the Ground Controlled Approach radar device. The leader of the MIT group, he says, was a young physicist named Luis Alvarez. "The pioneering struggles of the GCA 'talk down' system," he adds, "you'll find in my only *non*-science-fiction novel . . . though *Glide Path* certainly would have been science fiction had it appeared at any time before 1940."[35] And one further comment on this incident from Clarke's early adulthood drew my eye:

> Luis's brainchild provided me with the peaceful environment, totally insulated from all the nasty bombings and invasions happening elsewhere, which allowed me to work out the principles of communciations satellites in the spring of 1945.[36]

These were the clues enabling me to ponder more deeply the imagery of the geosynchronous comsat and to pinpoint the exact location of its origins at the abandoned airfields of St. Eval and Davidstow—right up the road, as it happened, from where the Goddess seemed present at the prehistoric holed stone, the Men-an-tol, and at the tiny settlement of Wicca. Therefore, while I did not know precisely what I expected to find at these disused sites, I did sense that my journey from a literary Serendip to a physical Cornwall (at the behest of an unwitting Arthur C. Clarke) could yield new data pertinent to the mythos—and the method—of reconnection to the earth.

CHAPTER EIGHT

GROUND CONTROLLED DESCENT AT THE DAWN OF THE SPACE AGE

> I am not indulging in false modesty—a concept which all my friends would reject with hysterical laughter—when I say that my contribution to satellite communications was largely a matter of luck. I happened to be in the right place at the right time.
>
> Arthur C. Clarke[1]

Aside from being Arthur C. Clarke's only non-science fiction novel, *Glide Path* does not have a great deal to recommend it aesthetically.[2] As a realistic fictionalization of his experiences in the RAF it is certainly not one of his best storytelling efforts. Nevertheless, my own fascination with those experiences, particularly as they helped induce Clarke's idea for the geosynchronous communications satellite—the comsat—made me an attentive reader of the novel.

It was *Glide Path* which described the development of the Ground Controlled Approach radar system in Cornwall in late 1943 and 1944, and gave me the notion of seeking out, some 35 years later, the actual sites where this had taken place. My reading of the novel was a search for clues to what might have been occurring in Clarke's imagination as a young RAF officer in those years, perceptions or preoccupations from his Cornish sojourn which might have resurfaced in the imagery of *Glide Path* in 1963 so as to suggest the shape of the comsat theory's genesis—or, indeed, to hint at any other element of the Space Age's larger implications.

This was, after all, the time of birth of the Space Age itself. Despite the tendency of many to date its start from the Soviet Union's launching of Sputnik in 1957 it seemed to me that the German V-2 rockets which achieved a height of over 100 miles in those war years truly ushered in the Age of Space, since "outer space" is generally judged to begin at the 100-mile altitude. Clarke's 1945 essay also cites the V-2 as the prototype of the long-range rocket required to launch his comsat into its "magic orbit".[3] To be sure, this was a time when bloody violence and destruction occupied the foreground of history; the Allies were advancing on Germany and Japan while Hitler's Holocaust was continuing and his rockets were exploding in southern England rather than exploring outer space.

But although the military uses of space are a continuing (or even increasing) threat, a more positive outcome for humankind of what began some 40 years ago can, I am convinced, still prevail. And this may depend, in turn, on whether people can find a right relationship to the earth. As far as I was concerned, the search for a mythic reconnection was a stop toward such a relationship.

FINDING THE GLIDE PATH

It has already been mentioned that *Glide Path* is dedicated to Luis Alvarez and the others who worked on the GCA system at MIT and later in Cornwall. Another bit of front matter for the novel is a not-surprising disclaimer by Clarke: He says that the characters in it do not in any way resemble the real-life originals and that "the sequence of events departs completely from historical facts." While respecting these warnings, I felt there were still some connections to be found between Clarke's actual experiences and their novelistic recollection, especially regarding the lenses of imagery through which the writer looked back at his life as he transmuted it into fiction. In any case I was persuaded that at least in broad outline the historical situation and the subject matter and setting of the story were the same.

Clarke's protagonist is named Alan Bishop, and since this character makes reference early on to being near the top of the alphabet when queuing up to get his paycheck it is fair to assume the name itself is a close facsimile of the author's. Beyond this, however, the choice of "Bishop" is noteworthy by itself: The word comes from the

Greek *episcopos*, which means "overseer", and the idea of seeing things from above, in a bird's-eye view, does figure significantly in the novel. Its first line is: "Flying Officer Alan Bishop found it singularly peaceful on this tiny metal platform a hundred feet above the North Sea". (p. 3)

From this radar station F/O Bishop is transferred to a remote airfield near Land's End — St. Erryn — to work on a secret radar device. In a brief flashback we learn that it was at Gatesbury on the Wiltshire moors that "he had said good-by to the simple, old-fashioned world of 'wireless' and had come for the first time face to face with the unsuspected marvels of radar" (p. 20). From my reading of Jeremy Bernstein's piece on Clarke in *Experiencing Science* I knew that he had in fact been stationed at Yatesbury (with a "Y" instead of a "G") in Wiltshire near the beginning of his RAF service, so this is the likely location for his first real-life encounter with radar.[4]

Interestingly enough, the "world of 'wireless'" was not entirely jettisoned from Clarke's later experience, for the title of the journal in which he published his 1945 comsat essay was *Wireless World*. Even more significant was the site of this base where Clarke entered the futuristic realm of space communications. The veritable Yatesbury is less than three miles from the most impressive megalithic complex in the British Isles: the Avebury circle of standing stones with the adjacent Silbury Hill and West Kennet Long Barrow burial chamber. In William Stukeley's early 18th century panoramic drawing of the area, looking north, the word "Yatesbury," with a hill and church tower, is clearly visible to the left of the main Avebury circle near Windmill Hill, an important prehistoric settlement.[5] As with the archaic earth images I had discovered earlier in future-oriented science fiction films, this juxtaposition again implied the centrality of ancient terrestrial data in assessing the meaning of the Space Age.

Certainly the development of radar, which began in the mid-1930s and intensified throughout the war, has been a major contributing factor in the Space Age's forward and outward thrust. In its fictionalized account *Glide Path* makes clear that Clarke played a worthwhile role in that development, while it also indicates the possibility for radar to point our priorities in a very different direction.

The site on the North Sea to which Alan Bishop is sent after his training at Gatesbury is one of a chain of radar stations all around the coasts of England which had detected incoming German aircraft and led to their defeat in the Battle of Britain in 1940. Later, in 1943-44, this same network of "Chain Home Stations" was used to warn of incoming

V-2 rockets. Since Clarke later speculated, in *The Fountains of Paradise,* about a "necklace" of satellites encircling the earth above the equator (pp. 248, 261), this image of a chain of radar towers around England implies that the latter can be seen as a geometaphor, a microcosm of the whole earth.

After F/O Bishop begins his work at St. Erryn in Cornwall he visits a friend at another of these stations and climbs one of its 300-foot towers. At the top, true to his name, he surveys the entire horizon and discerns "sea both to the north and to the south. He could tell at a glance that he was on the last tapering tongue of England as it jutted out into the Atlantic, and somehow this added to his sense of instability". (p. 89) It is important to note that in descriptions of the Cornish RAF operations the evocative qualities of radar come through as often as its technical characteristics:

> . . . the first signals were coming in, as the questing beams searched heaven and earth. Fuzzy, softly glowing pictures, meaningless except to those who knew how to read their messages of life and death, were appearing as if by magic. And it *was* magic; though he had watched countless radar displays, Alan had not yet lost his sense of wonder. He was seeing the world around him by waves a hundred thousand times longer than visible light. The images were blurred, and it would take him some time to interpret them, but that was to be expected. The patterns it perceives mean nothing to a baby when it first opens its eyes. (pp. 45-46)

This same incident also provides another instance of the hero's bird's-eye perspective, for one of the radar screens strikes him as though "he was really looking down upon the earth and the approaching aircraft from an enormous height". (p. 46)

Balancing this language, however, is the emphasis on control from the ground of planes coming in to land. The Ground Controlled Approach system first put into practice in Cornwall had been invented by Alvarez at MIT; that institution's Radiation Laboratory was the United States' wartime center for radar research. In the novel, Dr. Theodore Hatton, a world-renowned scientist, is described as having encountered the work of a Professor Schuster—Alvarez's surrogate, despite disclaimers—on what *Glide Path* calls GCD: Ground Controlled Descent. When Hatton had observed Schuster's team demonstrating the GCD technique at an airfield outside of Boston, "calling down aircraft from the sky with uncanny accuracy, it had been like a religious revelation". (p. 31) It was Hatton who had seen to it that the GCD scientific team and equipment were sent to St. Erryn.

As the RAF proceeds with its testing into 1944 it becomes obvious that the poor visibility on the Cornish coast, together with St. Erryn's having the world's widest runway and an absence of interference from German bombs, is responsible for Hatton's choice. Like the theme of glide path control being maintained from the ground — the person who talks to the pilots by radio is called the Approach Controller — this contribution of the Cornish mist seemed to me worthy of metaphorizing reflection.

During one of the GCD tests it is noted that "the mist still hid all reference points. . .". (p. 71) And when Bishop actually flies on a test himself he nervously realizes that "the fact that nothing in the skies of the whole world had its position pinpointed so accurately as S. Sugar did not help him in the least. *That* was theoretical knowledge; the reality was the wet and swirling fog beyond the windows". (p. 70)

Again in this experience, at least when the fog does not intervene, Bishop's lofty vantage point is stressed as he sees the St. Erryn airfield laid out below him. Later, on a leave for his father's funeral at Lyncombe on the Bristol Channel — there are an actual Lynton and an actual Lynmouth just west of Clarke's home of Minehead on this coast — he climbs the hill behind the town and looks down: "From this viewpoint, the whole town lay spread beneath him, as if in an aerial photograph . . . Alan knew every street and alley in the map spread out before him, for once this had been his entire universe. Now it seemed very small, and its smallness was not merely physical. He had outgrown his home; the ties that bound him to it were dissolving. There was no longer any place where he really belonged". (p. 161)

If we can transfer this last sentiment to Clarke — who wrote it in Ceylon — we recall his focus in *The View From Serendip* on finding his true home on a southern beach of that island nation. Here is another reminder that through Clarke's biographical journey Sri Lanka and the English West Country are interrelated as places of Space-Age significance.

It should be added that the theme of "over-seeing" in *Glide Path* is also extended to the figure of Professor Schuster. As portrayed in the novel, the inventor of the GCD system is crippled by childhood polio, and this coupled with his scientific brilliance leads Bishop to imagine him "soaring away like an eagle into realms where few other men could go". (p.80) Unlike Bishop, Schuster is also a pilot who actually assumes an eagle's viewpoint during a flight eastward from Cornwall: "Three thousand feet below, something strange caught his eye. A circle of stone columns, dull gray in the somber light of this cloudy afternoon, stood in lonely isolation on an open plain". (p. 109) He does not recognize the site, but his British copilot informs him it is Stonehenge, adding that it must be older than anything in America.

> Schuster was impressed; he banked the aircraft in a great circle, picking out the pattern of the immense slabs and wondering how they had been reared into position. In the face of such antiquity, his own problems seemed suddenly transient and trivial. A thousand years from now, these monoliths would still be defying the elements, while the only record of his existence would be a few articles in moldering scientific journals.
>   No—that was not true. Already he had made his mark upon history—upon *real* history, not the blinkered, myopic narrative that records only the doings of generals and politicians. He was a part, and no small part, of the forces that were shaping the future. (p. 109)

The conjunction of the futuristic with the archaic is presented in this passage even more directly than in the description of Alan Bishop's introduction to radar at Gatesbury (the connection of the latter to Yatesbury and Avebury not being obvious to the average reader). And since Schuster is depicted as an eventual Nobel laureate in physics—another characteristic he shares with the real-life Luis Alvarez—we truly have here a scientist "on the cutting edge" who is measuring his decidedly Space-Age life work against the most celebrated monument of ancient terrestrial religion and culture.

RADAR REFLECTIONS—THE LANDING FIELD AS GLOWING MAZE

The many images of *Glide Path* all appealed to me as clues to mythic meaning: the view from the sky above, the control from the ground below of an aircraft's approach and descent, the chain of towers around England, the evocative aspects of radar and the fog it required to prove its worth in the GCD system, the portentous intersections of the Space and the Stone Age, the prominence of Cornwall and the West Country. That they seemed significant to my search was largely because they repeated or complemented motifs and geometaphors I had uncovered earlier as aspects of a possible Space-Age mythos.

Another point to reiterate, however, is that these elements from *Glide Path* might constitute, at least in part a sort of imaginal seedbed out of which Clarke's geosynchronous satellite idea could grow. By exploring the former I hoped to see more deeply into the significance of the latter. Now I cannot, of course, maintain that Clarke was conscious of these ingredients himself when he put together the article he eventually published in 1945, or that they comprised any of his deliberate intention. But they did come from his own memories of Cornwall in 1943 and '44 as he composed the novel almost two decades later. An association between these motifs and the conception of the comsat was not, therefore, entirely farfetched, and I trusted that it would become a more and more meaningful one as I continued to pursue the text of *Glide Path*.

What I found when I did so was that the novel contained a further image which gathered together several of these earlier ones. It was not an image I had given much thought to within a Space-Age context, although I was certainly familiar with it from my general research on religious myth and symbol, and I had studied its appearance in Melville's writing. Once I became aware of its central role in *Glide Path*, however, it brought a surprising revelation regarding the outcome of my inquiry into the comsat.

Seven different times in his novel Clarke uses the term "maze". He employs it three times to describe the wiring of the radar equipment and once in referring to the calculations scrawled on Professor Schuster's papers. Of the other three instances, one pertains to ground reflections on a radar screen while the final pair concern the image of the St. Erryn runways. One of these last two also involves a radar display screen: "They had come at just the right moment, as an aircraft began its approach. There it was — a sharply defined blob of light at the limit of the tube. It was moving even as they watched; with every sweep of the scan it edged a fraction of an inch closer to the glowing maze that marked the airfield". (pp. 95-96) The second occurs when Alan Bishop has to bicycle across the field: "At night, or in heavy fog, it was easy to get lost on the airfield and to cycle around and around its vast concrete maze, unable to find a way out". (p. 73)

In this reference the close relation between a maze and a fog is made evident — one can be lost in either — and it can be seen that mazes inscribed on the ground are a kind of terrestrial equivalent of the atmospheric bewilderment experienced in the mists of Cornwall. Alan Bishop's last statement asserts that the maze is something to get out of, but if the St. Erryn landing field is the glowing maze on the radar screen, the objective for a plane on the glide path is to enter. Since the novel is fictionalizing the development of the Ground Controlled Approach system, an additional implication within Clarke's narrative is that the maze on the ground seems to be inviting this descent or re-entry, providing subtle guidance through its own convolutions.

Traditionally, the symbolism of mazes and labyrinths has to do with difficult but desirable transitions — the passage to adulthood in initiation, for example, or that of the dead person's spirit to the after-world — or what Gertrude Rachel Levy, in her insightful work from 1948, *Religious Conceptions of the Stone Age*, calls "the winding path of conditional entry".[6] The invitation to enter may be there, in other words, but it has conditions attached to it: the one seeking entrance must approach in a certain manner, avoiding false turns and blind alleys while also relinquishing the presumption of direct access to the center. The seeker must satisfy the demands of the labyrinth.

DOWN FROM DAVIDSTOW MOOR — CARVINGS AND CLUES IN ROCKY VALLEY

I have said in the previous chapter that I did not quite know what I expected to find at St. Eval and Davidstow. I had traveled there to supplement my reading of Clarke's writings — most especially *Glide Path* — and, in so doing, to gain some sense of whatever mythic import there might be in his conception of the geostationary satellite at the dawn of the Space Age. The images of *Glide Path* alone had not given me any single conclusive message about this matter; they offered a series of interconnecting clues which related provocatively to my overall project. But when I tried to add them up and get the deep meaning of the comsat I encountered the bewilderment of the maze instead.

When I was planning my 1979 trip to England I decided that actually seeing where Clarke had served could, in some unspecifiable way, help me put together the clues of *Glide Path* more successfully. The church at St. Eval — the novel's St. Erryn — as I have portrayed it earlier, had a large RAF flag hanging inside the sanctuary. The presence of the name Noel and the etymology of "Eval" (the possibility that through the Cornish it was derived from *humus*, or earth) were other suggestive findings at the once busy base just across the road. The red beacon light on the church tower was a reminder of all that had gone on when Clarke was here 35 years before. Now the only sound of life was the whine of a model airplane flown by a boy and his father on the empty and crumbling expanse of the airfield—once, according to the novel, the widest runway in the world.

What I found at Davidstow was a horizon containing the highest point in Cornwall to the south on Bodmin Moor, a large cheese processing plant due west, and a reservoir beyond pine trees to the southwest. Various abandoned buildings and mounds occupied the foreground. Decrepit runways connected by even more decrepit asphalt roads were all around me. The road from Launceston went right through the middle of this maze and headed for the Atlantic coast five miles away. After walking around for a few minutes and taking some pictures, I drove over to the Davidstow parish church. Aside from a few RAF headstones in its churchyard, it was similarly silent about any memories of World War II.

In sum, neither St. Eval nor Davidstow Moor revealed how Clarke had first dreamed up his comsat or what the mythic ramifications of its genesis might be. The comprehensive meaning I had sought in *Glide Path* was unfortunately not awaiting me at the two Cornish airfields.

What I did begin to see, paradoxically enough, was the message hidden in my own bewilderment. That is, in not knowing what I expected to find at these sites—not knowing how they were supposed to inform me about Clarke's satellite—and then in not discovering any recognizable answer, perhaps I was experiencing something more valuable to my search than a simple solution to a simple problem. Perhaps I had been straining against my lack of clear direction in my haste to get to the center and nail down the cause of Clarke's idea, instead of seeing that lack as an opportunity for opening up to the mystery of the unexpected, a chance to meet the conditions of true discovery.

My mind returned to the image of the maze in *Glide Path*. As I mulled over my lack of success at St. Eval and Davidstow it became, increasingly, a positive emblem for my perplexity, a reminder that my seeking would probably *need* to be labyrinthine, full of dead ends and false turnings for the ego's rational expectations. I was aided in this curious revelation by one of those clusters of coincidence I had begun to respect, for I knew that due west of Davidstow Moor a few miles— right on the glide path, so to speak—the labyrinth image itself was literally carved in stone for my further contemplation.

The location I am referring to was a narrow valley formed by a small stream which dropped quickly down to the Atlantic. I had first read about what was there in a strange little essay on Glastonbury Tor while studying the archaeological controversies over ancient sites in the English countryside (and well before my reading of *Glide Path*). The

West Country town of Glastonbury was felt by many to be the legendary place where Joseph of Arimathea introduced Christianity to Britain as well as a center of Arthurian associations. Along with a ruined abbey, "holy thorn" trees supposedly sprung from Joseph's staff, and a venerable healing well concealing some version of the Grail, Glastonbury features a striking 518-foot-high hill, called the Tor, with the tower of a former St. Michael's church on its summit.

Geoffrey Russell, the author of the essay, was intent on a particular aspect of the Tor. The story of how he acquired this preoccupation will also tell how I knew to head for the little valley after leaving Davidstow Moor.

An editorial preface to the essay supplies most of the information I found noteworthy:

> Mr. Russell's interest in his subject flows from a mystical experience in Ceylon in 1944. This was quite unexpected and unsought and involved the identification, in himself, of a pattern of concentric circles which had to do with the function of the brain. Mr. Russell was able to make a contemporary pencil sketch of the pattern, but he seldom mentioned his experience as he regarded its content to be incommunicable.[7]

Having had this vision in Ceylon while Arthur C. Clarke was serving in Cornwall, Russell discovered the meaning of the pattern in 1962 while Clarke, by then in Ceylon, was recalling his Cornish experiences for the writing of *Glide Path*. In the same "unexpected and unsought" fashion as the original epiphany, Russell, retired in Ireland, happened upon a photograph of two Cretan labyrinth figures in the correspondence column of the magazine *Country Life*. The patterns, said the caption, were carved on the slate wall of Rocky Valley, below the village of Bossiney on the Cornish Atlantic coast. The carvings were only found in 1948 — too late for Clarke to have seen them on a wartime outing from nearby Davidstow four years earlier — but they have been dated from the Bronze Age, around 1500 B.C. Whether they were actually produced by voyagers from ancient Crete is impossible to establish; the configuration of the two engravings, however, is very much the classic design of Daedalus's labyrinth shown on Cretan coins.

My initial fascination upon reading of Russell's experience had less to do with the maze motif *per se* than with a connection it permitted to another of the many guises of the Goddess: Ariadne. In her chapter on Ariadne as "Mistress of the Labyrinth", Christine Downing had stressed not Ariadne's guidance of Theseus—a solar figure like Daedalus—but her relationship to Dionysos, the bisexual alternative to Apollo whom Downing calls "the god of women". And the discussion of Ariadne's equal partnership with Dionysos is followed by Downing's treatment of a still earlier mythic stratum, one in which the Mistress of the Labyrinth is herself a divine being.

> Ariadne is one of the Great Mothers, a great goddess of Crete. As such she is titled the Potent One... the Untouched One. To ask who Ariadne is, to follow the thread all the way to the end, leads us to the center of a labyrinth and at that center we find Ariadne herself. In the beginning there is Ariadne, a goddess complete in herself, androgynous and self-perpetuating, creating out of her own being with no need of another.[8]

Here was the Goddess again, and the provocative figure of Dionysos was not far away. Coupled with Ceylon, Clarke, and Cornwall, through Geoffrey Russell's experience of the maze design, the appearance of these two mythic figures was surely some kind of clue to Space-Age significance. This seemed especially likely insofar as Ariadne, as Mistress of the Labyrinth, provided the ball of thread, or "clew", which was the originating image behind any findings of clues on any quest.

For Russell the discovery that his 1944 vision was embodied in the Rocky Valley carvings led not to Crete, Ariadne, and Dionysos, but to Glastonbury. While investigating instances of the maze pattern he came upon an aerial photograph of the Tor and saw encircling it what he took to be the remains of a three-dimensional labyrinth, the trackways for conditional ascent by generations of pilgrims. This he associated with the Welsh tradition of the *Caer Sidi*, or "Spiral Castle," drawing on the discussion of the latter in Robert Graves's *The White Goddess* (a work begun obsessively in 1944 in the West Country village of Galmpton, Devon, and involving "a chain of more-than-coincidences"[9]). Consulting that formidable volume myself, however, I was pointed back toward Ariadne, the Goddess, and Rocky Valley.

In his treatment of the *Caer Sidi* Graves compares it to the overlapping tradition of the *Caer Arianrhod*, the Castle of the Welsh goddess Arianrhod, whom he then goes on to identify with the Cretan Ariadne. He also sees these "castles" as sometimes being oracular caves with spirally-coiled serpents such as Delphi with its Python guarding the mysteries of Gaia.[10] These were stimulating linkages, again by way of labyrinth imagery (or its more abstract form, the spiral), to the role of the Goddess in my search. And to make matters even more enticing,

Graves includes the Bossiney maze carvings in a paragraph listing British survivals of the "Spiral Castle" tradition.[11] Together with Geoffrey Russell's experiences and their strange relation to the spaces and times of Clarke's life, this was enough to add Rocky Valley to my itinerary for the journey to Cornwall in 1979. But it was not until I actually got there, after my reading of *Glide Path* and my failure to find the definitive essence of the comsat at the wartime sites where it had been conceived, that I began to see that the labyrinth was my enigmatic answer, a central if exasperating finding rather than an adjunct to other lines of thought. Indeed, it drew those other lines of thought into its own convoluted message.

And so, a few minutes after departing from the disused airfield and neighboring church at Davidstow I pulled our Cortina into a carpark next to the coast road in Bossiney. We walked north along this road, following the detailed Ordnance Survey map. Down a modest hill past a Palomino grazing in a field it intersected with Rocky Valley, indicated by an unprepossessing sign. A footpath led down to the left toward the Atlantic. All we could see at first was some sort of fish hatchery which seemed, rather anomalously, to be designated as "Trevillett Mill". The path passed a substantial house on the left which was apparently associated with the fish hatchery (or the mill), and then, crossing and recrossing the valley's causative stream, began to descend in earnest.

There were no more houses now, and no other hikers were visible as my wife and daughters joined me in looking for some indication of the maze carvings. It was a hot day; dense vegetation kept out Atlantic breezes and the gravel path was occasionally steep and slippery. We came to a few ruined stone buildings, dry-walled affairs half covered with ivy—almost certainly a mill from an earlier age.

The path turned down to the left to avoid these buildings, which were close to the perpendicular valley wall on our right. Perspiring and intent on following the latest twist of the path, I failed to see, beyond the ivy-covered ruins, a green rectangle on the valley wall itself. Joanna caught it, though, and we hurried through the muddy area around the buildings.

This metal plaque announced in raised gold letters that we had found what we were looking for:

ROCKY VALLEY ROCK CARVINGS
'LABYRINTH' PATTERN CARVINGS PROBABLY
OF THE EARLY BRONZE AGE (1800-1400 B.C.)

One of the engravings was below the plaque and slightly to the right. The other was a few feet farther to the right and somewhat above the first. Aside from a rough sketch accompanying the Russell essay and the description of the carvings as following the Cretan design, I had had no precise idea of what these specimens would look like. The reality was impressive: The two figures were deeply and meticulously incised into the rock wall, defiant of the random scratches of recent visitors. I ran my finger around the coils of one of them, regular and concentric. The other was as close to identical in size and configuration as could have been possible without mechanical help.

I took the usual photographs, after which we descended the rest of Rocky Valley to meet the Atlantic. Sitting on a ledge watching the ocean and the seagulls, I considered the carvings. Among other things I wondered why there were two. At first I thought of them as portals for some invisible entrance to the underworld—the Cumaean Gate to that realm in Virgil's *Aeneid* had had a Cretan labyrinth inscribed upon it. Another such entrance in Virgil's epic, *The Gate of Horn*, had given access to true dreams, suggesting the connection between underworld and unconscious. *The Gate of Horn* had been the original title of Levy's *Religious Conceptions of the Stone Age*, where I had learned of the labyrinth as the way of conditional entry. (What I did not find out until I returned home was that the *Oxford English Dictionary* derives "Cornwall" from the same Latin root as "horn", suggesting a view of the Cornish peninsula from above as a "corner", a projecting headland like Cape Horn or the Horn of Africa.)

And then, recalling my reading of Christine Downing and Robert Graves, I daydreamed that one engraving was Ariadne's, the other her Welsh counterpart Arianrhod's. These Goddess-guises added to those I had already encountered down the Cornish coast at Wicca and the Men-an-tol. This hinted, further, that just as Gaia had given the metaphorizing process its mythic grounding, so she might be behind the labyrinthine path of unexpected and unsought discoveries my seeking had begun to take.

CONDITIONAL RE-ENTRY

I had come a long way in my search from the Vermont study where I had read Arthur C. Clarke's work, and as I sat cooling off by the Atlantic I realized how much farther I had come in imagination.

The relation of Clarke and the paradisal island of Ceylon, with its ancient name of Serendip and its future role—at least in Clarke's fiction—as terminal for the awesome Orbital Tower, had supplied several major images for a possible Space-Age mythos. But this relation had also pointed back to Clarke's childhood and early work in the English West Country, particularly to the RAF bases where he had helped develop the GCA system and hatched his theory of the geostationary satellite. This part of his life, recollected novelistically in *Glide Path*, took place at the very beginning of the Age of Space, and therefore invited interpretation if I wanted to understand the mythic significance of the latter.

Unhappily for this interpretive effort, while the imaginal motifs of *Glide Path* were suggestive enough individually, they were confusing in the aggregate. It was fitting, then, that the bewilderment of the maze was the most comprehensive image in the novel, and instructive to me beyond my disappointment once I started to appreciate its message of indirect access. Actually seeing the two maze carvings, which reflected back the inconclusiveness of the visits to St. Eval and Davidstow, deepened my realization that in these pursuits approach was paramount.

As Gertrude Rachel Levy had written, the labyrinth withheld its center unless conditions were met. For his part, Geoffrey Russell had claimed to find an ascending maze at Glastonbury Tor, a pilgrim's track up to the tower of St. Michael the Apollonic dragonslayer. Whether such an ascent to the skies and space, a prospective abandoning of earth, had met its own mythic conditions was not my primary concern. What did concern me was whether opportunities might still exist for Space-Age culture to meet the conditions for re-entry. And with this in mind I found it significant that the focus of Clarke's wartime activities was an approach—*Glide Path* had called it a descent—controlled from, or by, "the ground". That is, at the birth of the Space Age, in the work of its most Apollonic representative, we find this "ground" setting the conditions for what constitutes a proper "glide path", the requisite slope for a safe landing.

For me, of course, "ground" implied Gaia in her many manifestations, including the Mistress of the Labyrinth. And as Gaia, one of the conditions the ground was surely setting was the playful awareness of metaphor: metaphorizing, in other words, was here once more being recommended as the means of mythic reconnection, as a major condition to be satisfied if we seek that reconnection.

But as I reviewed all of this on the warm summer day of my pilgrimage to Rocky Valley, having climbed back up from the ocean for another long stare at the carvings, I thought that a possible further requirement for threading the maze deserved attention.

I had come to Cornwall looking for an answer to the inception of the comsat at Clarke's airfields and had discovered unexpected insights at another site nearby. Once I overcame my disappointment and learned something of the lesson of my bewilderment, a new openness became increasingly possible. This was an openness to the meaning of chance findings, the importance of surprising conjunctions. The curiously revelatory interchange between the questions raised by *Glide Path* and the answer offered by Rocky Valley would not have occurred to me unless I had begun to meet this condition of openness — another name for which might be serendipity.

Arthur C. Clarke's relationship with Ceylon, discussed in the previous chapter, involved his awareness that serendipity had its origins in that island's earlier designation as "Serendip" as well as in the mind of the 18th century English writer Walpole. Knowing this from my study of Clarke's work, and conjuring with the image of Serendip as the center of a terrestrial maze or labyrinth geometaphor, I imagined that serendipity was a principle of movement toward that center, one of the conditions, like metaphorizing, to be satisfied in approaching earth.

CHAPTER NINE

SERENDIPITY, SYNCHRONICITY, SPONTANEITY

It seemed to me that I was high up in space. Far below I saw the globe of earth bathed in a glorious blue light. I saw the deep blue sea and the continents. Far below my feet lay Ceylon, and in the distance ahead of me the subcontinent of India.

C.G. Jung (recounting a vision he had had while recovering from a heart attack in 1944).[1]

STARTING AT STRAWBERRY HILL

The guidebook had been only partially helpful. My daughters and I had taken a train in from our hosts' house in Surrey to London to watch the Changing of the Guard like good tourists (the band played the "Theme from *Star Wars*"), get our standby plane tickets back to Boston, and try to find Horace Walpole's country house, Strawberry Hill.

What the guidebook said was that Strawberry Hill was in Twickenham, once a quiet village on the north bank of the Thames but now a crowded western suburb of London. It did not say where in Twickenham the house was located, however, so that after a ride on the Underground and another on a double-decker bus, the three of us stood in the center of this suburb with no idea where to go.

The first few people we asked had never heard of Strawberry Hill, but finally a woman in a park overlooking the Thames pointed us toward St. Mary's College for Women a few blocks away. Our goal was supposedly within the grounds of this school.

After walking the required distance we found the main entrance of the college, but no one answered the doorbell. St. Mary's was apparently closed for the summer.

Despite this setback, we decided to inspect the perimeter of the school grounds for signs of Walpole's house. All I knew about it at the time was that it was a "mock-Gothic" affair, complete with fake turrets and towers. Retracing our steps toward the center of town, we found that a door to the last building on college property had a suspiciously ornate look, with an alcove containing several niches not unlike those to be found in imitation-Moorish movie theaters of the 1920s and '30s. A glance at the roof revealed a conical tower we had failed to see earlier, and then we glimpsed a small plaque on the wall near the door. It featured a profile of Walpole—this was indeed Strawberry Hill.

I had been under the impression that one could take a tour through the building, but it was shut tight like the rest of the college. However, someone had neglected to lock the high gate to the inner yard, and we nervously let ourselves in.

This yard—or garden, as the English would say—was a broad, flat expanse of thick green turf clipped very close: a cliche of the lawn as carpet. My daughters, tired from our travels, flopped prone on this luxurious ground. I wanted to join them. But first I roamed around the walls of Strawberry Hill. Peering through the lowest of the windows gained me nothing, so I took a longer view.

Walpole's "villa" was quite a structure—a rambling series of additions built at various times, with its infamous plaster turrets suggesting, in places, a Hollywood version of a medieval castle. Although I continued to feel furtive about being there, my feet ached and my daughters looked too comfortable on the lawn to ask them to leave. I lay down next to them and, chin in my hands, stared back at the building.

All I knew about the term serendipity at that point was the *Oxford English Dictionary* explanation Arthur C. Clarke had used in *The View From Serendip*: ". . .Walpole told one of his numerous correspondents that 'he had formed it upon the title of the fairy-tale *The Three Princes of Serendip*, the heroes of which were always making discoveries, by accident and sagacity, of things they were not in quest of.'" I knew nothing about the fairy tale—Clarke wondered whether Walpole had made it up—but, curiously enough, the guest room our friends in Surrey had given us contained a single print on the wall: three Middle-Eastern potentates on horseback. Neither of our hosts knew what the Persian words on the print meant; they assumed the script was Persian because they had been told the picture was copied from "a Persian miniature". They had no other information, and were certainly unaware of my interest in Horace Walpole and *The Three Princes of Serendip*.

I also recalled an incident during the brief trip I had taken to the Cotswolds, a range of rolling hills west and north of Oxford where the Rollright Stones are located. Having visited Cornwall and Rocky Valley a week earlier I had been preoccupied with the labyrinth image, so I had to have a look at a stone-walled maze recently constructed on the grounds of Ragley Hall near Alcester. This rectangular labyrinth, while lacking any ancient associations, was intriguing enough with its observation platform for lofty overviews. But what had turned out to be most arresting about Ragley Hall was inside the "stately home" itself. It was a portrait by Sir Joshua Reynolds over the fireplace, and it was of Horace Walpole.

These two occurrences could surely be called "happy accidents"— Clarke's minimal definition of Walpole's serendipity. I had not gone to our friends' house seeking a picture of the Three Princes. Nor had I visited Ragley Hall hoping to find Walpole's portrait. Of course I had been happy enough to happen upon such provocative and pertinent phenomena.

And I had encountered other coincidences in my other English wanderings and in my reading prior to that summer of 1979. Such conjunctions at least *felt* significant, and set me to wondering about their role in a Space-Age reconnection to earth— not to mention their meaning in my attempt to understand that reconnection from a mythic perspective.

I had come to Strawberry Hill as a sort of ritual beginning for my investigation into Horace Walpole's coining of serendipity. However, as I lay on his lawn I could not help thinking of another figure who had delved deeply into the interpretation of these accidental connections. Indeed, my knowledge of C. G. Jung's psychology greatly exceeded what I had thus far learned about the mind which produced the idea of serendipity, and even after returning home I was some time gaining the information I needed on Walpole.

JUNG'S MEANINGFUL COINCIDENCES

In graduate school at Drew University in the early 1960s one of my professors had been Ira Progoff. It was Progoff who introduced me to Jungian psychology and encouraged me in applying it to the life and writings of Herman Melville for my doctoral dissertation. It was also at his behest that I first became acquainted with Jung's elusive concept of synchronicity.

Progoff had actually consulted with the Swiss psychiatrist about this topic in 1952 and 1953 in Zurich, returning to the United States to write his own manuscript on synchronicity in 1954. He then went back to Switzerland the following year for further discussions with Jung. The latter's major essay on the concept, "Synchronicity: An Acausal Connecting Principle", had appeared in German in 1952 (a brief version, "On Synchronicity", had been given as a lecture the year before).[2] Delays in the English translation until 1955 gave Progoff, whose publishing schedule awaited this edition of the Jung essay, time to reconsider his own manuscript. He decided his treatment of synchronicity should be revised and expanded, but by then his practice of psychotherapy and his teaching at Drew monopolized his time, so that it was not until 1973—just as I began my research on earth images— that his book came out under the title *Jung, Synchronicity, and Human Destiny: Noncausal Dimensions of Human Experience.*[3]

At that juncture I saw no relevance to my explorations in Progoff's discussion. But after I got back from England in the fall of 1979, and while I hunted for details on Walpole's serendipity, I used the Progoff book, along with Aniela Jaffé's *The Myth of Meaning*[4] and Jung's own writings, to see what synchronicity might tell me about the mythic ramifications of the Space Age.

On the surface the concept seemed simple enough. "Synchronicity" was Jung's term for a principle of connection he thought applied between a psychic state and one or more external events which could have no causal relation to it but which nevertheless appeared to be "meaningfully" related. The short definition for such acausally connected phenomena, then, is that they are "meaningful coincidences", somehow possessing a significance beyond that of "mere" chance.

These coincidences can be of various sorts. They can be either simultaneous, or closely (but not exactly) corresponding in time of occurrence, or with the inner state being a precognition of a future event. Jaffé makes a noteworthy point about this range of instances and how it bears upon the precise meaning of the word "synchronicity" itself. Jung's essay had spoken of a "coincidence in time of two or more causally unrelated events which have the same or similar meaning." But Jaffé adds:

> the 'coincidence in time' does not refer to an absolute simultaneity determined by the clock, though such a thing can also happen. It is rather a question of the subjective experience or inner image through which the past or future real event is experienced in the present. Image and event coincide in a subjective simultaneity. Because of this Jung preferred the terms 'synchronicity' and 'synchronistic' to 'synchronism' and 'synchronous'.[5]

In playing with this terminology I was reminded of Clarke's conception of the communications satellite which was said to hover in a 22,300-mile-high "geosynchronous" orbit. The factor of geosynchronousness had to do with the satellite being high enough that it takes the same time (*syn–chron*) for it to complete one orbit as the earth (*geo*) needs for a single rotation on its axis. This renders the satellite effectively stationary in regard to what lies immediately below it on the earth's surface.

The *objective* simultaneity of Clarke's satellite clearly was not what Jung had had in mind with synchronicity. But I could hardly restrain myself from thinking about any similarities between the two concepts — especially since, as I knew, Jung himself had floated above Ceylon like a human satellite in a 1944 vision which not only overlapped suggestively with other happenings at the dawn of the Space Age but also "precognized" the exact perspective of the Orbiter 5 photograph of the whole earth 23 years later. Here was a dramatic example of one form of synchronicity, in other words, which also involved a kind of geosynchronousness.

I also recalled, in this regard, an image Jung borrowed from the philosopher Schopenhauer. He had written a treatise on the "simultaneity of the causally unconnected, which we call 'chance'", and this notion, Jung goes on, was illustrated "by a geographical analogy, where the parallels represent the cross-connection between the meridians, which are thought of as causal chains".[6] As Progoff's study emphasizes, the idea of separate causal chains running, as it were, "side by side" and leading to separate events which are then connected meaningfully, if noncausally, "across" time is a central one in Jung's thinking on synchronicity.[7] His use of the Schopenhauer analogy, moreover, reveals that the imagery implicit in the idea concerns the terrestrial globe as the mapmaker sees it, with lines of longitude and latitude, a cartographic geometaphor.

The first example of synchronicity that Jung cites from his own life experience pertains to his relationship with the Sinologist Richard Wilhelm. It was Wilhelm whose translation of the ancient Chinese book of divination, the *I Ching*, became the focus of Jung's effort to relate synchronicity to various "mantic" methods for interpreting the meaning of events or predicting the future, techniques such as horoscope-reading or pebble-tossing, as well as throwing yarrow stalks or coins in connection with the *I Ching* itself. Jung's encounter with synchronicity in this context turned out to offer yet another geometaphor, or whole earth image, of the sort I had been collecting and creating for several years in my search.

In 1928, as he recounts in his autobiography, Jung painted a mandala of a fortified, symmetrical castle, seen from above, with a star-shaped outer wall and a circular center. He says he had a sense of the picture being Chinese even though there was nothing overtly Chinese in it. Then he adds:

> it was a strange coincidence that shortly afterward I received a letter from Richard Wilhelm enclosing the manuscript of a Taoist-alchemical treatise entitled *The Secret of the Golden Flower*, with a request that I write a commentary on it. I devoured the manuscript at once, for the text gave me undreamed-of confirmation of my ideas about the mandala and the circumambulation of the center.

Because this synchronicity was so powerful for him, Jung added a caption to his painting: "In 1928, when I was painting this picture, showing the golden, well-fortified castle, Richard Wilhelm in Frankfurt sent me the thousand-year-old Chinese text on the yellow castle, the germ of the immortal body."[8]

The geometaphorical aspect of Jung's very meaningful coincidence here has to do with the bird's-eye perspective of his picture. It is a view one would get from an aircraft directly over the center of the vast and labyrinthine fortress with its concentric walls, roofs, and moats surrounded by bands of green and brown fields and yellow roads. A similar prospect can be seen not in China, or even in Frankfurt, but in an actual aerial photograph of a star-shaped walled town—Palmanova, near Udine—in northern Italy. The photograph appears in a collection of such views called *The World from Above*, and the Italian town is, if anything, even more symmetrical and mandala-like than the Jung painting.[9]

In any case, it was *this* coincidence which underscored for me how much the meaning of *Jung's* coincidence depended on a decidedly terrestrial image seen from a Space-Age vantage point.

While I continued to seek out the geometaphors implied by Jung's definition of synchronicity, I was also curious to probe the more complex matter of the *basis* for synchronistic events occurring at all. Jung's formulations in this area are not always easy to follow, and I appreciated the assistance provided by his commentators.

The conditions for the emergence of synchronicity, conditions which can never be deliberately planned or willed owing to synchronicity's noncausal nature, lie with the meaning which the subject finds in what is otherwise a mere coincidence or pure chance. According to Aniela Jaffé, Jung began his researches on synchronicity by inferring that when coincidences were experienced as meaningful it was due to their participation in a "transcendental meaning independent of consciousness".[10] He also wrote of "latent meaning" existing in the synchronistic situation.[11] Both of these early renditions rely on our subjective sense that because such situations occasionally befall us there must be a structure of meaning "out there", apart from ourselves, which is responsible.

But Jaffé points out that in Jung's later writings on the topic, "the concept of *pre-existent meaning* as characteristic of such phenomena was gradually replaced by the more objective concept of *acausal orderedness*." She thus concludes that "the concept of 'meaning' remains just as characteristic of synchronistic phenomena as before, but it now takes on . . . the quality of something created by man: the orderedness that comes to light in acausal events can be experienced as meaningful, or else dismissed as pure chance and therefore meaningless."[12]

Jaffé's distinctions were helpful, but she seemed to shift the problem right back again to the enigma of how the meaning arises in these situations in the first place. Whatever the abstract implications of an underlying "orderedness" might be, it was nevertheless true, on her assessment, that if we, as experiencing subjects, happened to find no meaning in such coincidences any theorizing about their transcen dental significance remained empty. In other words, she was indicating that synchronicity could not provide reliable evidence for a hidden order or blueprint in the world because it depended, finally, on fleeting human experiences of meaning—or more unreliably still, on the subjective human *creation*of meaning.

The only way to move the explanation of synchronicity beyond the dead end of subjectivity, it seemed, would be to look at the role of what Jung called "archetypes"—from the Greek for "prime imprint" or "prime imprinter"—in the creation of meaning, especially in the creation of the meaningfulness sometimes experienced as characterizing certain coincidences (which thereby become "synchronistic events"). For Jungian psychology, archetyupes, as inherent predispositions in the human psyche, influencing perception and behavior and manifesting themselves indirectly in the imagery of dream and myth, are in themselves "irrepresentable". That is, archetypal images of various sorts can be grouped and labeled according to common traits but an archetype *per se* can neither be named nor pictured.

Aside from their always indirect manifestation in dreams and myths, however, the presence of archetypes in given circumstances is often signalled by a heightening of emotion, a growing or sudden sense of awe. And it is this situation, with its suggestion of the nearness of an archetype, which is apparently a more-than-merely-subjective source of the meaning in a meaningful coincidence. As Jaffé puts it, "experience has shown that synchronistic phenomena are most likely to occur in the vicinity of archetypal . happenings like death, deadly danger, catastrophes, crises, upheavals, etc. One could also say," she goes on, "that in the unexpected parallelism of psychic and physical happenings, which characterizes these phenomena, the paradoxical, psychoid archetype has 'ordered' itself: it appears here as a psychic image, there as a physical, material, external fact."[13]

With this last statement Jaffé introduces a factor in addition to the emotional intensity of a situation. She speaks of the nature of the archetype which seems present in such situations as "paradoxical" and "psychoid": in other words, as able to affect both a psychic state and a physical event, bringing them into correspondence for the subject, who then finds the conjunction meaningful. It is the idea of the archetype as psychoid—as quasi-psychic or psyche-like, but not necessarily limited to the psyche—that was the major development of Jung's late writings on archetype theory. Jaffé points out that "the concept of the psychoid archetype added an altogether new dimension, for the possibility of an archetypal 'imprinting' of the physical and inorganic world, and of the cosmos itself, had also to be taken into account. Jung went even further and saw in the psychoid archetype the 'bridge to matter in general.'"[14] This provocative comment, in turn, is amplified when Jaffé quotes Jung's 1940 essay "The Psychology of the Child Archetype" regarding the psychoid quality of archetypes:

> The deeper 'layers' of the psyche lose their individual uniqueness as they retreat farther and farther into the darkness. 'Lower down,' that is to say as they approach the autonomous functional systems, they become increasingly collective until they are universalised and extinguished in the body's materiality, i.e.,in chemical substances. The body's carbon is simply carbon. Hence 'at bottom' the psyche is simply 'world.'[15]

These complexities of Jungian thinking on the underlying basis of synchronicity were most supportive for my searching. The downward imagery of Jung's language, as well as the archetypal connection to the material world of body and nature, implied that the occurrence of meaningful coincidences might have some inherent relation to earthward movements of consciousness and culture.

"DEEPENING" AND THE PSYCHOID ARCHETYPE

Ira Progoff's treatment of the psychoid archetype in his book on synchronicity contributed further to my feeling that here was a significant component to include in my findings. He sees the intensification of emotion and awesome atmosphere accompanying the manifestation of archetypes as the direct corollary of their psychoid nature. The emotional heightening, he explains, makes possible a compensating "lowering of mental level" in the subject, a lowering of the threshold between the conscious and the unconscious thereby making conscious deeper levels of the unconscious.[16] It is this psychic lowering, then, which allows the psychoid to come into play, for the latter—the bridge to materiality—functions at the deepest "level" of the personality, "the depth beneath the transpersonal *collective unconscious*".[17]

Although Progoff would agree with Jung that synchronistic phenomena cannot, by definition, be produced by an effort of the willful ego, he notes that his own work with persons writing autobiographical journals often leads to a "deepening of atmosphere." This in turn seems to assist in the lowering of mental level and leads to a consequent activation of the psychoid factor. Because of these effects of the "deepening" which accompanies his journal-writing approach to therapy he can go on to claim that it is of "the greatest importance for establishing an environment in which synchronistic experiences can occur and for increasing the individual's sensitivity to them."[18]

Progoff's imagery of depth, like Jung's, was a linkage for me between the intricacies of synchronicity and the needed reconnection with the earth and the earthy. His formulation, together with Jung's own description of the psychoid archetype, echoed an idea I had inferred from William Barrett's *Time of Need* at the outset of my project: that ancient myth, expressed through art and religion, repeated the patterns of the earth itself, the ecological rhythms and priorities of natural history.

This impression was reinforced by another piece of Jung's description, not noticed by any of his commentators. In 1959, two years before his death, he wrote to Wilhelm Bitter, a psychiatrist, replying to the latter's question about the causes of so-called miracle cures. Jung's answer was that "in some cases of psychotherapeutic treatment, contact with the sphere of the archetypes can produce the kind of constellation that underlies synchronicity. Naturally in these circumstances anything that borders on the miraculous, or actually is miraculous, may be expected, because for the life of us we cannot discover exactly how a synchronistic result comes about."[19] While he does not go into detail here about the mysterious workings of the psychoid factor, he implies a dramatic extension of his thinking about that factor at the end of the letter. Speaking again of synchronistic events, Jung writes:

> It is clear that such things do not happen only under inner psychic conditions; very often they also need an external ambience to happen in, for instance a numinous spot. At Lourdes, where Mary appears as a kind of rebirth-giving Earth Mother, it is the cave and the underground spring. The latter is actually one of Mary's appellatives: *page pagon*[source of sources].[20]

Not only was this passage replete with terrestrial images — in particular imagery of the depths of earth — but it also brought in the familiar figure of the Earth Mother. Here was the "bridge to matter" indeed and, as I had found in my exploration of feminist spirituality, the mythic grounding for the workings of metaphor which were so crucial a means of mental reorientation in the Age of Space. By saying that, at Lourdes, Mary appears as the Earth Mother, Jung also suggests the reverse: that Mary is yet another guise of the Goddess.

And so, in probing the imagery infusing the idea of meaningful coincidence, I had found several areas for relevant reflection: the implicit geometaphors in various formulations of synchronicity itself, the earth-oriented implications of the psychoid archetype, and even the role of a "numinous spot" on the planet, a place of sacred awe where the Great Mother, as Mary, held sway.

It was this last cluster of images underlying synchronicity which prompted me to think once more of Walpole's Strawberry Hill. Enduring within the protection of St. Mary's College for Women, it hinted to me that perhaps serendipity, too, harbored hidden geometaphors, imagery which commented playfully on the nature of earth and how we might return to it from our space odyssey. When I tracked down the requisite information on the origins of the Walpole concept I was surprised to discover my suspicion corroborated even more strikingly than I had imagined it would be.

WALPOLE'S ACCIDENTAL SAGACITY

In the early fall of 1961 Theodore G. Remer visited Strawberry Hill and noted that there was "little outward change in the eighteenth-century part of the house". At that time Remer, a Chicago lawyer, had been pursuing the topic of serendipity for six years. Before another four had passed his book, *Serendipity and the Three Princes*, was published by the University of Oklahoma Press.[21] It took me some time to locate a copy, but the effort was worthwhile.

Drawing on the magisterial Walpole scholarship of Wilmarth Sheldon Lewis as well as research on oriental tales pertinent to the background of *The Three Princes of Serendip*, Remer had assembled a valuable reference volume. From his study I learned that Walpole, whose life spanned the rationalistic eighteenth century from 1717 to 1797, was in several ways an unlikely inhabitant of the Age of Enlightenment. He was the first Englishman of that classicist era to revert, in his preferences, to the Gothic architecture of the Middle Ages and, by implication, to the outmoded superstitions infesting its gloomy castles. The remodeling of Strawberry Hill between 1749 and 1770 into what Walpole referred to as a "castellino" reflected most graphically this anachronistic fondness for things medieval. Not only did he supervise the building of the fake turrets and towers I saw over two centuries later, but he filled it with "Gothic fragments," medieval artifacts brought back from the Crusades by Sir Terry Robsart, a supposed ancestor whose name reveals he was actually Walpole's own witty invention.

Such doings were quite out of keeping with eighteenth century tastes, as was his novel, *The Castle of Otranto*, written in 1764 on the basis of a dream. This was, in fact, the first "Gothic" novel, initiating a long line of romantic fiction culminating in Poe and the mystery novel.[22]

Beyond these rather eccentric achievements Walpole produced admirable works on politics, art history, and gardening—I was intrigued to note that at one point he planned a "bower" for the back garden at Strawberry Hill, deciding against a full-sized hedge labyrinth only because he lacked the room for a proper "clew" or winding path.[23] But it is the thousands of letters he wrote on social and political matters which constitute Walpole's most acclaimed legacy. There were 1800 letters to Horace Mann alone, and one of these is serendipity's source.

Walpole had met Mann during his "grand tour" of Europe from 1739 to 1741. The latter was the English envoy to Tuscany and remained in Florence for the entire forty-five years between meeting Walpole and his death. Indeed, after 1741 the two men never met again, but they had become close friends and were faithful correspondents.[24]

On January 28, 1754, Walpole wrote to Mann to report the arrival of a sixteenth-century portrait of "Her Serene Highness the Great Duchess Bianca Capello" which Mann had sent him as a gift from Italy. Walpole had admired this portrait thirteen years earlier in Florence and was delighted to have it. In his letter he discusses his intention to have a proper frame built for the painting and describes what he calls "a critical discovery" made in researching the Capello coat of arms which would decorate the frame. In an old book of Venetian heraldry he had found two coats of Capello, one with a device which he knew also occurred in the Medici arms, thus allowing him to put both the Capello and Medici arms on the frame.

"This discovery," Walpole continues, "I made by a talisman, which Mr. Chute calls the *sortes Walpolianae*, by which I find everything I want *a point nommé* wherever I dip for it." This "talisman," he then adds, suggests a whole new category of discovery, and here, in Remer's transcription of the letter to Mann, is where I found the authentic origin of the term toward which Arthur C. Clarke and my trip to Strawberry Hill had pointed me:

> This discovery indeed is almost of that kind which I call *serendipity*, a very expressive word. . .you will understand it better by the derivation than by the definition. I once read a silly fairy tale, called *The Three Princes of Serendip*: as their highnesses travelled, they were always making discoveries, by accidents and sagacity, of things which they were not in quest of: for instance one of them discovered that a mule blind of the right eye had travelled the same road lately, because the grass was eaten only on the left side, where it was worse than on the right — now do you understand *serendipity*?[25]

If Horace Mann failed to understand the new word Walpole had coined — and there were confusions in the letter which could easily block understanding — countless people up to the present who have not seen his letter, according to Remer, assume they know the exact meaning of serendipity. More than one dictionary or writer on scientific investigation has departed from the definitional ingredients Remer finds in Walpole's language, which are summed up as "a gift for discovery by accident *and* sagacity while in pursuit of something else".[26] Often the element of "sagacity" is simply ingored in faulty definitions. An example would be the common use of Walpole's word to denote a "happy accident".

One difficulty with the letter is that although farther along Walpole himself underscores the idea that serendipity must involve "*accidental sagacity* (for you must observe that *no* discovery of a thing you *are* looking for, comes under this description)",[27] his initial example of the three princes and the blind mule does not support his later emphasis particularly well. In addition, he has already almost equated serendipity with the gift for critical discovery by which he finds whatever he *wants*. This gift, which his friend Chute calls the *sortes Walpolianae*, seems thus at odds with the requirement for serendipity that one not be *looking for* what one happens, through accidents and sagacity, to discover. And yet Walpole has suggested that serendipity and the *sortes Walpolianae* are virtually the same; certainly Remer writes as though they were identical.

The term *sortes Walpolianae* is itself enigmatic, and while "the Walpole luck" is serviceable as a loose translation, a deeper probe would want to know more about these two Latin words. The first one, *sortes*, refers to one's "lot" or "fate", as in casting lots, while the addition of the adjective implies the specific form of divination known as bibliomancy; one points at random to a passage in the Bible or some other worthy book and interprets the passage as a message about what the future holds or what action one should take. Thus, for example, the *sortes Virgilianae* would employ Virgil's *Aeneid* for the divination.

But what can it mean to have Walpole's own name as the adjective? Surely this cannot suggest he finds what he wants in his own works, although it could carry the connotation that the Walpole luck involves his gaining what he wants, or lacks at the level of consciousness, by delving into himself, into his own psychic depths. Whether Walpole truly had a sense of his own subconscious mind as a divinatory text—or whether his friend Mr. Chute merely misapplied the Latin term to Walpole's knack for finding needed information through a half-accidental browsing—is impossible to decide with any certainty.

In any case, it is by means of this conceivably mantic "talisman", or magic charm, that Walpole says he makes his critical discoveries. And he makes them, the letter states, at the critical moment, *à point nommé*, in the nick of time—a saying which echoed the "lucky hit", the sudden connection cutting across causal chains in Jung's notion of synchronicity.

Indeed, the connection between the term *sortes Walpolianae* and bibliomancy put me in mind of another aspect of Jung's principle: its manifestation in the context of a divinatory text like the *I Ching*. Moreover, there was also the similarity of a painting being central in both Jung's experience and Walpole's (not to mention my own encounters with the latter's portrait and the print of what I took to be the three princes).

There was yet another linkage in that Jung's mandala painting related to Richard Wilhelm's translation of an ancient alchemical text, for alchemy—an increasing preoccupation of Jung's later writings— also enters into the coining of serendipity. Remer cites a letter of September 10, 1789, in which Walpole seeks to clarify the concept he had first introduced 35 years earlier:

> Nor is there any harm in starting new game to invention; many excellent discoveries have been made by men who were *à la chasse* of something very different. I am not quite sure that the art of making gold and of living forever have been yet found out—yet to how many noble discoveries has the pursuit of those nostrums given birth! Poor Chemistry, had she not had such glorious objects in view![28]

For Remer this almost Jungian endorsement of the serendipitous advantages of alchemical activity shows Walpole's "understanding of and appreciation for the magnificent definition that he had coined".[29] The insinuation is that in the original letter to Mann back in 1754 Walpole had been demonstrating as much confusion as clarity about his own concept.

However, despite his attention to definitional rigor Remer makes the mistake, as noted earlier, of equating the willful use of the *sortes Walpolianae* with the unsought occurrence of serendipity. Additionally, for all his close reading of Walpole's language he neglects what I found to be the most significant factor in the 1754 letter.

"A VERY EXPRESSIVE WORD"

While reading Remer's account of the birth of serendipity I wondered why a "silly fairy tale" Walpole read in childhood—he had turned 21 in 1738—would be recalled twenty or more years later. What was there about the experience discussed in his letter that made Walpole think of *The Three Princes of Serendip*?

With the term *sortes* I saw that the act of opening a text at random, dipping into a passage selected by chance, might itself be a factor in Walpole's gift of discovery. By this talisman, he writes, "I find everything I want *à point nommé* wherever I dip for it," and it is in the very next sentence after using the word "dip" that he says "this discovery indeed is almost of that kind which I call *serendipity*, a very expressive word . . ."

The fact that Walpole consciously highlights the expressiveness of his new word adds greater force to the conjecture that using the word "dip"—from the Anglo-Saxon for "deep"—helped trigger the memory of the tale with Serendip in its title, and thus gave rise to the neologism "seren-dip-ity". The latter term, after all, combines "dip" with "serenity", and Walpole had opened the letter by referring to the noblewoman whose portrait he was about to discuss: "Her Serene Highness the Great Duchess Bianca Capello." This suggests, further, that the contrast between "dip" ("deep") and "high-ness" (a term Walpole also used to describe the three princes: "their highnesses") played a part in the genesis of serendipity. The capacity for word play certainly need not be read into Walpole's character. Remer cites his invention, in another context, of

"triptology"— repeating the same thing three times — and "Sharawadgi"—
a pseudo-Chinese term for "the quality of beauty to be found in an
unintentionally picturesque arrangment of apparently irreconcilable
features."[30] Even more to the point, though unnoticed by Remer, is the
evidence right in the 1754 serendipity letter of Walpole's playful self-
consciousness about the interaction of sound and sense in the syllables
of words. He writes to Horace Mann, "if you will suffer me to conclude
with a pun, content yourself with your *Mannhood*. . ."[31]

From all these confusions and conjectures regarding the origins
of serendipity I inferred that chief among the latter's messages about
the mystery of new discovery was the strong sense of a dipping back
down to earth from the serene heights of space — perhaps, in our day,
from Apollo 11's Tranquillity Base on the moon. Given my mythic or
metaphorizing perspective, of course, the preferred place for this dipping down would be the island once called "Serendip": it is an Arabic
name in which the syllable "dip" is derived from the Pali word for
"island". The ancient inhabitants of Serendip apparently considered it
the island *par excellence*.[32] Accordingly, I could consider it the *pars
pro toto* geometaphor for our global island in space.

DIPPING DOWN TO EARTH AND THE PUER-PSYCHE MARRIAGE

Along with its own provocative connotations, the imagery of "dipping down" from "serene high-ness" in the idea of serendipity also led
back to Jungian thought. It was, in particular, through James Hillman's
creative modification of Jung's theories that I saw this interrelation,
for it was Hillman who had written in detail of the "inner" figure Jung
called the *puer aeternus*, the eternal boy or youthful spirit.
In Hillman's view the puer, represented mythologically by someone like Icarus who flies so near the sun that his wings catch fire and
he plunges back down to earth, illuminates the qualities of "spirit"
generally. His 1976 essay "Peaks and Vales" distinguishes importantly
between spirit and "soul" (*psyche* in the Greek) on the basis of the
imagery attaching to each — imagery which struck a familiar note for
someone who was playing with the parts of Walpole's very expressive
word. Hillman speaks of spirit, including the puer, as having a penchant
for "peak experiences" and "highs", conceptual abstraction and tran-

scendence. Soul, he says, is characterized on the other hand by down-to-earth involvements and depressions, concreteness and immanence, and the fantasy-language of metaphor.[33]

The Hillman essay is far-ranging and difficult to summarize beyond its basic spirit-soul distinction. But what appealed to me most in connection with my study of serendipity is easy enough to pinpoint: it was Hillman's description of "finding connections between the puer's drive upward and the soul's clouded encumbering embrace".[34] He calls this goal "the puer-psyche marriage", and his account resonated at many points with an appropriately peculiar reading of Walpole's playful concept. Moreover, it seemed to contain the sort of large implications I was seeking in my project. For if the astronaut can be seen as carrying us on a puer-trip to the moon, then the move back toward terrestrial re-entry would be akin to Hillman's hoped-for marriage between puer and psyche, spirit and soul.

With this possibility in mind it was instructive to follow what else Hillman has to say about this psychologically healthy liaison. "The puer," he warns, "takes its drive and goal literally unless there is reflection which makes possible a metaphorical understanding of its drive and goal. By bearing witness as the receptive experiencer and imager of the spirit's actions, the soul can contain, nourish, and elaborate in fantasy the puer impulse, bring it sensuousness and depth. . ."[35] Here was an endorsement of metaphoric activity as part and parcel of a "deepening" which psyche affords the puer. Beyond this, Hillman maintains that in the marriage with psyche each puer inspiration or idea "will first be drawn through the labyrinthine ways of the soul, which wind it and slow it and nourish it from many sides. . .developing the spirit from a one-way mania for 'ups' to *polytropos*, the many-sidedness of the Hermetic old hero, Ulysses".[36]

In another discussion of the puer he reiterates the maze image to which my investigations of Arthur C. Clarke's life had led me — and hints at Ariadne's presence as well — when he stresses that the soul, the "feminine" partner in this marriage, "has the thread and knows the step-by-step dance that can lead through the labyrinth, and can teach the puer the subtleties of left-hand/right-hand, opening and closing, accustoming and refining his vision to the half-light of ambivalence."[37] This ambivalence, he adds, "finds echo in many familiar phrases from Lao Tzu, but especially: 'Soften the light, become one with the dusty world' "[38] — an imperative I found, in turn, all too fitting for an age dominated by Apollo's blinding clarity and remoteness, the distancing calculations necessary to a cultural "space program" in which we were all, willy-nilly, "caught up".

Other aspects of soul suggest other possibilities for the puer and, by analogy, for a dipping back down to earth, a coming home, of Space-Age consciousness. At one point in the "Peaks and Vales" essay Hillman turns to E.M. Forster's discussion of what he labels the fantasy genre of novel-writing in order to illustrate the further qualities of soul: ". . . let us now invoke all beings who inhabit the lower air, the shallow water, and the smaller hills, all Fauns and Dryads and slips of memory, all verbal coincidences, Pans and puns, all that is medieval this side of the grave."[39] These are Forster's words; they could almost be describing Walpole's imagination.

But it was Hillman's own extrapolations from Forster's words which I found most applicable to my purpose: "Here," states Hillman, "I think of the free associations of Freud as a *method* in psychology, or of Jung's mode of writing where no paragraph logically follows the one preceding, or of Lévi-Strauss's figure, the '*bricoleur*', the handyman and his ragtag putting together of collages. . ." This improvisatory soul-style of fantasy also includes an appeal to history:

> . . . I too am speaking soul language in going back all the time to historical examples such as old E.M. Forster, little fussy man in his room in Cambridge, now dead, and dead Freud and Jung, back to old myths and their scholarship, to etymologies and the history in words, and down to specific geographic localities, the actual vales of the world. For this is the way the soul proceeds.[40]

"Only connect", Forster had once written, and Hillman's discussion of the puer-psyche union as simultaneously entailing the earthly conjunctions of metaphor—its ambivalence, its associativeness, its specificity—served as an edifying elaboration of the imagery I had drawn from Walpole's language. Tracing such ramifications was an exciting as well as useful segment of my search. However, I found that the more conventional senses of serendipity, as of synchronicity, might also be deepened and perhaps deliteralized by taking account of Hillman's insights.

In "Notes on Opportunism," an earlier piece on the puer figure, Hillman explains how central to the existence of this boyish spirit is the taking of chances, the seizing of opportunities. The word "opportunity" comes from the Latin for "entrance", "passage through", or "opening". According to the OED it is related to the Roman god of harbors, Portunus. According to Hillman it also has to do with doors and windows, including the *porta fenestella*, "a special opening through which Fortune passed". He notes further that the English phrase "nick of time"—Walpole's *à point nommé* and the image of synchronicity as an event "cutting across time" between separate causal chains—carries the same feeling: "that slot in the system of law and order through which an opportunity can be seized".[41]

Operating on his own, Hillman continues, the puer moves with his luck, his hunches, resourceful and stealthy. And in this spirit—for he *is* this spirit—the puer sees with a truly opportunistic eye for which "every wall and every weave presents its opening. Everything is porous. As the surrealists say: 'There exists another world. But it is assuredly in this one.'"[42] This kind of talk solicits the metaphorzing vision of René Magritte once again, and is to that extent a postive direction. On the other hand, it also leads Hillman to speak of a tie between synchronicity and surrealism's predecessor, Dada, a movement which supposedly chose its name through bibliomancy, opening the dictionary at random and dipping to the French word for hobbyhorse.

Dada and synchronicity, he says, share a shortcoming with puer consciousness, which worships opportunity, unfortunately,

> . . . at the altar of chance: *I Ching*, a dream, even someone else's dream, spot words on a page will send one off to California. The Dadaist movement elevated chance to a law. . . How much like the new Puer Religion. . . of Synchronicity. These two Zurich schools, Dadaism and Synchronicity, use similar methods: 'When Surrealism interrogates chance, it is to obtain oracular replies.'[43]

The problem with all this puer opportunism, as with the Dada, surrealism, and synchronicity which proceed so similarly, is the tendency to literalize—which is exactly spirit's temptation in the absence of soul. Elevating chance to a rigid law, actually moving to California on the basis of a chance occurrence, can be, as Hillman puts it, "opportunity literalized into a venture".[44] Or, in a psychotherapeutic formulation from the later "Peaks and Vales" essay he asserts that the paranoid fixity of meaning which the soulless puer may attach to coincidence or accident becomes a disorder: "The disproportion between the trivial content of a synchronistic event on the one hand, and on the other, the giant sense of meaning that comes with it, shows what I mean. . . Part of this disorder is the very systematization that would by defensive means of the doctrine of synchronicity, give profound meaningful order to trivial coincidence."[45]

It is not the occurrence of synchronistic events *per se* that is prob-lematic but the implicit appeal to doctrine, to law, "congealing this play into paranoid monuments of eternal truth".[46] The difficulty, that is to say, comes when psyche's metaphorizing approach is missing.

By the same token, when puer opportunism is able to connect with psyche it can avoid the literalistic paranoia of unbridled spirit and enjoy coincidence and accidents as openings for more down-to-earth mean-ing, entertained lightly rather than acted upon compulsively or taken as absolute truth. A final insight from E.M. Forster stimulates Hillman to make a comparison which reveals more of what the puer-psyche marriage would do to puer opportunism:

> Here we return to Mr. Forster, who reminded us that the spirit's voice is humble and the soul's humorful. Humility is awed and wowed by meaning; the soul takes the same events more as the puns and pranks of Pan. Humility and humor are two ways of coming down to *humus*, to the human condition. Humility would have us bow down to the world and pay our due to its reality. Render unto Caesar. Humor brings us down with a fall. Heavy meaningful reality becomes suspect, seen through, the world laughable — paranoia dissolved, as synchronicity becomes spontaneity.[47]

SERENDIPPING — SEIZING OPPORTUNITIES TO METAPHORIZE

As with his words on the nature of myth and metaphoric imagery, which I had drawn upon earlier in my research, Hillman's discussion of the puer-psyche marriage and what it would do to puer opportunism proved to be a valuable resource. Although it was taken from the midst of his psychological theories — always subtle and sometimes arcane — and adapted to my somewhat different purposes, this discussion en-abled me to discern the deep relevance of both serendipity and syn-chronicity to a hoped-for homecoming in the Space Age. Seen from the perspective provided by Hillman's language, the message of my search through Jung and Walpole (and, less directly, of my wanderings from Clarke's Serendip to the coast of Cornwall) was no single, settled con-clusion, to be sure. While the volatile idea of spontaneity might be said to sum up all my findings starting at least at Strawberry Hill, the message more fully elaborated would contain other components, notably an encouragement to metaphorize more emphatic than any I had received from my initial explorations, an encouragement which came with enhanced opportunities for doing so.

I had been aware as early as my use of William J.J. Gordon's book on creativity, *Synectics*, that what he calls "play and irrelevance" are central to the process of inventing and appreciating metaphoric meanings when offered the earth's imagery. Indeed, I had learned in this connection that his book recommends "a willingness to entertain the possibility that any accident, distaction, or interruption may be revealing". Certainly reading that Gordon had begun his research at the Space Age's dawning in 1944 with a problem of altimeter design—a problem, in other words, of determining ascent and descent—had been enough of a revelation to have me heed his advice about how metaphorizing thrives on the unexpected.[48]

But it was only later, while moving from Clarke's work into Jung and Walpole, and then more completely with Hillman's assistance, that I began to understand the spaced-out experience of meaningful coincidences and accidental sagacities as involving the "mystery of new discovery". (It was the encounter with this mystery, according to Norman Mailer's book on the Apollo 11 moon mission, which would force us to perceive the world again with the primitive eye of metaphor.) I also came to see in my more recent searchings that the causeless connections of serendipity and synchronicity, in addition to sharing the imaginal grounding in earth of metaphoric activity generally, had their own telltale terrestrial roots revealed through the imagery used to explain them.

Such unsought conjunctions, I therefore concluded, were especially powerful means to make meaning which could fulfill the deliteralizing conditions of re-entry, the cognitive requirements for a return to the planet. Situations as often as single images or geometaphors, these chances and happenstances offered no final answer from earth. Instead, they held out subtle and elusive openings for reconnection if we were open to metaphorizing our way back.

Consequently, finding synchronicity deliteralized into spontaneity and pondering the surreal birth of serendipity, I arrived at another very expressive word: serendipping—expressive enough, I felt, to encompass Walpole's humor and puer's descent to psyche's winding ways. Serendipping became my preferred name for what needs doing in the Age of Space to make meaningful our trivial coincidences and accidental discoveries. The sagacity we want here is less the prepared mind of the trained researcher or even the disciplined serenity of the stereotyped mystic than a nose for novel conjunctions, a nondoctrinaire Dadaism, or what Melville meant when he said that in some matters a careful disorderliness is the true method.

To speak in terms of serendipping is to take more seriously than those scientists who praise serendipity as a tight safe principle the reality that Walpole's word emerged from a silly fairy tale about a farfetched kingdom, an implausible synectic principality. Awareness of serendipping thus remembers that its deepening operations in metaphor are grounded not by the geopolitical actuality of the modern day republic of Sri Lanka but in the fabulous domain of Sinbad the Sailor, that fictive realm from which three royal pueri launched their long-ago peregrinations in search of new discovery. In an additional work I consulted on Jung's synchronicity Marie-Louise von Franz notes that she has "never found a single fairy tale which began 'A king had three sons. . .', where the problem was not to integrate the feminine".[49] Perhaps through Walpole's dealings with the portrait of Bianca Capello we gain a picture of such an assimilation.

A sense of serendipping instructs us not to stay with her serene highness, however, but to see a deeper feminine, to dip down, for instance, to the "holy jug" of clouds and coastline held by May Swenson's woman in the earth. This is Gaia's center, the omphalos or world-navel, terminus for the *axis mundi* of Mircea Eliade's myth studies and for the Orbital Tower of Clarke's science fiction, terminus — and, more than that, transformation — of the patriarchal questing which the Space Age culminates and in which we are all caught up as pilot or reluctant passenger.

While sticking with Walpole's hidden imagery and exploiting James Hillman's help I could imagine a redirection and deepening even of Apollo's distancing mission: three princes bound for the moon this time, daredevil fly-boys with "the right stuff", riding out the century's and the civilization's dream of soaring above and beyond. But looking back now at that accidental planet like Columbus headed for India, surprised by another New World, offering it to us for viewing as they could not view it: with soulful vision, surrealism or savage poetry, following Ariadne's tangled clew in all our clues, to see through the technological coming-true to the old amazements, respecting the mists and mystery, finding the bridge to what matters, willfully serving Gaia, skillfully playing with the opportunities for coming home, a Ground Controlled Descent to safe harbor in Ceylon or Cornwall or East Calais, Vermont — or any trivial terrain, any numinous spot, in the center of anyone's earth.

V
FINDING A MYTHODOLOGY
FOR THE SPACE AGE

CHAPTER TEN

AERIAL ARCHAEOLOGY AS MODEL: RADICAL DEPARTURES, BEAUTIFUL VIEWS

Barre, Vermont, calls itself the Granite Center of the World. I live less than 20 miles from the quarries, straight up north on the state highway. Almost every day in the summer of 1980, as I sat outside working on my manuscript, the big flatbed trucks would rumble past toward Hardwick and the Canadian border. I never learned what their exact destination was, whether they were headed for some huge building project in Quebec City or Montreal. But the single enormous blocks of granite each truck carried fascinated me. I imagined Stonehenge was being transported for reassembly at some secret North Country ritual space, and was continually reminded to wonder about what made sacred stones sacred. Just as I was writing about the reappearance of prehistoric earth images in the mass media, these particular archaic specimens were being paraded by my house.

But another association was kept before my mind by the sight of the evocative blocks from the Granite Center of the World. I had been following the "Ancient Vermont" controversy for several years, starting just before a disputatious conference on the topic at Castleton State College in October 1977. I have written in Chapter Three about my reactions to the arguments over possible pre-Columbian megalithic structures in the Vermont woods and similar debates about "geomantic" alignments or patterns of "sacred geometry" in the ancient stone sites of the British Isles. However, I have yet to comment on the "Ancient

163

Vermont" disputant whose work had intrigued me most and who returned to my thoughts as I began to write my book in earnest after some seven-and-a-half years of impressionistic research.

NOEL RING'S REMOTE SENSING

Several factors contributed to my recalling Noel Ring's work that summer. In addition to the daily reminders of Vermont's stone enigmas trucking past my house there was the aerial photograph I had received for my birthday a few months earlier. While I was away from home teaching in Syracuse an enlargement had been made of a section of the latest state aerial survey which included our property. Taken from approximately 30,000 feet and measuring almost three feet square in its blown-up version, the photograph centered on East Calais village. Included as part of its overview was everything within roughly two miles of the village, which allowed for our house and barns with the horizontally familiar fields and woods nearby.

Every time I looked at the picture I thought of Noel Ring's research as presented at the Castleton conference. She was a geographer whose specialty was using aerial and satellite photographs to determine the cultural impact of past uses on the landscape. In the context of the "Ancient Vermont" debate she was analyzing the shapes of field patterns in portions of the state where alleged pre-Columbian sites had been discovered and in sections of Europe near confirmed megalithic complexes to assess whether there were trans-Atlantic correlations. Her slide lecture at Castleton had been hard to follow, but I was tantalized by her name alone — it seemed to offer some personal clue to me, some "magic ring" for my search. Moreover, she had alerted me to the possibility that the uses of aerial imagery in geography, or in archaeology, might have implications for understanding the mythic meanings of the Space Age.

When the printed papers from the conference came out I was able to read her lecture carefully and take a more leisurely look at the single aerial photograph accompanying it in the volume. The editor's caption for the photograph summarizes much of the sort of thing her slides had presented too rapidly:

> Pentagonal field and stone walls in the shape of a lance head, socket and shaft, two miles from Calendar Site II, one component

or 'fingerprint' of a repetitive constellation of curiously-shaped features, a cultural 'handprint' which Professor Noel Ring has identified in aerial photos in over twenty Vermont townships, often near slab-roofed chambers, and perhaps a diagnostic of additional sites.[1]

Using "multispectral high-altitude NASA U-2 type photography matched by low-altitude oblique photography", Ring had sighted not only "spearhead" field patterns—sometimes called "keyhole" patterns—but also various "horn" or "cornucopia" shapes, "holster" shapes, and so forth.[2]

Aside from these provocative patterns, with their suspiciously projective character, Ring's method of finding them attracted me: She describes her efforts generally as "identifying relict traces of ancient landscape disturbance via space age remote sensing techniques".[3] Although my daily contemplation of the aerial photograph of East Calais revealed none of the shapes favored by Ring—my own back pasture did look a bit like a horse's head, or was it a dragon's?—the idea of "remote sensing" from above sounded extremely pertinent. I became more and more curious about aerial archaeology.

Then, in England in 1979, I happened upon Leo Deuel's *Flights into Yesterday*, a history of the use of aerial photography by archaeologists. Deuel's title induced reflection all by itself, and his account of aerial archaeology's emergence and distinctive contribution was filled with opportunities for my metaphorizing.

ARCHAEOLOGY'S RADICAL DEPARTURE

Deuel states that aerial archaeology involves a "radical departure in the study of antiquities", one which "entails a new vision of the past".[4] Certainly "radical departure" was an apt term for a method which depends on the historically recent development of techniques for rising above the earth. The idea that the very new can have a fresh relationship with the very old from this elevated perspective also echoed my interest in the unlikely conjunctions between the futuristic and the archaic appearing in the popular media.

Thinking back on it, the cartoon I had seen at the outset of my search—of the astronaut looking down through the lunar porthole to

the Easter Island megaliths—seemed a good illustration of the point
Deuel was making, while also graphically suggesting the nature of the
opening offered to Space-Age opportunism. *Flights into Yesterday*
follows up this last point in saying of the new approach to archaeology
that "its lofty medium defines its opportunities just as it dictates its
methods."[5] Not surprisingly, I wondered how much the same might be
said about a metaphorizing-and-serendipping approach to earth imagery. And when I found Deuel pursuing the matter in a series of questions I could not help applying them to my own search:

> What is it that makes observation from the air unique? Without
> even direct physical contact with relics on and in the ground, how
> is it that the past may be revealed with an amazing clarity never
> beheld before? Why the paradox that distance rather than proximity
> can be a boon for students of buried yesterdays?[6]

For the author the answer to all three questions has to do with the
advantages of a bird's-eye perspective, recalling for me the "episcopal"
overviews experienced by Clarke's Flying Officer Alan Bishop in *Glide
Path*, or the mythic remoteness of Apollo and the puerile flights of
spirit discussed by James Hillman. As I read on I became convinced that
aerial archaeology contained a wealth of imaginal possibilities in its
lofty viewpoint as long as the formidable excesses of Apollonic and puer
consciousness could be avoided. The ability to see ancient and forgotten
human impressions on the earth for the first time since they were made
millennia ago felt epochal—as if the race were remembering at last a
deep dream, or opening a letter from long ago meant to be delivered
only when we had achieved our radical departure into the skies.

Flights into Yesterday devotes an entire chapter to O.G.S. Crawford,
founding editor of England's leading archaeological journal, *Antiquity*.
It was Crawford who was, more than any one person, responsible for
there being an aerial archaeology at all. Raised in Hampshire, southwest of London, he was attracted to archaeology by a childhood visit
to Stonehenge and Avebury. Although Stonehenge seems to have been
the first ancient site photographed from above in 1906, the event was
a sheerly accidental occurrence, a chance shot taken by a military
officer during practice with war balloons. Crawford's pioneering contributions did not begin until over a decade later. However, they, too,
involved the famous megaliths on Salisbury Plain and "made Britain",
as Deuel puts it, "the very *locus classicus* for discoveries from the air".[7]

Crawford's career as an archaeologist began just before World War
I, and he realized that wartime aerial reconnaissance photographs

would contain valuable data for his work. It was the chance to see such previously inaccessible photographs in 1922—by which time he was working for the Ordnance Survey map-makers—that he himself called the birth of aerial archaeology. The pictures were taken by pilots from an RAF aerodrome in Weyhill, Hampshire, and showed crop marks indicative of ancient field patterns, invisible for centuries. Crawford was then able to make his most significant discovery a year later while reviewing pictures of the Stonehenge area taken during the dry year of 1921.[8]

What he found was the long lost true course of the so-called "Avenue", a 70-foot wide road leading out from the main Stonehenge circle past the Heel Stone and toward the summer sunrise point on the horizon. After some reconnaissance photographs revealed a thin pair of parallel lines turning abruptly southeastward and stopping at West Amesbury—a direction none of the experts had anticipated—Crawford confirmed the sighting with careful digging on the ground. Because of the widespread interest in Stonehenge, this was the particular discovery which insured the acceptance of the new archaeological technique. Commenting later on in his major book, *Wessex from the Air*, about the effect of different angles of sunlight on the visibility of subtle earth markings from above, he notes that "on a June morning before breakfast the greater part of Salisbury Plain is seen to be covered with the banks of abandoned Celtic fields, but afterwards they 'fade into the common light of day.'"[9] Assuming the overview Crawford has in mind includes the Stonehenge circle, I had the strange revelation upon reading his statement that the time and place described as optimum for archaeology have also been the time and place, for thousands of years, of "something magical and important about to happen"—in the words of Stanley Kubrick comparing the summer solstice sunrise at Stonehenge with the alignments of heavenly bodies in his *2001*.

These episodes from O.G.S. Crawford's career were extremely evocative ingredients in the story of aerial archaeology. But so were the episodes involving Charles Lindbergh.

Lindbergh, of course, had been the very avatar of aviation. His trans-Atlantic flight in 1927 is the achievement with which the Apollo 11 mission 42 years later is most often compared. Indeed, in its issue of July 4, 1969, *Life* magazine asked Lindbergh to assess the upcoming moon landing. And while this *Life* piece notes his support of the early rocket experimentation of Robert Goddard in the '30s, it neglects to mention what Deuel chronicles: that our astronaut of an earlier day was the pioneer of aerial archaeology in the New World.[10]

Lindbergh's activity in this realm began with what *Flights into Yesterday* calls "an accidental venture into American antiquities".[11] In February of 1929, after completing a mission for Pan American Airways to chart an airmail route to Panama, he was flying over the Yucatan in search of emergency landing fields when, serendipitously, he saw the overgrown pyramid-mounds of an abandoned pre-Columbian city, perhaps a lost Mayan center. Lindbergh was quickly caught up in the potential for aerial archaeology in Mesoamerica. Later that year he photographed sites in New Mexico and then was back over southern Mexico, northern Guatemala, and what was then British Honduras with his new wife Anne Morrow as photographer. Among the many sites which were surveyed was Tikal, one of whose temple-towered pyramids became the "rebel base" for the filming of *Star Wars* almost half a century later.[12] The Lindbergh-led expedition of October 1929, says Leo Deuel, "fell far short of the work carried out by contemporaries in Europe and the Near East . . . Nevertheless," he grants, "for the Americas it was in every sense a trail-blazing achievement."[13]

By the time of *Star Wars* and its sequels, satellites were taking infrared photographs of ancient canal systems hidden from view by the Central American jungle or radar views of settlement remains under several feet of desert sand in Egypt. The final chapter of *Flights into Yesterday*, published the year of Apollo 11, looks ahead to such developments. In addition to describing the use of aerial archaeology to identify submerged port cities—with the help of techniques perfected during World War II in "photographic experiments off such far-flung places as Cornwall and Ceylon"[14]—and the increasing relevance of ethnological studies—such as in Noel Ring's area of cultural geography—Deuel imagines the advent of *spatial* archaeology:

> Non-archaeological aerial photography has already stepped out into space. Pictures from man-made satellites depicting entire continents have become a common feature of our daily papers. Meanwhile space crafts have been charged with detecting mineral and oil deposits, finding fishing grounds, or investigating plant disease. Perhaps it is only a question of time till artificial stars will be made to screen the past and relay to us from far away its long-muted messages.[15]

Deuel does not say which one of aerial archaeology's founders claimed that it has made "as vital a contribution to archaeological investigation as the invention of the telescope did to astronomy".[16] But his book supports this grandiose claim most persuasively.

LITERALISM IN AERIAL ARCHAEOLOGY

The appeal of aerial archaeology lay in the large clue it held out about the significance of the Space Age. The rather bizarre local activities of Noel Ring no less than the world-circling exploits of Crawford, Lindbergh, and their human or mechanical successors implied a possible evolutionary trajectory for the era which began in 1944. That is, the futuristic technological leap into space might be giving us, first and foremost, fresh and deeper access to the archaic earth, the earth which patterned our earliest mythic sense of reality while we were imprinting it with the shapes of human culture and agriculture.

But if an inherent opportunity, so to speak, of the Age of Space were to make the radical return suggested by aerial archaeology, it was important not to take the latter literally, or take to its literalism. When Noel Ring spoke of lancehead, keyhole, and cornucopia patterns during the "Ancient Vermont" debate she was surely aware that these were metaphorical designations. However, like the other disputants she failed to follow up the implications of her reliance on nonfactual constructs, to play along with her own vision, to ask what the lance was piercing, what could be seen through the keyhole, what nourishment the cornucopia offered. Her training as a scientific researcher had led her to discount the nonliteral factors in her inquiry. Moreover, her involvement in aerial archaeology—so rich with metaphoric images as chronicled by *Flights into Yesterday*—exerted its own literalizing force on her imagination.

This last point was not evident at the outset, but as I reflected upon Leo Deuel's account I realized that the dependence of the new method on the technology of flight lent a necessary literalism to the enterprise—despite the poetic associations flying could have if differently seen. And, more subtly, the *way* archaeologists were trained to regard earth from their recent bird's-eye perspective was an additional guarantee that their own sensing would probably remain remote: Apollonic and literalistic rather than reconnective by means of metaphoric vision. In a textbook introducing remote sensing techniques—for which Noel Ring has coauthored a chapter on "Manned Spacecraft Imagery"—the editor offers a description whose language bespeaks the literalism of this viewing:

Remote sensing, imaging the earth's features from suborbital and
orbital altitudes, in various parts of the visible and invisible spectrum, and converting data to information by visual and digital processing is a new and powerful method of acquiring knowledge
about targets, scenes, and events at the surface of the earth. As a
research tool, remote sensing methods of technology transfer have
broadened the vision of scientists to the point where many facets
of the earth's atmosphere, hydrosphere, lithosphere, and culture-
sphere, which previously were unobservable for study, now have
become discernible.[17]

Clearly the "imaging" indicated here is not the imaginal thinking
of primitive, poet, or dreamer. Like Arthur C. Clarke's seeming space
mythos in *The Fountains of Paradise*, the imagery involved in aerial
archaeology's approach is treated as a univocal denotative affair, a
literalistic coding without nuance or mystery.

Beyond the technology of flight and the scientific protocols of
archaeology, however, the major reason for the antimetaphorical bias
of remote sensing may simply be its roots in photography. This likeli-
hood was one I had already considered in connection with May Swenson's "Orbiter 5 Shows How Earth Looks from the Moon." The contrast
between her vision and that of the satellite photograph was a dramatic
demonstration of the move from the literal to the metaphoric. Another
source of reflection on this issue was a little book from 1977, *The Clam
Lake Papers*.

I had corresponded with its author, Edward Lueders, earlier in the
'70s concerning our views on the relation of religion to literature. Our
letters expressed a shared sense of the nature and role of nonliteral
language in these realms, so that while I was delighted, later on, with
the discussion in his book of what is termed "the metaphorical imperative",[18] I found little there to add to my own previous notions about
metaphor. The correspondence with Lueders had not, on the other
hand, dealt with the matter of meaningful coincidence in its relation
to the metaphorizing process, so I was surprised to find confirmation
for the pertinence of what I called serendipping in *The Clam Lake
Papers*: "We are pleased to regard coincidence as mysterious, fortuitous,
remarkable, yet we immediately begin to search for a causal relationship. In the first instance we are following the metaphorical imperative;
in the second, the analytical need to explain."[19]

But what I found most enlightening were Lueders' insights into
how "the photograph has revolutionized our image-making habits."[20]

He does not go on at great length, and yet his comments on the subject powerfully impinged upon my concern for the literalizing dangers of photography. He points out, for instance, that

> such metaphorical phrases as 'to look on the face of God' become ludicrous in the context of a photographed world. In this respect, the poetic image, the mental juncture in metaphor of word and thing, and the figurative expression of a truth become increasingly important to balance for us (maybe I mean to *offset*) the strong claim of the photograph upon our belief, as if it did not also in its own way lie.[21]

The photographic mendacity to which Lueders refers here complicates but does not deny the threat of literalism, or naive realism, in photography. It is by seeming to cancel out the interpretive involvement of human cognition and emotion in the act of seeing that photograhy can foster a literalizing vision. Certainly the photographer pursuing the medium as a serious artist knows the creative distortions which occur between the click of the camera (or before) and the finished picture: setting up the shot, choosing the film, developing and cropping it, and so forth. Such procedures hardly suggest a literal copying of an unaltered external reality. Nevertheless, used as a recording device for capturing what is prejudged as beautiful by the amateur or simply as data by the scientist, photography's general cultural influence appeared to me to be in the direction of literalism: the one-to-one correspondence between reality and image implied in terms like "documentary".

THE AMBIVALENCE OF PHOTOGRAPHIC SEEING

Lueders' remarks about photography, which seemed to support my fear that its development was such as to hinder the emergence of a metaphorizing perspective toward the earth, led me to the fuller discussion in Susan Sontag's *On Photography*, published the same year as *The Clam Lake Papers*.

Reading Sontag's book, rich to the point of convolutedness and replete with historical examples, at first challenged my suspicion about photography's inherent literalism. She does acknowledge that at its birth in the early 19th century the medium was taken to be a mere copying maneuver, a process of faithful recording which would free painting to be nonrepresentational. However, very soon serious photographers wanted to be accepted as artists themselves, and argued for their creative equality with painters.

The difficulty with this latter claim, as Sontag herself admits, is that "the formal qualities of style—the central issue in painting—are, at most, of secondary importance in photography, while what a photograph is *of* is always of primary importance."[22] Later she adds that "while the authority of a photograph will always depend on the relation to a subject (that it is a photograph *of* something), all claims on behalf of photography as art must emphasize the subjectivity of seeing."[23]

Photography's achievement of aesthetic status has thus entailed a reorientation of the viewer: photographs needed to be regarded as instances of creatively subjective "photographic seeing" rather than as images dependent on their subject matter (as more or less objective reproductions). To the extent that this counterthrust against the medium's literalizing origins and continuing functions has been successful, several factors are contributory. One of these factors is the inclusion of photographs in museum collections: "When viewed in their new context, the museum or gallery," says Sontag, "photographs cease to be 'about' their subjects in the same direct or primary way; they become studies in the possibilities of photography."[24] Another component in the establishment of an aesthetically-prized photographic seeing is that the choice of subject matters has shifted away from those which are conventionally beautiful or significant—that is, those which would underscore the dependence of the photographer as technical copyist on the subject. The aspiring art photographer increasingly selects subjects "because they are boring or banal. Because we are indifferent to them, they best show up the ability of the camera to 'see'."[25]

Sontag's argument was powerful, but the whole earth photographs, ascribable to no single human *auteur*, hardly seemed to be candidates for a serious museum collection. Certainly their subject matter was far from boring or banal. Accordingly, they were apparent prisoners of photography's literalistic mediation unless deliberately adapted to the metaphorizing purposes of a poet like May Swenson (or of the poet in any of us). Much to my disappointment, Sontag nowhere comments on the whole earth photographs or on the role of photography in aerial archaeology. It was therefore up to me to draw my own inferences on these topics, and the ascription of a literalistic vision seemed to follow from her complex premises in both cases. In addition to the determinative subject matter of the whole earth views, aerial archaeology's strictly utilitarian use of the camera scarcely suggested the photographic seeing of the avowed artist.

My reading of Sontag's book, a sometimes confusing but frequently enlightening experience for someone unfamiliar with the history and aesthetic theories of photography, left me even more convinced than I had been after encountering Edward Lueders' observations that the problem of the literalism of the camera lens was a real one. Near the end of *The Clam Lake Papers* Lueders points out that "those hauntingly whole photographs of our planet from space are really portraits, the most up-to-date portraits available, of *us*, the first complete group photographs we've ever had."[26] The question raised for me by *On Photography*, however, is whether this photographic seeing is a way to "know thyself" or, on the contrary, to "mistake thyself"—as Franz Kafka voices it in a mordant quotation Sontag includes at the close.[27] The crucial metaphorizing contribution exemplified by May Swenson's poem would be precisely to prevent such a mistaken self-perception of earth, and rather to see in our planetary portrait, as she did, that "hidden life which glimmers through the outlines of things like a play of light and shade", the qualities Kafka felt photographs could never capture.[8] Metaphorizing provides, where the photographer does not, the feelingful groping for which Kafka called.

But sometimes, I also found, the photographer can engage in his or her own metaphorizing, or at least can help to instigate ours.

GEORG GERSTER AND THE DELITERALIZING
OF AERIAL PHOTOGRAPHY

In 1978 Paddington Press brought out *Flights of Discovery: The Earth from Above*, an abridged version of Georg Gerster's lavish book of photographs entitled *Grand Design*.[29] Gerster, a Swiss journalist, had spent the decade from the mid-'60s to the mid-'70s—a period of manned space exploration—photographing terrestrial patterns all over the world from airplanes. When I ran into Gerster's book late in the summer of 1980 it served as a final footnote to my examination of the role of photography in effecting, through aerial archaeology, a Space-Age reconnection with the earth.

The photographs in *Flights of Discovery* are, first of all, stunning enough to suggest that Gerster's subject matter contained its own metaphorizing impetus, overwhelming the literalism of even the merely accurate copy. These "beautiful views", as he calls them in his Introduction, reminded me of something Sontag had written: that the same man who first successfully photographed the earth from above in a balloon in 1858, Nadar, also "took the most authoritative celebrity portraits of his time and did the first photo-interviews". Her point with this example is that both "photography as art" and "photography as document" (i.e., photography as metaphorizing and as literalizing medium) are "logical extensions of what photography means: note-taking on, potentially, everything in the world, from every possible angle".[30] Gerster echoes Sontag's appraisal of an inherently *dual* tendency within the note-taking of photography when he describes the aerial employment of the camera:

> Certainly, town and country planners, geologists and generals, tax assessors and realtors, cartographers, foresters, agricultural and civil engineers have long been making good use of aerial photography in their respective fields. For them, as for a number of other specialists, it is everyday fare and certainly no cause for emotion. If these specialists and technicians have no wish to get excited, that is their business. As I see it, however, an aerial photograph is a unique vehicle for wonder, vexation, joy, wrath—it never leaves one cold.[31]

Here again was something I had not realized in my reading of Lueders' and Sontag's books, something I welcomed. If Gerster were right, the aerial perspective *per se* could offer a feelingful overplus beyond its practical utility.

Assuming that the emotional impact cited by Gerster could counteract literalism and ignite metaphor, I wondered if the same might be said of the aerial photography used in archaeology. I had, to be sure, been impressed by the vividness of Leo Deuel's imagery in recounting the development of that technique. I even saw the rise of aerial archaeology as a promising paradigm, a "radical departure" through the technology of flight which surprisingly revealed heretofore hidden patterns of archaic interaction between humankind and its home, carrying us back in imagination to the earth of our origins.

I had been worried, however, by the rhetoric of "remote sensing" and the evidently utilitarian assumptions underlying aerial archaeology's reliance on photography: The threat of literalism seemed clear and present. In this regard, the photographs in *Flights of Discovery* were reassuring. Gerster even includes a section on "Biblical cities and sites from the air" in which the visions of aerial archaeology are directly addressed. Noting that Palestine was one of the earliest areas to be photographed from above (in World War I), he says that "since then, the airplane—or sometimes just a balloon or kite—has become indispensable for archaeological work, particularly in a country where high places have always had a religious significance". While Leo Deuel might contest his further comment that "the flight into the past is more rewarding over Palestine than anywhere else",[32] Gerster's beautiful views themselves testify that the photographic mediation of buried yesterdays by way of space flight need not always be literalistic. Quite to the contrary, the use of aerial photography in archaeology might itself constitute an overarching metaphor for the very process I had been exploring, the mental approach to earth made uniquely possible by entertaining and inventing metaphoric images.

But Gerster's support for the notion that aerial archaeology could be a model of the metaphorizing reconnection was not his only contribution to my search. In remarks introducing his final section of photographs he asks: "How far from the earth can an astronaut travel without losing sight of all signs of earthly life? And how near must a visiting astronaut come to be able to recognize signs of life on our planet?" His answer to these questions ends enigmatically: "Only when resolution is better than 100 yards can such traces be recognized for what they are. But even then there may be misunderstandings about the type of life assumed to exist on our planet. . .We have to take a step nearer to the earth, and then suddenly the patterns of living creatures are joined by their monumental question marks."[33]

What does Gerster mean when he refers to the "monumental question marks" involved in the patterns of living creatures? The fourteen photographs in this section of his book suggest an answer. Among these there are aerial views of Ayers Rock, a mountain sacred to the aborigines of central Australia (and not unlike the Devil's Tower of *Close Encounters*); a rock temple in Ethiopia; Mont-Saint Michel near the coast of Normandy; Stonehenge; the Great Mosque of Samarra, Iraq; the Tower of Babylon, also in Iraq; the Shinto shrine of Ise in Japan; a bell-shaped stupa, or dagoba, in Sri Lanka housing relics of the Buddha; the huge radar radiotelescope in Arecibo, Puerto Rico; the Parisian-style Teatro Amazonas in remote Manaus, Brazil; and a baroque Benedictine abbey in Switzerland. Such sites—even the astronomical facility in Puerto Rico could be compared to Stonehenge if the latter indeed served as a neolithic observatory—all bespeak humankind's concern with religious questions regarding the purpose of life and death in a cosmos which may or may not contain "intelligent life" or a deity who cares about the third planet from the sun. These are, in other words, monuments to the deepest perplexities of earthlings, massive reminders that starting before Stonehenge and extending beyond the telescope at Arecibo we have directed our yearning to the skies: here we are—where are you?

Moreover, if the latter question continues to go unanswered, the prior statement of terrestrial presence asks its own question. After millennia of striving for solutions in the stars, striving which culminates in all our Space-Age exploits, do we any longer even realize that we are *here*, that we are rooted in the earth and have our identity in the dark wet soil from which we raise our monuments and our rockets?

At the outset of my inquiry I had encountered William Barrett's conclusion that "art seems to say no" to the success of our efforts at breaking our ties to earth. Two of Gerster's other aerial photographs of "monumental question marks" deepen the point made by Barrett and suggest another metaphoric paradigm for the needed homecoming from space, another model characterizing in the largest terms the method I had found for terrestrial reconnection. The first of these is a view of *Double Negative* by Michael Heizer, an "Earth Art" construction at the edge of Mormon Mesa in Nevada. Heizer, the son of a leading scholar of Mesoamerican archaeology, has made a straight cut— or two cuts, since the line is interrupted by crossing the space beyond the uneven cliff edge—30 feet wide, 50 feet deep, and 1,640 feet long. According to Gerster, a reputable art critic calls *Double Negative*, created by displacing 200,000 tons of rock during the year following the Apollo 11 moon landing, "the greatest sculpture in the history of Western art—and its turning point too." Gerster also quotes Heizer, who observes that "one of the implications of Earth Art might be to remove completely the commodity status of a work of art and allow a return to the idea of art as. . . more of a religion."[34] That "return," exemplified in Heizer's massive earthwork, takes us back to the archaic structures, the enigmatic monuments, from a time when art and religion were not separate and conjointly expressed the mythic patterns of humankind's relation to the environment.

Rechecking Leo Deuel's *Flights into Yesterday*, I noticed a brief remark on earth sculptures such as Heizer's. With them, Deuel says, "modern art has embraced instant aerial archaeology."[35] Certainly here was a forceful aesthetic rejoinder to the literalistic seeing I feared. If Earth Art were truly "instant aerial archaeology"—strictly speaking a contradiction in terms—it would give us views of a *nonliteral past*, a metaphorically human imprint on the earth. Such a contribution would include not only Heizer's *Double Negative* but also *Spiral Jetty*, a huge causeway of rubble in the red algae-stained water of Utah's Great Salt Lake. Built in 1970 by Robert Smithson, this was Gerster's other instance of Earth Art.[36]

CHAPTER ELEVEN

EARTH ART AS MODEL: EADEM MUTATA RESURGO

As it happened, I had encountered *Spiral Jetty* several times since the early days of my project. I first saw pictures and an essay on it by Smithson in 1972 in an anthology called *Arts of the Environment*.[1] The shape of the construction was arresting by itself. Like the maze and labyrinth patterns from which they seemed an abstraction, spirals had long intrigued me; they conveyed the sense of a successive movement back to beginnings on a new basis. In my dissertation research on Melville's imagery during the mid '60s I had run across Swiss mathematician Rudolph Bernoulli's epitaph: *Eadem mutata resurgo*, or "Likewise I return, changed." These words were inscribed on his tombstone along with a logarithmic spiral and came to seem, a decade after my Melville work, an apt statement of what should happen with humankind's odyssey to the moon and back. In Smithson's earthwork these nuances of the spiral image were further dramatized by the view from above which was a major component of the piece for artist and audience alike.

Although at the time I had absolutely no prior acquaintance with Earth Art, I was very impressed with Smithson's 1972 *Spiral Jetty* essay. Here were thoughts paralleling my own dawning preference for "geo-metaphor" rather than "geometry" in these matters, for the earthly serendipities and sensuous indeterminacies of image as a contemporary channel back to myth's mysteries. Smithson says, for instance, that

179

> . . . in the Spiral Jetty the surd takes over and leads one into a world that cannot be expressed by number or rationality. Ambiguities are admitted rather than rejected, contradictions are increased rather than decreased — the *alogos* undermines the *logos*. Purity is put in jeopardy. I took my chances on a perilous path, along which my steps zigzagged, resembling a spiral lightning bolt.[2]

Such words certainly indicated the possible relevance of *Spiral Jetty*. But despite seeing, in mid-decade, Smithson's film about the construction of his project (with a striking visual evocation of conjunctions between the postmodern and the prehistoric), my lack of knowledgeability in either Earth Art or sculpture and painting generally blocked any further probing until 1979. That was when I saw an article on "New Landscapes in Art" in *The New York Times Magazine*.

The author, Kay Larson, begins by discussing the radical return to the past effected by the new earthworks, citing one critic's appraisal that "some of them have a majesty, a simplicity and an enduring value that connect back thousands of years".[3] She then speaks of Smithson in particular, recounting a recent visit to the *Spiral Jetty* site with Nancy Holt, an Earth Artist herself and Smithson's widow:

> The jetty had been swallowed by the rising waters of the warm shallow bay, which was dyed the color of pink lemonade by swarming microorganisms — some of the oldest life forms on earth. Smithson, she told me, had welcomed the notion that the flooding lake would sometimes 'borrow' his art. But if the water rose another five feet, she said, it would also inundate the Salt Lake airport. The thought seemed apt. All human actions succumb to time, which makes them mysterious. The pyramids, the stone temples of the Mayas, the 'Spiral Jetty' and the Salt Lake airport — all of them swamped by time.[4]

This passage pointed to another aspect of the "monumentality" characterizing both prehistoric remains — some of them only visible with the advent of aerial photography — and the instant archaeology of Earth Art. The tension between time and human temples built to speak to a remote future is what gave these monuments their mystery, according to Larson. And among them she listed a contemporary airport, suggesting a Space-Age vantage point might be involved in the new aesthetic landscapes exemplified by *Spiral Jetty*.

While Larson's article, popularly written for nontechnical readers like me, inspired the purchase of a collection of Smithson's writings which Nancy Holt published later in 1979, it was only several years

after that that I could study it in earnest. Having worked through—
with major interruptions—the Arthur C. Clarke connections and the
similarly balanced literalizing dangers and metaphorizing opportunities of aerial archaeology, I was brought back around to Earth Art by
Georg Gerster's *Flights of Discovery*. Seeing again his aerial photograph
of *Spiral Jetty* finally prompted me to work through the volume of
Smithson's writings and thereby to realize, at last, how central this
remarkable artist's vision could be to my concerns.

TAKING OFF WITH EARTH ART—
ROBERT SMITHSON'S AERIAL PERSPECTIVE

The Nancy Holt collection of published and unpublished pieces
contains an Introduction by Philip Leider, Smithson's editor at *Artforum* magazine and a friend who had delivered a eulogy at his funeral
in 1973. From Leider's Introduction I gained a glimpse of that context
I had lacked: the New York world of painting and sculpture out of
which—and away from which—Smithson's art developed. This world,
in the 1960s, was operating in the aftermath of Jackson Pollack, rigidly
adhering to what Leider calls the "rational categories", exemplified in
the sculpture of Anthony Caro. By 1966 Smithson's sensibility had
begun to depart from this paradigm. He had already written some
stinging criticism of Caro and, says Leider, "Smithson's own faith in the
'rational categories' was considerably shaken by his experience that year
as an art consultant to the firms then engaged in planning the immense
Dallas-Fort Worth Regional Air Terminal. A 'sculpture garden' did
not seem adequate in the face of runways the length of Central Park:
'Simply looking at art at eye-level is not a solution.'"[5]

From this project until his death Smithson was able to fashion an
amazing career in only seven years. "At the end of them," Leider claims,
"he stood at the head of a wholly unexpected development in mid-
century American art," and "the 'touchstone' that Anthony Caro's *Prairie*
never became was instead Smithson's *Spiral Jetty*".[6]

While I was admittedly in no position to confirm or refute Leider's
glowing appraisal of Smithson's historical significance, I was favorably
influenced to find an editor of *Artforum* advancing it at all. What particularly appealed to me, however, was the major role in Smithson's
career played by his involvement in the Dallas-Fort Worth airport. It

was in 1965 at a Yale University conference on "Art in the City" that he applied his growing preoccupation with the imagery of crystal structures (which he saw as "the structure of matter itself"[7]) to the idea of the city. An architect in the audience later asked him if he would like to participate in the planning of the immense Texas facility "in terms of trying to figure out what an airport is". He accepted the offer and, as he goes on to recall, "that's where the mapping and the intuitions in terms of the crystal structures really took hold in terms of areas of land—I was dealing with grids superimposed on large land masses, so that the inklings of the earthworks were there."[8]

The connection between mapping and the crystalline structure of matter is that, for Smithson, the grids and coordinates of the former—the abstractions of latitude and longitude, for instance—are a kind of metaphor drawn from the geological realities of the latter. In other words, instead of *imposing* an abstract geometrical grid upon the earth, Smithson's crystalline mapping metaphorizes with data provided by the actual physicalities of place.

Along with this, the vast scale of the airport prompted Smithson to deal for the first time with an explicitly aerial perspective. In fact, in one of two essays on the project he refers to the "aerosurveying" of the SECOR satellite (a photograph of which accompanies the essay) and adds, characteristically, that "mapping the Earth, the Moon, or other planets is similar to the mapping of crystals".[9] Then, working with a site slightly less global than these bodies, he proposes several pieces in a genre he has invented and calls "Aerial Art". Since he has already indicated that his involvement in the Dallas-Fort Worth airport planning was decisive for his move into earthworks, this regard for the bird's-eye viewpoint suggests a familiar Space-Age relationship of reconnection. Smithson almost says as much directly in his article on Aerial Art: "Art today is no longer an architectural afterthought, or an object to attach to a building after it is finished, but rather a total engagement with the building process from the ground up and from the sky down."[10]

The primary art work devised by Smithson for the airport combines several of these elements while introducing another which was new to his development at the time. He entitles the piece *Aerial Map* and describes it as "a progression of triangular concrete pavements that would result in a spiral effect. This could be built as large as the site would allow, and could be seen from approaching and departing aircraft."[11] Here the aerial perspective, monumental scale, and crystalline structure come together in a "map" which is also a spiral. This feature looks ahead to the upright sculpture *Gyrostasis*, in 1968, as well as to *Spiral Jetty* two years after that and to several other important late works. This form evidently fascinated Smithson as it does me, and as I read the Holt collection of his writings—along with a comprehensive 1981 commentary, *Robert Smithson: Sculpture*, edited by Robert Hobbs —I wondered why this was so. I also wondered how the airport project in particular helped make the evocative spiral such an important ingredient of his Earth Art.

SPIRALLING

I was able to find a few answers to my questions in the materials I was studying. Robert Hobbs, for example, observes that

> the triangular spirals of *Gyrostasis* and *Aerial Map* have a prototype in an alternative design for the regional airport's 'Clear Zone': the *Spiral Reflecting Pool* (1967), a 4-foot-deep concrete container for a rectangular spiral 150 feet in width. The importance of this shape resides not only in its foreshadowing *Spiral Jetty* but also in its being a direct reference to a fairly frequent mode of crystal extension —spiral growth from a single rupture . . . [12]

This insight was helpful in pointing again to the importance of crystallography as a resource for Smithson's abstract mapping, his metaphorizing with what he took to be the structure of earthly matter itself. Hobbs's observation only indirectly illuminated the issue of why the Dallas-Fort Worth airport project prompted Smithson to see the spiral form, however.

Turning back to Smithson's own essay, "Aerial Art", I encountered several comments which at least deepened my sense of the context within which he made his choice of this form. First he speculates that "just as our satellites explore and chart the moon and the planets, so might the artist explore the unknown sites that surround our airports." With this manifestly Space-Age vista in mind, he goes on to fill in some details:

> The naturalism of seventeenth-, eighteenth- and nineteenth-century art is replaced by non-objective sense of site. The landscape begins to look more like a three dimensional map rather than a

rustic garden. Aerial photography and air transportation bring into view the surface features of this shifting world of perspectives. The rational structures of buildings disappear into irrational disguises and are pitched into optical illusions. The world seen from the air is abstract and illusive.[13]

Smithson's stress on the irrational and illusive suggests a hyper-metaphoric viewing. The earth approached from above yields not only naturalistic geometaphors like the garden, which retain significant aspects of literal perception, but also reveals or allows for even more thoroughly nonliteralistic imagery. The image of a three-dimensional map, for instance, is in Smithson's viewing related to the fanciful cartography of Lewis Carroll as well as to the configurations of crystallography.

A year after he proposed *Aerial Map* and *Spiral Reflecting Pool* for the Dallas-Fort Worth project in 1967, but a year before the publication of the "Aerial Art" essay, Smithson's piece "A Museum of Language in the Vicinity of Art" appeared in *Art International*. The final section of this rich and witty commentary on the writing surrounding the art scene of the '60s is called "Mapscapes or Cartographic Sites". It discusses how the map has for centuries "exercised a fascination over the minds of artists" and includes, as a current example, "electronic 'mosaic' photomaps from NASA".[14] The reference to Carroll which I found so relevant to the image of the three-dimensional map concerns an episode in Chapter 11 of *Sylvie and Bruno Concluded*. There, as Smithson relates it, "a German Professor tells how his country's cartographers experimented with larger and larger maps until they finally made one with a scale of a mile to a mile. . .The Professor said, 'It has never been spread out, yet. The farmers objected: they said it would cover the whole country, and shut out the sunlight! So now we use the country itself, as its own map, and I assure you it does nearly as well.'"[15]

Smithson sees this story as a parable for the fate of painting since the '50s and a signal that museums and galleries should perhaps plan square-mile interiors. But of course in his Dallas-Fort Worth airport proposals just that sort of vast scale presented itself. The literal landscape became an abstract and illusive landscape, or a "mapscape" in Smithson's sense, a "cartographic site" so immense when seen from the skies that it returns the viewer to "the country itself".

How, then, did his conception of mapscapes issue in his use of the spiral? There seemed to be no simple and direct relation, but again on the level of context an awareness of the way in which Smithson employed cartography provided me with an enhanced feeling for his radical vision of the landscape from the air.

I became convinced, for one thing, that his artist's sense of mapping *denies* the distancing and geometric distortion usually associated with that cognitive operation. A long 1972 interview points this up. He explains how he had become interested in "an area of abstraction that was really rooted in crystal structure" and had been led from there to the grids of mapping. He adds: "So I began to see the grid as a kind of mental construct of physical matter, and my concern for the physical started to grow. Right along I had always had an interest in geology as well."[16] He makes clear, however, in a reflection which also applies to crystallography, cartography, and geometry, that his attraction to geology grew out of his perception as an artist: "It wasn't predicated on any kind of scientific need. It was aesthetic."[17]

Having gathered all this background information on the role of crystals and maps in Smithson's art, I was eventually able to see a bit farther into the origins of what can be called his aerial discovery of spirals. Robert Hobbs points out, in this regard, how the free-standing spiral sculpture *Gyrostasis* developed out of the geometry of the non-spiral piece *Hexagonal Clock*.[18] Moreover, comparing *Aerial Map* and *Spiral Reflecting Pool* with some of the works from the same period which deal in circular and polygonal forms it is possible — once having understood Smithson's unique use of aerial viewpoint, mapping, and crystallography — to see the spirals as likewise concerned with the relation of circumference to center. Indeed, spiralling seems to function here as a way to get from one to the other while stressing, with its asymmetry, that one cannot count on the fixity of either. It is as though the spiral deliteralizes the circle, a deliteralizing Smithson often appears to be doing with his symmetrical figures as well.

One of the first of these pieces was *A Nonsite, Pine Barrens, New Jersey* in 1968. As with the Dallas-Fort Worth works an airfield is a crucial component. Smithson's own description of this "indoor earth-work"— the "nonsite"— mentions that the outdoor site to which it points centers on "a hexagon airfield. . .which lent itself very well to the application of certain crystalline structures which had preoccupied me in my earlier work." Not surprisingly, the image of the Pine Barrens airfield seen from above, along with aerial photographs from Dallas-Fort Worth, drew him into his own kind of map-making. "I decided to use the Pine Barrens site," he says, "as a piece of paper to draw a crystalline structure over the landmass rather than on a 20×30 sheet of paper. In this way I was applying my conceptual thinking directly to the disruption of the site over an area of several miles. So you might say my non-site was a three-dimensional map of the site."[19]

The upshot of this procedure in Smithson's hands is the sort of self-cancelling map concocted by Lewis Carroll's German Professor. Additionally, the actual nonsite gallery piece itself indicates the vacuous nature of the center. Smithson's way of expressing this verbally is to say that "the map of my *Non-Site #1* (*an indoor earthwork*) has six vanishing points that lose themselves in a pre-existent earth mound that is in the center of a hexagonal airfield in the Pine Barren Plains in South New Jersey."[20]

The vanishing or void-like center of many of Smithson's constructions has one source in the consulting work for the Dallas-Fort Worth airport, as does the concern for a dialectic between center and periphery. His essay on Aerial Art discusses the relation between the central terminal buildings of the airport—which could include a museum housing a nonsite—and its boundaries, the "clear zones" where his earthworks, or sites, would be located. This is among other things a sly comment on the New York gallery world at the center of art-as-commodity: he is identifying this center as a nonsite in contrast to the actualities of the remote or run-down sites he generally preferred. In the case of the Aerial Art essay he combines all of this with the element of vastness, suggesting with what can be taken as a spiral image that the art on the boundaries of the airport "is remote from the eye of the viewer the way a galaxy is remote from the earth".[21] He infers from this that the center is almost invisible, in effect infinitesimal and certainly unreachable in any sense of literal arrival.

Acknowledging for an interviewer the fact that his Dallas-Fort Worth pieces were never actually built, Smithson nevertheless maintains that "it was very worthwhile for me because it got me to think about large land areas and the dialogue between the terminal and the fringes of the terminal—once again, between the center and the edge of things. This has been a sort of on-going preoccupation with me, part of the dialectic between the inner and the outer."[22] That the spiral is, so to speak, the shape of this dialogue or dialectic is underscored by another comment to the same interviewer about the site/nonsite works which followed *Aerial Map* and *Spiral Reflecting Pool*: "Although the nonsite designates the site, the site itself is open and really unconfined and constantly being changed. And then the thing was to bring these two things together. And I guess to a great extent that culminated in the *Spiral Jetty*."[23]

BACK TO *SPIRAL JETTY*

As explained earlier, I had run into Smithson's statement about this work early in my project, had seen his film on its construction, and had read Kay Larson's article on Earth Art in 1979. But it was not until after seeing a picture of *Spiral Jetty* in Georg Gerster's book of aerial photographs and almost completing my manuscript in early 1983 that I engaged in a more thorough investigation of Smithson's writings together with the essays on him collected by Robert Hobbs. My more detailed study, focusing on Smithson's use of spiral forms in the context of aerial perspectives — and his related adaptations of crystallography, cartography, and the dialectic between circumference and center — eventually led me back to his foremost construction, the one which is acknowledged to represent the entire enterprise of Earth Art.

One thing these repeated probings of mine accomplished was to reveal the pertinence of statements in the *Spiral Jetty* essay which had not been clear to me earlier. For example, Smithson recalls that when he first saw the specific locations for his giant earthwork he realized how determinative the role of site would be:

> As I looked at the site, it reverberated out to the horizons only to suggest an immobile cyclone while flickering light made the entire landscape appear to quake. A dormant earthquake spread into the fluttering stillness, into a spinning sensation without movement. This site was a rotary that enclosed itself in an immense roundness. From that gyrating space emerged the possibility of the Spiral Jetty.[24]

This description of the genesis of the work underscores how, for Smithson, even what seems like an imposition on the environment of forms drawn from crystallography, mapping, or geometry is actually a metaphorizing maneuver, an extrapolation from the site itself (just as his nonsite pieces include physical materials from their corresponding sites).

Another point worth noting is the obvious relationship between the motionless rotary feeling Smithson got from the lakeside location and the title of his 1978 spiral sculpture *Gyrostasis*. The immensity of the roundness he encountered also restates the vast scale of the Dallas-Fort Worth Air Terminal, and elsewhere in his essay he discusses how this factor operates on the viewer of *Spiral Jetty*. Working from the etymology of the word "scale" as a ladder or flight of stairs, he says that "after a point, measurable steps. . .descend from logic to the 'surd state.' The rationality of a grid on a map sinks into what it is supposed to define. Logical purity suddenly finds itself in a bog, and welcomes the unexpected event."[25]

Here was the sense of the ambiguous and alogical, the openness to serendipitous discovery, which had first attracted me to Smithson's Earth Art as relevant to my own search. His awareness was one which approached what I saw, following James Hillman, as the essence of the mythic viewed from a Space-Age vantage point, and it somehow fit with the spiral form Smithson felt was dictated for his most famous construction. That form, as he had developed it in several important works between 1967 and 1971, seemed to me a turning away from the purity of the circle, from the static relation of fixed circumference to fixed center, which paralleled my many rejections of literalistic purity for the muddy thinking of metaphor. Just as the center of my "mandala earth" was a fanciful Serendip which fostered a eccentric serendipping, and its far edge was a fog-bound Cornwall vaguely discerned at one boundary of a fortuitous satellite photograph, so Smithson's writing had speculated on center and periphery in art by referring to "marginalia at the center" and exploring minimalist painter Ad Reinhardt's 1955 cartoon for *Art News*, "A Portend of the Artist as a Yhung Mandala."[26]

The essay on *Spiral Jetty* culminates many of these themes, or comments on their culmination in the 1970 earthwork itself. Smithson allows that "the flowing mass of rock and earth of the Spiral Jetty could be trapped by a grid of segments". However, he stresses that such segments would only be a mental construct and concludes, as noted earlier, that ". . . in the Spiral Jetty the surd takes over and leads one into a world that cannot be expressed by number or rationality."[27] For Smithson the burning glare off the reddened water forces metaphors of blood pumped by the heart of the lake. It also evokes the imagery of solar activity: not only the heat and brightness of the sun reflected back from the spiral's center, but the spiral itself as a solar prominence, a boiling storm of collapsing matter. Indeed, the metaphorizing is manifold in Smithson's interactions with the site. He remembers:

> Once, when I was flying over the lake, its surface seemed to hold all the properties of an unbroken field of raw meat with gristle (foam); no doubt it was due to some freak wind action. Eyesight is often slaughtered by the other senses, and when that happens

it becomes necessary to seek out dispassionate abstractions. The dizzying spiral yearns for the assurance of geometry. One wants to retreat into the cool rooms of reason. But no, there was Van Gogh with his easel on some sun-baked lagoon painting ferns of the Carboniferous Period. Then the mirage faded into the burning atmosphere.[28]

Again and again Smithson emphasizes the unaccountable or "surd" quality of the site and of the spiral, not to mention the irrationality of his attempts to make them add up in words: "The equation of my language remains unstable, a shifting set of coordinates, an arrangement of variables spilling into surds. My equation is as clear as mud—a muddy spiral."[29]

Beyond the swamp of sensuous imagery into which the jetty throws Smithson himself, Robert Hobbs quotes a large portion of the entry on spirals in Cirlot's *Dictionary of Symbols*, a work the artist owned. Hobbs especially focuses on one signification in the Cirlot account: "Going right back to the most ancient traditions, we find the distinction being made between the creative spiral (rising in clockwise direction, and attributed to Pallas Athene) and the destructive spiral like a whirlwind (which twirls round to the left, and is an attribute of Poseidon)."[30] The second of these two symbolic traits, according to Hobbs, dominates Smithson's earthwork, "the counterclockwise whirl of the *Jetty* itself connoting entropy and destruction."[31]

Undeniably entropy and destruction were concerns of Smithson. But whether he built his jetty as a counter-clockwise spiral with this symbolic element in mind is far from clear. His two spiral works proposed for the Dallas-Fort Worth airport are clockwise, as is the *Gyrostasis* sculpture (at least as pictured). Moreover, in commenting on his own masterwork Smithson exclaims that "following the spiral steps we return to our origins, back to some pulpy protoplasm, a floating eye adrift in an antideluvian ocean."[32] Contrary to Hobbs's view, in other words, the notion that spiral steps lead back to our origins implies a destination for even the counterclockwise whirl which need not be seen as negative. Since, in the northern hemisphere, the rotation of the earth on its axis is responsible for this direction of water's flow in a vortex, it could even be imagined that the movement of terrestrial reconnection entails this sort of spiral.

Of course, there *can* be a negative face as well to such earthward returns. In the caption to his aerial photograph of *Spiral Jetty*, Georg Gerster speaks of Smithson's experience, "when walking along the spiral from the outside, of the swirl and suction of life, which spirals in irreversibly and ever faster toward the point of final truth—death."[33] Through this association it is possible to discern, in the midst of Space-Age sophistication, the primordial mystery of personal extinction, the return to earth we all make. Whether or not the artist felt that this "final truth" was his destination when he traveled the coils of his earthwork, as Gerster insinuates, he faced it three years later in a tragically literal fashion.

AMARILLO RAMP AND THE PREHISTORIC FUTURE

On July 20, 1973, the light plane carrying Robert Smithson on a photographing survey of his *Amarillo Ramp*, staked out in a shallow West Texas lake, hit an air pocket, stalled, and crashed. The pilot, a photographer, and Smithson were all killed.

He and Nancy Holt had been visiting with a friend, Tony Shafrazi, in New Mexico when they happened to learn of a ranch near Amarillo with desert lakes and a receptivity to art, and went to investigate. The ranch owner, Stanley Marsh, agreed to let Smithson build an earthwork at Tecovas Lake Dam on his property and hired a plane for Smithson's use in surveying the site. Later, after her husband's funeral, Holt decided to accept Richard Serra's offer to help in completing *Amarillo Ramp*. In August Holt, Serra, and Shafrazi returned to the Marsh Ranch, saw to the draining of the lake, and in about three weeks finished the project according to Smithson's plans.[34]

Seen from above, the red and white rocks comprising the Ramp form an incomplete circle like *Broken Circle*, the artist's 1971 construction. However, unlike *Spiral Hill*, the companion piece to the latter work, the helix of *Amarillo Ramp* ascends in a clockwise direction. Smithson's final work is therefore a so-called "creative spiral", a seemingly positive statement about the move up and off the earth. The manner of his dying suggests otherwise, though, and in one of the contributions to the Hobbs anthology John Coplans remarks that only after climbing *Amarillo Ramp* and returning, and looking back, does one gain the deeper significance of the work: ". . .you are reminded that even if you think you know the pattern of the world, you still have to move through it to experience life".[35] Ascent and safe re-entry are evidently both required to receive the statement made by *Amarillo Ramp*, a statement which also needs to be seen in the light of *Broken Circle/Spiral Hill* two years before.

This double piece, built in an abandoned Dutch sand quarry, is the most important of Smithson's works between *Spiral Jetty* and *Amarillo Ramp*. Although he disliked fixed centers, he was forced to deal with one in this case because a boulder too large to move occupied the middle of the *Broken Circle* site. He referred to it as the "accidental center" of his construction, finally accepting it as "a kind of glacial 'heart of darkness'—a warning from the Ice Age."[36] Lucy Lippard, in another essay for the Hobbs volume, notes of boulders like this one that "in the Bronze Age they were used to make huge dolmens or passage tombs. . . . Smithson," she continues, "passed such a 'Hun's Bed' each day on his way from town to his site and it became very important to him."[37]

Because of its configuration—a semicircular canal interrupted by land balanced with a semicircular jetty interrupted by water—*Broken Circle* seems to be "facing" in a clockwise direction (it can read as a stylized capital "S") and qualifies, according to Lippard's idea of spiral symbolism, as a clockwise movement into the future.[38] If so, in view of its central megalith the future it moves into may be the "prehistoric future" Smithson often hypothesized. And for the artist himself this future came to pass, sadly enough, through *Amarillo Ramp*, which in one work combined the major elements of the double *Broken Circle/ Spiral Hill* construction—i.e., the incomplete circuit, the helical ramp, the relation to water and damming—and led to his death as in fulfillment of the threat Smithson felt in the Hun's Bed boulder. The "accidental center" of the earlier work, a gravestone, can, in other words, be seen as a foreshadowing of the grim accident at the heart of the final one.

The accident which killed Robert Smithson, all are agreed, robbed us of a giant talent who, at 35, had become the most original spokesman for an artistic vision focused on the earth. Perhaps it is because of his vision and the grisly appropriateness of his death that Georg Gerster's photograph of *Spiral Jetty*—the caption to which cites the tragedy of *Amarillo Ramp*—is followed by one more aerial view in *Flights of Discovery*. It is a picture of a cemetery in Indonesia for well-to-do Chinese, a series of tombs oddly arranged in accordance with an ancient divination technique. As Gerster explains, "the striking and studied irregularity in the direction of the graves is the work of the geomancer, a wise man skilled in *feng-shui*.[39] Like the "ley lines" theories of unorthodox observers of the landscape in old and New England, this ancient Chinese concept perceives sacred forces in various topographical features.

It was the art of *feng-shui* that was responsible for the layout of

China's Great Wall[40] — supposedly the only human structure visible from an orbiting space craft[41] — and a magnificent candidate for "site selection" in one of Smithson's Earth Art projects: a dam under construction in California he appreciated as a "functionless wall".[42] Admittedly the Great Wall did have a military function, as do many space projects starting with the German V-2 rocket. But such fortifications also had sacred purposes; they were "magical defenses", according to Mircea Eliade,[43] which little resemble our narrowly utilitarian notions of function and thereby approach the functionlessness of Smithson's art. Conversely, his work qualifies him as a kind of supreme postindustrial geomancer, one who left a legacy of earth wisdom which I found indispensable for concluding my quest.

SMITHSON'S LEGACY—
THE SENSE OF A MYTHODOLOGY

As a young reporter for the Zurich weekly *Weltwoche* in 1954, Georg Gerster was assigned to interview C.G. Jung about his long-standing interest in "flying saucer" phenomena. Jung declined to be interviewed, but wrote to the newspaper that

> in the course of years I have accumulated a voluminous dossier on the sightings, including the statements of two eye-witnesses well-known to me personally (I myself have never seen anything!) and have read all the available books, but I have found it impossible to determine even approximately the nature of these observations. So far only one thing is certain: it is not just a rumour, *something is seen*.[44]

Four years later Jung followed up this response to Gerster with a little book on the saucer sightings. It was subtitled *A Modern Myth of Things Seen in the Skies*, and set forth his theory that the round, spherical, or disk-shaped phenomena were archetypal symbols of order and wholeness projected upon the heavens by a politically tense and divided world populace. More specifically, the things seen in the skies in Jung's modern myth were analogous, as he puts it, "with the symbol of totality well known to all students of depth psychology, namely the *mandala* (Sanskrit for circle)".[45]

For me, as I worked through the implications of Robert Smithson's Earth Art in 1983, Jung's discussion came to mind as a curious parallel. The connecting link was Gerster's involvement with both men, but building on this coincidence I felt more than once that Smithson was offering a fitting twist to Jung's statement on flying saucers.

It had occurred to me that since the first whole earth photographs in the late '60s the planet itself had become a "flying object" in our skies, and was actually the least adequately identified one of all: the quintessential UFO. The metaphorizing and serendipping approach I had developed, leading to geometaphors grounded in Gaia and played with in defiance of the dominant literalism of Apollo, was partly an attempt to locate this hidden face of earth in the Age of Space. But very soon it became clear that a definitive mythos of terrestrial identity would not be forthcoming. What I had discovered instead, in addition to a line of sight back down toward the planet, was the way itself, the approach. Rather than a simple circle of meaning, a static mandala summing up all the many things seen in the earth — Jung's Cold War scenario transferred from the skies — here was a *mythic* (or, more precisely, a *neomythic*) *way of seeing*.

In other words, a method had emerged for actually "seeing things": for imagining a planetary picture more akin to a kaleidoscopic display than to any fixed and factual viewing. Being able to see earth in this way answered to the question "What do you see in her?" It was a means of valuing the variousness of terrestrial imagery, sensing a dancing lady in the misty outlines of a satellite photograph one time, interpreting our home as a sacred stone or garden another, regarding the world in every sighting as a savage or poet would do, seeking reconnection through this metaphoric vision.

And so my growing sense was that this approach, inferred over several years from the earth's own surprisingly insistent images and chance revelations in the Space Age, furnished the only mythic significance I would find. Not until I was propelled by aerial archaeology and Gerster's photographs into the "instant aerial archaeology" of Smithson's art, however, did I fully understand what it was that I had discovered in my search: a *mythology* for seeing things in the earth.

Put specifically, the use of aerial photography by archaeologists showed me a gathering of scientific data, unwittingly imaginal but prone to literalistic readings, which provided a large metaphor or model for my method, allowing me to realize its mythic qualities. Likewise — but even more conclusively given its endemic resistance to literalism —

Smithson's legacy of Earth Art helped me stand outside my metaphorizing and serendipping while still engaging in them on another level. I was able to follow his aesthetic geomancy far enough to gain an overview of my own approach and see that it was characterized by the same sort of perception. This approach was not, after all, a neutral tool to probe a mythos outside itself, but through the mini-myths of metaphor and the metaphorizing openings of serendipity sought to build its own imaginal avenue from the Space Age to the Stone Age — that is, toward the ancient matrix of religion and art in myth as we move onward.

Responding to humanistic psychologist Jean Houston's witty insinuation that we have yet to do so, my approach was an attempt to "put the first man on earth" by counterbalancing the consciousness needed to put one on the moon[46] — seeking the path along which, like the spiral's coils, we return, changed. To the extent that the method constituted a Space-Age approximation to a mythic style of seeing, its implications could best be understood, I decided, through the coining of another new term at the close.

ON OUR WAY OUT INTO SPACE,
A TIME FOR SEEING THINGS IN THE EARTH

Robert Smithson once told an interviewer that ever since he had collected snakes as a boy he had felt "reptilian, cold and earthbound".[47] Perhaps this partly accounts for an art that went so thoroughly against the grain of the Apollonic mindset motivating the NASA space program throughout the seven years of his major projects. He died four years to the day after Neil Armstrong's historic lunar step. By then, what I would call the first phase of the Age of Space was over.

It is certainly not that the impulse to blast off and explore the universe ended in 1973. NASA's work goes on, and now includes female and black astronauts as well as plans for a space station and an eventual return to the moon, while President Reagan's dubious "Star Wars" proposal insures that the militarization of space will continue to threaten us. The Soviets, for their part, seem to be moving toward a permanent orbiting platform, and many other nations participate in various satellite ventures. Moreover, the popular media have hardly stopped producing space-related books and films and television shows; although not without their own striking terrestrial imagery,[48] these are generally upbeat treatments of the move out from earth. Two examples would be James Michener's huge novel and TV mini-series *Space*, about the origins and activities of NASA, and Arthur C. Clarke's predictably literalistic sequel to *2001*, brought slickly to the screen by producer-director Peter Hyams.[49]

Nor will this move out to the stars cease in the future. It is unquestionably a noble enterprise, worthy of the worshipful adulation accorded it by champions like Clarke, Michener, or Carl Sagan, not to mention their millions of admirers.

But shortly before Smithson died there began a lull in space exploration which offers another opportunity. The four years between Apollo 11 and *Amarillo Ramp* now seem, with a decade's hindsight, to have been the high plateau achieved in the first stage of our push into space. The initial landing on the moon was succeeded by five other Apollo lunar missions (plus Apollo 13, which had to abort before reaching its goal). All told, twelve men walked on the moon. By July 20, 1973, however, manned flights beyond earth orbit, which had never begun for the Soviets, were finished for America in this century. Funding for the NASA projects diminished during the '70s; priorities were rearranged. There would probably not be another man—or a woman—on the moon during the lifetime of most of those adults who watched Neil Armstrong's feat on television.[50] The recent death of seven astronauts in the Challenger shuttle explosion also gives pause to our outer-space enterprise even while pointing up, in tragic fashion, its non-utilitarian factors, the "human considerations" of subjective aspiration and judgement which NASA's technological efficiency has often seemed intent on suppressing.

On the day after the lunar landing of Apollo 16 in April 1972, Robert Smithson spoke with Bruce Kurtz. The conversation is included among his writings edited by Nancy Holt. Smithson begins:

> I described the moonshot once as a very expensive non-site. It keeps people working, you know. To an extent I thought that after they got to the moon there was a strange demoralization that set in that they didn't discover little green men, or something. It's on that level. I was watching the one last night, and there was kind of a forced exuberance. There was this attempt to try to confer some meaning onto it, and to me it's quite banal.

Kurtz's response continues this criticism of NASA:

> One thing that amazed me about the first moonshot was that you saw Mission Control in Houston with all those incredible com-

> puter stations, that incredible technology, with hundreds of people
> facing toward a kind of altar, like at the movies, and above the altar
> was a picture of Snoopy. There had to be some way in their minds
> of attaching a mascot to the whole experience, in other words to
> symbolize the experience to make it more comprehensible, and the
> image was so regressive that it denatured the experience. There was
> no awareness of the meaning.

Smithson then adds a final comment: ". . .it's sort of like they're so
abstracted that they. . . their imagery would draw from Snoopy, or Porky
Pig, or something."[51]

Although he stressed the banality of the space scientists' symbolism, their tendency thereby to impose an inappropriate meaning on
the moonshot, he did not deny that there might be meaningful images
for it. Rather, he apparently agreed with Kurtz that at Mission Control
"there was no awareness of the meaning". His remark that he saw the
lunar mission as "a very expensive non-site" was more than a critical
point about the costliness of the space program, a point many were
beginning to make by the early '70s and a factor in the reduced support
for NASA thereafter. What Smithson was referring to was the process
of collecting rock samples from the moon for analysis and display back
on earth. Such a process paralleled his own practice in the site/nonsite
works, where a gallery or museum piece referred to, and contained
physical material from, an actual site at some distance. For Smithson,
that is to say, Houston had become a nonsite referring to the moon
as site.

This interpretation was unwittingly echoed a few months after the
plane crash at *Amarillo Ramp* when the National Cathedral in Washington commissioned a stained glass "Space Window" with a tiny lunar
sample in its center,[52] suggesting the entire nation had become a nonsite. A further implication of this reading of the Apollo program is that,
by contrast, Smithson's work represents an "Earth Window", an aggregate nonsite pointing not away from the earth but toward it, drawing
out its aspects instead of "denaturing" experience. Here again his Earth
Art supplies appropriate imagery, possible meanings— and a reminder
that the word "art" occupies the middle of the word "earth". Moreover,
in so doing it suggested a suitable purpose for the post-Apollo lull in
outer-space activities.

To be sure, if our aspirations toward the stars were suffering from
more than a temporary setback we would be facing a bleak future indeed for the human spirit, whose Apollonic needs are irreducible and

deserve their due. Such is the prospect worrying James Michener, the last chapter of whose best-selling *Space* consists of a series of lamentations over the past decade's slowdown of space exploration. He evidently sees this slowdown as part of a popular revulsion against the whole tradition of scientific thought. His main character at the end of the novel, speaking in Vermont to a conference on extraterrestrial life, warns that "when the mind of man ceases to thrust outward, it begins to contract and wither."[53]

But the outward—one might say phallic—thrust Michener recommends is not the sole direction for the mind's creativity. On the contrary, if this thrust is not being permanently diminished the time seems apt for exploring other humanly important options and directions beyond an oversimplified either/or. The most dramatic instance of science's outward push is, of course, the flight into space, and it is here that the temporary slackening is most obvious. Accordingly, it is also here, in terms of these themes and thought-styles, that alternatives may be most readily available for exploration.

To reiterate: Apollo will not die. Nor will his space program, under whatever name, cease its lofty strivings. But Dionysus, as well, deserves proper respect along with his sometime spouse Ariadne of the Labyrinth and, of course, Gaia, who undergirds our savage or poetic seeing. A turn back toward earth and non-scientific kinds of consciousness need not deny the value of science or its future in space. Indeed, some scientists themselves acknowledge other modes of knowing in what they do. As early as 1974 I ran across a letter to *Science* magazine by a Nobel laureate biochemist, Albert Szent-Gyorgyi, which emphasized the role of "Dionysian thinking", a reliance on intuition and serendipity, in scientific research.[54] And quite recently, in July of 1983, I noticed a *New York Times* headline announcing "Metaphor Getting Its Due As a Wellspring of Science".[55] The major focus of the *Times* piece is a book called *Physics as Metaphor* by a physicist, Roger S. Jones, who draws heavily, I found, from Owen Barfield's writings on metaphor.[56] Neither of these scientists evidences a recognition of how the activities I have called metaphorizing and serendipping are rooted in the earth and lead back to earth. Both, however, include such activities as integral to a deeper view of science.

No, it is only when science itself sounds exclusivistic and self-congratulatory, ignorant of its own excesses or of the nobility characterizing other directions of thought (including the intuitive thinking in its own midst), that it rightly begins to incur censure. In terms of its Space-Age comportment this means that the necessary literalism

of scientific calculation must not be allowed to override modes of seeing
and saying which connect us to our home, must not be allowed, in other
words, to foster the abandonment of earth.

When William Barrett wrote, near the end of the Apollo moon
missions, that "art seems to say no" to the probable success of our efforts
to break ties with our primitive cultural roots (and, implicitly, with
the earth), he was not saying art and space travel must be incompatible.
Robert Smithson's Earth Art makes an even more emphatic statement
than Barrett about the impossibility of divorcing ourselves from our
archaic origins and from the planet of those origins. And yet, again, the
crucial point concerns the utter break, the complete divorce, which
the space scientists often seem to be intending. This would indeed,
Barrett and Smithson caution, leave art behind along with everything
else which makes for a recognizably human existence. Stated more
drastically, such a prospective abandonment, however subtle and slow
moving, or couched in attractive propaganda for space colonies, only
serves the forces of planetary pollution and nuclear annihilation. But
conversely, they are suggesting, it is a regard for art—and, through art's
vision, the earth-grounded values of traditional peoples, their mythic
sensibility—which can forestall such a fate while allowing for science
to move forward more circumspectly into space.

This, as I came to see it, was what the Space Age was for. Checking
the OED I learned that one of the obsolete meanings of "space" is "time,
leisure, or opportunity for doing something", linking it at last with the
imagery of opportunism: openings, harbors, and portholes. This meaning was far from obsolete for my purposes. The "Age" of "Space" was a
period in which to take advantage of the new line of sight our astronauts
and scientists have given us to look at ourselves and our earth in ways
they were not prepared to do, a chance to return changed. Although I
was hardly conscious of it at the outset, my search had been an attempt
to use the years beyond the last moon landing to probe the opportunity
the age offered.[57]

And the approach I had developed in this attempt was certainly
strange enough to merit its new name: launched by a cartoon and the
curious conjunctions of the futuristic with the archaic in popular
media; inspired by the advice of the antifeminist Mailer and the manifestly amythic William J.J. Gordon, but grounded in sacred stones,
feminist spirituality, and the mythic attributes of the Goddess; spurred
on to spontaneity by the lifework of Arthur C. Clarke in literalistic
science and fiction; consulting at key points the antiliteralistic scholar-

ship of Mircea Eliade and James Hillman or the aesthetic vision of René Magritte and May Swenson; finding its model through Space-Age innovations in archaeology and art; all along handling the images, exploring the geometaphors, learning to see things in the earth. My metaphorizing, my recourse to chance connections as a "serendipping" extension of metaphorizing, my skirmishes with what I saw as the threat of literalism to such mental activities — in short, the components of my "mythodology"—were all conceived and applied to direct us away from the exclusively outward thrust science might make on its own. They were my eccentric but, I felt, appropriate means of countering that would-be abandonment while seeking to move toward its opposite: the re-establishment in Space-Age consciousness of the connection to earth once effected in the artistic and religious expressions of ancient myth.

In other words, the mythodology which had emerged from my search for the mythic significance of the Space Age was a beginning for this needed re-entry into earth — or re-entry of earth into us — as we paused in our pursuit of worlds beyond. I finished the manuscript which set forth the search late in 1983 in the hills of Vermont (where James Michener had closed out his novel), with over a year of revisions, negotiations, footnotes and finagling still ahead. But a paradoxical sense of closure had come months earlier and several thousand miles to the east.[58]

EPILOGUE

On Friday, the 13th of May, I was standing at dusk next to the Men-an-tol on a moor near Land's End in Cornwall. I had not done more than pass through Dartmoor, the bleakly fascinating upland in Devon to the east. But seeing those misty hills with their granite tors had been enough to remind me of Lucy Lippard's book.

Lippard, one of the essayists in the collection I had consulted on Robert Smithson, had spent 1977 on a farm in South Devon. During one of her frequent walks on Dartmoor she literally stubbed her toe on a small standing stone in what turned out to be a ritual alignment, a sacred avenue of menhirs. This inspired her to study the archaic relationship the stones seemed to exemplify between art, nature, and society. The result was her book, *Overlay: Contemporary Art and the Art of Prehistory.*[1] I had read it with great interest just before this brief return trip to England in the spring of 1983 which I hoped would help me end my search and my book.

One striking addition to her earlier commentary on Smithson was the cover illustration for *Overlay*. It was a view of the sun on the horizon through the lengths of two aligned concrete pipes: Nancy Holt's *Sun Tunnels*. Constructed in the Great Basin Desert of Utah in the three years following her husband's death, Holt's massive project underscored the newly appreciated role of women in art together with Lucy Lippard's commitments as a feminist critic. Moreover, where Lippard's aesthetic and feminist preoccupations intersected with her Dartmoor-inspired interest in megalithic sites there was a theme I had not previously considered in relation to Earth Art: the many guises of the

Goddess — not only in prehistoric artifacts but also in contemporary women's art.

This is a theme which runs throughout *Overlay* in hundreds of pictures as well as in its text. It is most specifically treated in a separate chapter, "Feminism and Prehistory", where I found Lippard echoing Patricia Berry's thoughts on matter/*mater*/Mother and agreeing with Susan Griffin and Carol Christ that, despite the dangers of negative stereotyping, the positive strengths of the woman-nature relationship should be affirmed. And Lippard further declares that the implications of doing so within the context of contemporary art are *Overlay*'s major concern:

> The debate about the advantages, disadvantages, and sources of women's identification with nature is important to this book because of the profound influence of prehistoric myth and imagery on contemporary women's art, due in part to the convergence of the latest wave of feminism and the upsurge of interest of avant-garde artists in 'primitivism.' This combination is no coincidence. It testifies to a basic need, expressed by men as well as women, to reevaluate the socio-esthetic structures and values of the society in which we live.[2]

Two new impressions came to me upon reading this statement. One was that if the recent convergence of feminism and aesthetic primitivism was "no coincidence", the simultaneous U.S.-Soviet "space race" of the 1960s and '70s was at least a *meaningful* coincidence: a project of patriarchal earth-abandonment being countered, perhaps, by the deep terrestrial grounding of feminism and art.

A second reaction, however, was to Lippard's comment that not only women were involved in the impulse toward "socio-esthetic" rethinking going on in the last few years. Indeed, a footnote to the passage just quoted suggests that "such an urge, with its respect for values traditionally attributed to women, seems to be behind both Paul Shepard's *Man in the Landscape* and Philip Slater's almost obsequiously feminist *Earthwalk*. Robert Smithson was also interested in 'psycho-ecology.'"[3] The inclusion of Smithson's work in this trend was of course noteworthy, as was the reference to Shepard's book, which I had drawn on in discussing the "garden" and "woman" geometaphors. I had not found Slater's *Earthwalk* particularly helpful in my research, but I now saw him making a sort of backhanded contribution by way of Lippard's remark.

The idea that male humility in the face of feminist priorities — an imperative implied by Naomi Goldenberg's presentation of witchcraft — might be excessive, even approaching servility, was a provocative one. It called to mind James Hillman's assertion that "humility and humor are two ways of coming down to *humus*, to the human condition," and his preference for the latter, for the pratfall instead of the low bow. I wondered how much my own humbling experience at Wicca and the Men-an-tol in 1979 (which assuredly contained humorous components as well) had happened due to the kind of obsequiousness Lippard discerned in Slater's feminism.

Beyond this I was intrigued to discover that, in her chapter on feminism, males were not at all incidental to the goals sought in women's art. She gives over several pages to artists such as Dennis Oppenheim and Charles Simonds as positive partners to women, developing by way of necessarily male psychosexual predilections a new, nonbelligerent reconnection to the earth. In a later chapter Lippard illustrates this tendency by quoting a sample of what she has called Smithson's "psycho-ecology":

> It is possible to have a direct organic manipulation of the land devoid of violence and 'macho' aggression. . .The farmer's, miner's or artist's treatment of the land depends on how aware he is of himself as nature. After all, sex isn't all a series of rapes.[4]

The role of the male Earth Artist as a paradigm for the feminist vision of *Overlay* was fascinating, and it insured that the book's other themes would stay with me as I left for England.

My return to Cornwall in May, 1983, included visits to Arthur C. Clarke's RAF airfields at St. Eval and Davidstow Moor — both looking more wind-raked and forlorn than ever, and presenting a chilling geo-metaphor of the earth as a vast abandoned runway from which the last vehicle has departed. In between these two depressing locations, which I tried to enliven with thoughts about Smithson's airport earthworks, I stopped again at Rocky Valley.

Going back to this numinous spot proved to be inconclusive for finishing my work on the Space-Age mythos, despite being even more evocative, if anything, than in my previous visit. The stream which had formed the valley was more impressive in May than in early August's tame flow four years earlier. The two Cretan labyrinth carvings still stared out from the north wall across the five feet or so to the closest part of the ruined mill. I took several pictures, including one which focused on a vertical crack in the rock face dividing the two engravings. Out of this crack a small leafy plant was growing, drawing the metaphoric eye to see a green tunnel between the grey mazed portals. No more definitive access to the underworld was evident, however, so I set myself the task of meditating on the slide of this elusive entryway, this Cornish gate of true dreams, until I fulfilled its psychic conditions.

On an intellectual level Lippard's book had helped prepare my return to Rocky Valley, for the maze or labyrinth is perhaps the most pervasive visual motif in *Overlay*. This motif is examined, for instance, in the chapter "Time and Again: Maps and Places and Journeys", where she includes a photograph of the coin from Knossos, Crete, which is our source of the classic labyrinth pattern. The caption for the picture mentions that "an identically formed labyrinth is carved on a rock at Tintagel, Cornwall"—a reference to the Rocky Valley engravings—and her chapter adds a listing of the multiple symbolic attributes of this shape.[5] When coupled with her linkage of labyrinths to spirals (recalling Smithson's preferred configuration), Lippard's mention that the former often served as "a dance floor, a ritual place",[6] brought to mind *The Spiral Dance*, a book on contemporary witchcraft by the practitioner named Starhawk.

The title of Starhawk's book is an image she uses to convey the prehistoric pantheistic sensibility informing witchcraft's nature worship, "the dance of the double spiral, of whirling into being, and whirling out again".[7] By the time Christianity came to the British Isles, she claims, this "Old Religion" of the Great Goddess was concentrated in small groups within rural communities: "The covens, who preserved the knowledge of the subtle forces, were called *Wicca* or *Wicce*, from the Anglo-Saxon root word meaning 'to bend or shape.' "[8] But a further meaning of this word, I knew in thinking back to Starhawk's rendering, might be "to weave", thus moving it into the imagery of the labyrinth from another direction, by way of Ariadne and her thread, the spindle and the clew.

These were the thoughts that had accompanied me on another visit to Wicca, up the coast a few miles from the Men-an-tol, on that same May day.

A closer inspection than I had been capable of making in 1979 quickly revealed that Wicca was even smaller than the semihamlet I had supposed it to be. It was in truth a single farm which the guidebook for the closest church at Zennor implies was there as early as 1470, the date when a sailor named Quick drowned in nearby Wicca Pool, or Cove — long before the word *wicca* would acquire currency in the witch-craft revival of this century.

There were no black feathers or holy cows to humble me this time. I set off down the lane and came to a house with a large trailer in the yard, a strutting rooster, and "Wicca" on the front door. Unfortunately or otherwise, no one was home, so that my investigation of this site as the imagined primal home of witchcraft, like my exploration of the Rocky Valley carvings, could not be brought to a close.

But if no clinching finding was forthcoming at Wicca Farm on Friday the 13th, I had high hopes for a consummation at the Men-an-tol before dark. By the time I knelt in front of the opening of the hole-stone at twilight the weather had become blustery and very chilly for even a Cornish May on the moors. I felt my string had finally run out; that was the element in Lippard's catalogue of labyrinth symbolism which remained most vivid among all my other recollections of her book. Her enumerating of the weaving associations of the labyrinth had not only pertained to my concern with the etymology of *wicca* but also related to my sense of an ending, a recapitulation and closing out of all the many connections I had made or mused upon in my search. Lippard had alluded to the figure of the Spider Woman in treating the labyrinth as a spinning or weaving image. She pursues this figure more closely in a chapter on ritual, where she looks at the art of Donna Henes, who actually calls herself "Spider Woman": ". . . continuing the winding, wrapping, swaddling process that has characterized the work of many women abstract sculptors, Henes uses line to transform land-scape, trees, herself, and others."[9]

In ancient folk practice, the leaving of cloth or string near wells or "fertility stones" was clearly meant to reinforce the regenerative and curing powers of such sites, since the "weaving" of a child in the womb was one of the connotations of the spinning of the thread deposited in this way. As part of her survey of women's web-weaving art Lippard refers to the fertility and healing traditions of "holed trees and holed stones, with their obvious birth imagery".[10] Here next to her text she places a half-page photograph, one she had taken herself, of the Men-an-tol.[11]

I had seen another picture of the Men-an-tol on the late afternoon of my arrival at the lane leading up to it. At the head of this lane, on the paved road between Madron and Morvah, there was an establish-ment not present four years earlier. The building — a century-old schoolhouse—had been there, to be sure, but its use had changed. It was now occupied by the Men-an-tol Studio, actually a combined studio and printmaking workshop. I had taken a quick tour around the small interior before walking up to the holestone site itself. Anxious not to lose the daylight I had hurriedly purchased a small woodcut of the Men-an-tol from the artist, Ian Cooke, a soft-spoken man about my age with a crew cut and a cigarette. I tossed the picture in my rented car and headed up the slight rise toward the point where a narrow path led across the moor from the farm lane to the stones.

It was about as difficult to squeeze through the doughnut-shaped megalith as I had imagined. A small stone had been placed on either side of the opening to facilitate this passage, although these props were unsteady enough in the muddy ground to provide a taste of travail as well. The two phallic menhirs a few feet in front of and behind the holestone reminded me of the Easter Island statues in *The New York Times* cartoon at the beginning of my search over a decade before. I was now the cartoonist's astronaut, more humorous than humble, not only staring through his porthole but seizing the Space-Age opportunity for a decisive re-entry.

When I stood up after this presumed consummation, however, taking care to turn "widdershins", or counterclockwise, and benefit from any ritual healing which might want to happen, something suggested otherwise. In one of the prickly gorse bushes surrounding the stones a blob of purple shone in the fading light. A tangled piece of thread, another labyrinth, wound through the gorse branches.

This small sign from Ariadne insisted that terrestrial reconnection was not to be achieved in a mere ten years of journeying through books and across an ocean. We had been about the business of abandoning earth for very much longer: manned flight was celebrating its bicentennial this very year, and those who had been born when a V-2 rocket first reached "outer space" would soon be 40, entering middle age. Of course Apollo had usurped Gaia's shrine at Delphi several millennia earlier, and NASA's curtailing of lunar missions after 1972 hardly constituted a conclusive antithesis to his distancing domination. The whole culture had become a "space program", and we had a long way to go to return.

The purple string threaded through the gorse bush led me back to the Men-an-tol Studio. I was afraid Ian Cooke would have closed up for the weekend, but the door to the old schoolhouse was unlocked. I had returned to exchange the print I had bought. Despite my haste during the first visit, an image from his wall had stayed with me enough to be triggered anew by the purple thread. It was a larger picture than the little woodcut of the Men-an-tol, a circular band of wavy red lines on a green background. In the center of this circle, as though framed by a dowser's perception of the holestone's emanations or a henge of standing stones seen from above, one of the red lines, entering at the right from the peripheral swirl, described a stylized Cretan labyrinth.

Ian Cooke had been taking notes on a book called *The Celtic Heritage* when I interrupted his privacy. He was agreeable to accepting the Men-an-tol print as partial payment for the larger picture. As he wrapped it for the long trip to Vermont he explained that he had had the Rocky Valley maze carvings in mind when producing the central pattern, and had superimposed the red line as "earth energy" (collected by the human arrangement of ancient stones) on the green background of vegetable life which this energy had vitalized. For me these colors seemed custom-made, since I had begun celebrating my last name a bit by using Christmas red and green.

At first I had trouble reading the title of the silkscreen print behind the glare of its glass frame, but I eventually saw what it was and came to the paradoxical closure of which I have spoken: "Continuity."

In other words, at what had seemed the end of my search, at the very end of England, I learned with finality a lesson only hinted at by the inconclusiveness of my return to Rocky Valley and Wicca. The work I had done, from the last year of Robert Smithson's brilliant life in art to the realization a decade later that the vision of that life was a model for my method, had followed a winding path of clues and come up with a "mythodology". It would now become available, I hoped, for anyone to apply.

But having provided this mythodology by recounting the rambling search I had made was not, after all, the end of the line. Aside from my own preliminary efforts the application had not yet begun. And it was clear that others all around this beautiful and beleaguered planet would need to use the mythodology, or something like it, on their *own* imagery, producing their *own* geometaphors so as to see things in the earth and contribute to the coming home of human consciousness — even as my personal metaphorizing and serendipping would surely continue beyond the covers of a single book.

NOTES

Prologue

1. "Editor's Introduction," *Michigan Quarterly Review*, Special Issue on "The Moon Landing and its Aftermath," XVIII, 3 (Spring 1979), 153.

2. Joseph Campbell, "The Moon Walk—the Outward Journey," in his *Myths to Live By* (New York: Bantam Books, 1973), p. 246. Although brief and less direct than Campbell's, another early acknowledgement of the evolutionary turning-point represented by our being able to leave the planet—and come back—occurred in the last chapter of Loren Eiseley's eloquent *The Invisible Pyramid* (New York: Charles Scribner's Sons, 1970).

Chapter 1.   A LINE OF SIGHT

1. Joseph Campbell, "The Moon Walk—the Outward Journey," in his *Myths to Live By* (New York: Bantam Books, 1973), p. 243.

2. Campbell,*The Mythic Image* (Princeton: Princeton University Press, 1974), p. 499.

3. Stewart Brand, "The First Whole Earth Photograph," in Michael Katz, William P. Marsh, and Gail Gordon Thompson, eds., *Earth's Answer: Explorations of Planetary Culture at the Lindisfarne Conferences* (New York: Lindisfarne Books/Harper & Row, 1977), p. 186.

4. Cf. C.G. Jung, *Mandala Symbolism*, trans. R.F.C. Hull (Princeton: Princeton University Press, 1972), *passim*.

5. William Barrett, "The Leap Into Space," *The New York Times*, Op-Ed page, Sunday, December 3, 1972. The accompanying cartoon is by Roland Topor.

6. Barrett, *Time of Need: Forms of Imagination in the Twentieth Century* (New York: Harper Torchbooks, 1973), p. 360.

7. Ibid., p. 357.

8. Ibid., p. 358.

9. Jerome Agel, ed., *The Making of Kubrick's 2001* (New York: Signet Books, 1970), pp. 76, 80. Cf. also Arthur C. Clarke, *2001: A Space Odyssey* (New York: Signet Books, 1968), and Clarke, *The Lost Worlds of 2001* (New York: Signet Books, 1972).

10. Mircea Eliade, *Patterns in Comparative Religion*, trans. Rosemary Sheed (Cleveland: Meridian Books, 1963), p. 216.

11. Ibid., p. 234.

12. Ibid., p. 216.

13.   Aniela Jaffé, "Symbolism in the Visual Arts," in C.G. Jung, ed., *Man and his Symbols* (New York: Dell Books, 1968), p. 257.

14.   Ibid., p. 258.

15.   Ibid., p. 259.

16.   Cf. Peg Bubar, "Tikal: The First Skyscrapers," *The New York Times*, July 17, 1977, Section XX, p. 7.

17.   Vincent Canby, "'Close Encounters' Has Now Become a Classic," *The New York Times*, August 30, 1980, Section 2, pp. 10, 17.

18.   While it does not focus upon the terrestrial imagery I am emphasizing, Gregor T. Goethals' 1981 study, *The TV Ritual*, was helpful in showing how televised science fiction and coverage of space exploration have presented an "icon," or sacred image, of our deeper relationships to nature (which could, of course, include my earth references) and especially to technology in a secular age. Cf. Goethals, *The TV Ritual: Worship at the Video Altar* (Boston: Beacon Press, 1981), Chapter II.

19.   Barrett, *Time of Need*, p. 386.

20.   Ibid.

Chapter 2.   A WAY OF SEEING

1.   Cf. Erich von Däniken, *Chariots of the Gods? Unsolved Mysteries of the Past*, trans. Michael Heron (New York: G.P. Putnam's Sons, 1970), *passim*, and von Däniken, *Gods From Outer Space: Return to the Stars or Evidence for the Impossible*, trans. Michael Heron (New York: G.P. Putnam's Sons, 1971), *passim*.

2.   Ian I. Mitroff, "Science's Apollonic Moon: A Study in the Psychodynamics of Modern Science," *Spring: An Annual of Archetypal Psychology and Jungian Thought* (1974), 102-112.

3.   Ibid., p. 110.

4.   James Hillman, *The Myth of Analysis: Three Essays in Archetypal Psychology* (Evanston, IL: Northwestern University Press, 1972), p. 250. The paradox of Apollo's presence today may be that while he sets us off from what we need to regain and dictates the distance we have to travel to do so, he also (perhaps unwittingly, if gods can be unwitting) clarifies that need and shows us our chance for reconnection.

5.   Ronald Story, *The Space-Gods Revealed: A Close Look at the Theories of Erich von Däniken* (New York: Harper & Row, 1976), p. 4.

6.   Norman Mailer, *Of a Fire on the Moon* (Boston: Little, Brown and Company, 1979), p. 471-72.

7.   Ibid., p. 470.

8.   Ibid., p. 471.

9.   William Barrett, *Time of Need: Forms of Imagination in the Twentieth Century* (New York: Harper Torchbooks, 1973), p. 361.

10.   Herbert Read, *Icon and Idea: The Function of Art in the Development of Human Consciousness* (New York: Schocken Books, 1965), Chapter I and *passim*.

11.   Stanley Burnshaw, *The Seamless Web* (New York: George Braziller, 1970), Part II and *passim*.

12.   Cf. Owen Barfield, *Poetic Diction: A Study in Meaning* (New York: McGraw-Hill, 1964), Chapters III and IV, Appendix III, and *passim*. It is noteworthy that in distinguishing between what he calls "true" and "accidental" metaphors Barfield gives as an example of the latter "when I ask you to think of the earth as a great orange with a knitting needle stuck through it" (p. 197) — an indication, perhaps, that my own metaphorical operations with whole earth imagery would be of the accidental (playful, exploratory) variety as a necessary step toward the true (metaphysically certain).

13.   Cf. Philip Wheelwright, *Metaphor and Reality* (Bloomington: Indiana University Press, 1962), *passim*. Like Barfield, Wheelwright stresses the connection between metaphor and myth, adding the terminological advice that "in order to avoid the implication of falsity that is attached in many people's minds to the words 'myth' and 'mythical,' there is reason to prefer the neutral noun *mythos* and the neutral adjective *mythic*" (p. 132). This rationale has influenced my own usage.

14.   William J.J. Gordon, *Synectics: The Development of Creative Capacity* (New York: Collier Books, 1961), p. 3.

15.   Ibid., p. 33.

16.   Ibid., p. 114.

17.   Ibid., pp. 114, 115.

18.   Ibid., p. 122.

19.   Ibid., p. 126.

20.   Ibid., p. 128.

21.   Ibid., p. 138.

22.   Ibid., p. 92.

23.   Ibid.

24.   Ibid., p. 115.

25.   Ibid., p. 109.

26.   Hillman, *Re-Visioning Psychology* (New York: Harper & Row, 1975), pp. 149, 150.

27.   Ibid., p. 156.

28.   Ibid.

29. Ibid., p. 153.

30. Ibid., p. 155.

31. Ibid., p. 142.

32. Ibid., p. 158.

33. Hillman, *The Dream and the Underworld* (New York: Harper & Row, 1979), p. 106. There are *many* theories and definitions of myth, to be sure, and my predilection for its metaphoric, ambiguous, mysterious qualities would not be reflected in all of them. One scholar who has instructed me in these complexities is William G. Doty, a friend and former colleague at Goddard College. His 1980 essay, "Mythophiles' Dyscrasia: A Comprehensive Definition of Myth," allows that myths are "(3) imaginal (4) stories, conveying [their meanings] by means of (5) metaphoric and symbolic diction, (6) graphic imagery, and (7) emotional conviction and participation . . ." However, in addition to these five elements, which he goes on to discuss adroitly and in detail, Doty's definition includes a dozen others. In any case, I took comfort from his statement—in the course of an explanation of the need for myths to be "culturally important"—that "it is sometimes possible to spot junctures where contemporary persons and events are considered so important that they are mythicized, as North Americans witnessed . . . after the first emplacement of cosmonauts on the moon's surface . . . but we lack compelling broad-based analyses of contemporary culture from mythological perspectives." It was encouraging to infer that any contribution my own search could make, even if it were less broad-based (and less analytical) than was necessary fully to remedy this lack, would nevertheless be breaking new ground. Cf. Doty, "Mythophiles' Dyscrasia," *Journal of the American Academy of Religion*, XLVIII, 4 (December 1980), 533, 536. This valuable essay was eventually incorporated into Doty, *Mythography: The Study of Myths and Rituals* (University, Ala.: University of Alabama Press, 1986).

34. Mailer, op. cit., pp. 133-34.

35. Cf. René Passeron, *René Magritte*, trans. Elisabeth Abbott (Chicago: J. Philip O'Hara, Inc., 1972), p. 26.

36. David Sylvester, *Magritte* (New York: Frederick Praeger, 1969), p. 2.

Chapter 3.   MEGALITHS BEYOND MEASURE

1. Warren L. Cook, ed., *"Ancient Vermont": Proceedings of the Castleton Conference, Castleton State College* (Rutland: Academy Books of Rutland, 1978).

2. Barry Fell, *America B.C.: Ancient Settlers in the New World* (New York: Quadrangle/New York Times Book Co., 1976).

3. Cf. Giovanna Neudorfer, "Vermont's Stone Chambers: Their Myth and Their History," *Vermont History*, 47, 2 (Spring 1979), 79-146.

4. Glyn Daniel, "Pop Goes Archeology," *The New York Times Book Review*, March 13, 1977, pp. 8, 12-13.

5.   Cf. Katharine Briggs, *British Folktales* (New York: Pantheon Books, 1977), p. 245.

6.   Cf. Janet and Colin Bord, *Mysterious Britain* (London: Garnstone Press, 1972), p. 39.

7.   Cf. Francis Hitching, *Earth Magic* (New York: William Morrow, 1977), p. 217.

8.   Alfred Watkins, *The Old Straight Track* (New York: Ballantine Books, 1973).

9.   John Michell, *The View Over Atlantis* (New York: Ballantine Books, 1969).

10.   Cf. Paul Devereux, "Operation Merlin," *The Ley Hunter*, No. 88 (Spring 1980), 16-19.

11.   Keith Critchlow, *Time Stands Still: New Light on Megalithic Science*, colour photographs by Rod Bull (London: Gordon Fraser, 1979).

12.   Anthony Roberts, ed., *Glastonbury: Ancient Avalon, New Jerusalem* (London: Rider and Company, 1978).

13.   Briggs, op. cit., p. 245.

14.   Brian Wicker, *The Story-Shaped World* (Notre Dame: University of Notre Dame Press, 1975), pp. 4-5.

15.   Bruno Snell, *The Discovery of the Mind: The Greek Origins of European Thought*, trans. T.G. Rosenmeyer (New York: Harper Torchbooks, 1960), p. 221.

16.   Ibid., p. 220.

17.   Robert Graves, *The White Goddess: A historical grammar of poetic myth*, amended and enlarged ed. (New York: Farrar, Straus and Giroux, 1966), p. 283.

18.   Critchlow, op. cit., p. 7.

19.   Anthony Roberts, *Sowers of Thunder: Giants in Myth and History* (London: Rider and Company, 1978).

20.   Ibid., p. xvi.

21.   Ibid., pp. xv-xvi.

22.   Ibid., p. vii.

23.   Ibid., p. ix.

24.   Watkins, op. cit., p. 167.

25.   Katharine Briggs, *The Vanishing People: Fairy Lore and Legends* (New York: Pantheon Books, 1978), p. 7.

26.   Ibid., p. 74.

27.   G. Rachel Levy, *Religious Conceptions of the Stone Age* (New York: Harper Torchbooks, 1963), pp. 146, 146 n. 5.

28.   John Michell, *The Earth Spirit: Its Ways, Shrines and Mysteries* (New York: Avon Books, 1975), p. 86.

29. Graves, op. cit., p. 185.

30. Briggs, *The Vanishing People*, p. 7.

31. Roberts, *Sowers of Thunder*, pp. 140, 144.

32. Snell, op. cit., p. 224.

Chapter 4. MORE AND MORE GEOMETAPHORS

1. Norman Mailer, *Of a Fire on the Moon*(Boston: Little, Brown and Company, 1969), p. 431.

2. Arthur C. Clarke, *2001: A Space Odyssey* (New York: Signet Books, 1968), p. 220.

3. Cited in Gyorgy Kepes, "Art and Ecological Consciousness," in Kepes, ed., *Arts of the Environment* (New York: George Braziller, 1972), p. 10.

4. Mailer, op. cit., p. 413.

5. C.G. Jung, *Memories, Dreams, Reflections*, recorded and ed. Aniela Jaffé, trans. Richard and Clara Winston (New York: Vintage Books, 1961), p. 227.

6. José and Miriam Argüelles, *Mandala*(Berkeley: Shambhala, 1972), p. 23.

7. Ibid., p. 24.

8. Mircea Eliade, *Patterns in Comparative Religion*, trans. Rosemary Sheed (Cleveland: Meridian Books, 1963), p. 373.

9. Quoted in Argüelles and Argüelles, op. cit., p. 84.

10. Ibid., p. 42.

11. Olivier Marc, *Psychology of the House*, trans. Jessie Wood (London: Thames and Hudson, 1977), p. 104.

12. Ibid., p. 106.

13. Eliade, op. cit., p. 100.

14. Ibid., p. 101.

15. Cf. Barbara Nimri Aziz, "Maps and Mind," *Human Nature*, August 1978, pp. 50-59.

16. Quoted in Argüelles and Argüelles, op. cit., p. 84.

17. Edgar Allan Poe, "The Landscape Garden," in his *Works*, The Cameo Edition, Vol. Seven (New York: Funk & Wagnalls, 1904), p. 57.

18. Joseph Campbell, "The Moon Walk—the Outward Journey," in his *Myths to Live By* (New York: Bantam Books, 1973), p. 245.

19. Argüelles and Argüelles, op. cit., pp. 60, 63.

20. Quoted in Eliade, op. cit., p. 377.

21.   Quoted in John Woodcock, "The Garden in the Machine: Variations on Spaceship Earth," *Michigan Quarterly Review*, XVIII, 2 (Spring 1979), 309. Cf. also R. Buckminster Fuller, *Operating Manual for Spaceship Earth* (New York: Simon and Schuster Clarion Books, 1969). A year after Fuller's book Loren Eiseley, too, referred to the earth as "a space ship of limited dimensions." But he also called it "an incredibly precious planetary jewel" and at least by implication identified it with what he termed the "sunflower forest" of our biological origins. Cf. Eiseley, *The Invisible Pyramid* (New York: Charles Scribner's Sons, 1970), pp. 150-55.

22.   Ibid.

23.   Ibid., p. 315.

24.   Ibid., p. 316.

25.   Ibid., pp. 316-17.

26.   Lewis Thomas, *The Lives of a Cell: Notes of a Biology Watcher* (New York: The Viking Press, 1974), p. 94. Thomas's geometaphor was noticed a few years later in an essay by Thomas Berry which also stresses the feminine qualities of earth I explore below: "When we speak of earth, we are speaking of a numinous maternal principle in and through which the total complex of earth phenomena takes its shape. Recently the biologist Lewis Thomas, when considering the integration of life systems of the earth, suddenly saw the total life process of earth as a single cell." I was heartened to realize that despite our different backgrounds (Berry's was in Roman Catholic theology and the history of world religions) and sources of inspiration (his included Chinese philosophy and the visionary Jesuit paleontologist Teilhard de Chardin) the findings of our two quests seemed to converge at several points. Cf. Thomas Berry, "Spirituality of the Earth," *Anima*, 6, 1 (Fall 1979), 16.

27.   James Lovelock and Sidney Epton, "The Quest for Gaia," *The New Scientist*, February 6, 1975, pp. 304-306. Also cf. William Golding, *The Inheritors* (New York: Harcourt, Brace & World, 1963).

28.   Paul Shepard, *Man in the Landscape: A Historic View of the Esthetics of Nature* (New York: Alfred A. Knopf, 1967), p. ix.

Chapter 5.   THE MANY GUISES OF THE GODDESS

1.   Eleanor Bertine, *Jung's Contribution to Our Time* (New York: G.P. Putnam's Sons, 1967), p. 70. Cf. also M. Esther Harding, "The Early Days," in Michael Fordham, ed., *Contact with Jung* (Philadelphia: J.B. Lippincott Company, 1963), pp. 180-81, and Barbara Hannah, *Jung: His Life and Work* (New York: G.P. Putnam's Sons, 1976), p. 141.

2.   William Bottrell, *Traditions and Hearthside Stories of West Cornwall* (Newcastle upon Tyne: Frank Graham, 1970 reprint), p. 45.

3.   Ibid., p. 24.

4.   Ibid., p. 46. Bottrell does not mention what I did not learn until a later trip: that "Zennor" may after all derive from a saint's name: St. Senara. According to a pamphlet at the village church, this is its patron saint, by legend a Breton princess named Asenora.

5.   Robert Hunt, *Cornish Customs and Superstitions* (Truro, Cornwall: Tor Mark Press, n.d.), p. 21. Cf. also Bottrell, op. cit., pp. 72-89.

6.   *Cornish Charms and Witchcraft* (Truro, Cornwall: Tor Mark Press, n.d.), pp. 7-8.

7.   David L. Miller, *The New Polytheism* (New York: Harper & Row, 1974).

8.   *American Academy of Religion: 1977 Annual Meeting Program*, San Francisco, (Missoula: University of Montana Printing Department, 1977), p. 49.

9.   Carol P. Christ and Judith Plaskow, eds., *Womanspirit Rising: A Feminist Reader in Religion*(San Francisco: Harper & Row, 1979).

10.   Starhawk, *The Spiral Dance: A Rebirth of the Ancient Religion of the Great Goddess* (San Francisco: Harper & Row, 1979).

11.   Naomi R. Goldenberg, *Changing of the Gods: Feminism and the End of Traditional Religions* (Boston: Beacon Press, 1979).

12.   Ibid., p. 96.

13.   Ibid., p. 97.

14.   Ibid., p. 98.

15.   Ibid., p. 99.

16.   Ian Mitroff, "Science's Apollonic Moon," *Spring* (1974), 109.

17.   James Hillman, *The Myth of Analysis*(Evanston: Northwestern University Press, 1972), p. 248.

18.   Goldenberg, op. cit., p. 103.

19.   Carol P. Christ, *Diving Deep and Surfacing: Woman Writers on Spiritual Quest* (Boston: Beacon Press, 1980), p. 47. Cf.also Christ, "Margaret Atwood: The Surfacing of Women's Spiritual Quest and Vision," *Signs*, 2, 2 (Winter 1976), 316-30.

20.   M. Esther Harding, *Woman's Mysteries: Ancient and Modern* (New York: Bantam Books, 1973), pp. 123-24.

21.   Christine Downing, "A Poetics of the Psyche," *The American Poetry Review*, July 1976, p. 35.

22.   Hannah, op. cit., pp. 141, 149ff., 209, 211, 249, and Harding, "The Early Days," pp. 180-82.

23.   John Layard, *The Virgin Archetype: Two Papers*, Dunquin Series 5 (Zurich: Spring Publications, 1972).

24.   Elizabeth Gould Davis, *The First Sex*(Baltimore: Penguin Books, 1972). Cf. also Rhoda Lerman, "In Memorium: Elizabeth Gould Davis," *Ms.*, December 1974, pp. 74-75, 95.

25.   Rhoda Lerman, *Call Me Ishtar* (New York: Holt, Rinehart and Winston, 1973), pp. xi-xii.

26.   Ibid., p. 229.

27.   Harding, *Woman's Mysteries*, pp. 188-89.

28.   Ibid., p. 192.

29.   Ibid., pp. 185, 207-208.

30.   A version of this novel was indeed published five years after my Cornish encounter. On its dust jacket are a stylized map of Iona and, in the lower right, an emblem containing a crescent moon and a leaping cow. Cf. Lerman, *The Book of the Night* (New York: Holt, Rinehart and Winston, 1984).

31.   Goldenberg, op. cit., pp. 111, 114.

32.   Christopher Bice, compiler, *Names for the Cornish: Three Hundred Cornish Christian Names* (Padstow, Cornwall: Lodenek Press, 1970), p. 13.

Chapter 6.   EARTH AS THE MOTHER OF METAPHORIZING

1.   Naomi R. Goldenberg, *Changing of the Gods: Feminism and the End of Traditional Religions* (Boston: Beacon Press, 1979).

2.   Ibid., pp. 116-17.

3.   Simone de Beauvoir, *The Second Sex*, trans. and ed. H.M. Parshley (New York: Bantam Books, 1970).

4.   Sherry B. Ortner, "Is Female to Male as Nature Is to Culture?" in Michelle Z. Rosaldo and Louise Lamphere, eds., *Woman, Culture, and Society* (Stanford: Stanford University Press, 1974), pp. 67-87.

5.   Carol P. Christ, *Diving Deep and Surfacing: Woman Writers on Spiritual Quest* (Boston: Beacon Press, 1980), p. 22.

6.   Susan Griffin, *Woman and Nature: The Roaring Inside Her* (New York: Harper Colophon Books, 1978),pp. 217-27.

7.   Ibid., p. 227.

8.   Christ, op. cit., p. 53.

9.   Ibid., p. 129.

10.   Ibid., p. 130.

11.   Goldenberg, op. cit., p. 124.

12.   Ibid., p. 125.

13.   Ibid., p. 126.

14.   Cf., for example, James Hillman, "Peaks and Vales: The Soul/Spirit Distinction as Basis for the Differences between Psychotherapy and Spiritual Discipline," Hillman, *et al.*, *Puer Papers* (Dallas: Spring Publications, 1979), pp. 54-74.

15.   Cf., for example, Hillman, *The Dream and the Underworld* (New York: Harper & Row, 1979), *passim*.

16.   Ibid., p.36.

17.   Patricia Berry, "What's the Matter with Mother?" Lecture No. 190 (London: Guild of Pastoral Psychology, 1978), p. 6. While I shall continue to cite this original published version, the lecture was later incorporated into a collection of Berry's essays and is currently available there. Cf. *Echo's Subtle Body: Contributions to an Archetypal Psychology* (Dallas: Spring Publications, 1982), pp. 1-16.

18.   Ibid., p. 7.

19.   Ibid., p. 16.

20.   Ibid., p. 13.

21.   Ibid., p. 16.

22.   Ibid.

23.   Ibid., p. 17.

24.   Ibid., pp. 17-18.

25.   Ibid., p. 10.

26.   Quoted by Berry in "An Approach to the Dream," *Spring: An Annual of Archetypal Psychology and Jungian Thought* (1974), 61, and by Hillman in *The Dream and the Underworld*, p. 194.

27.   Christine Downing, *The Goddess: Mythological Images of the Feminine* (New York: Crossroad, 1981), p. 147.

28.   Ibid., pp. 143-44.

29.   Margot Adler, *Drawing Down the Moon: Witches, Druids, Goddess-Worshippers, and Other Pagans in America Today* (New York: Viking Press, 1979).

30.   Adrienne Rich, *Of Woman Born: Motherhood as Experience and Institution* (New York: W.W. Norton, 1976), p. 284 and *passim*.

31.   Cf. Mara Donaldson, review of Adler, op. cit., *Journal of the American Academy of Religion*, L, 2 (June 1982), 304.

32.   Adler, op. cit., p. 46.

33.   Goldenberg, op. cit., p. 89.

34.   Adler, op. cit., p. 66.

35.   Ibid., p. 84.

36.   Ibid., p. 67.

37.   Ibid., p. 83. Adler is here quoting an unpublished manuscript by Kelly, "The Rebirth of Witchcraft: Tradition and Creativity in the Gardnerian Reform," p. 274.

38.   Ibid., p. 169. In this case Adler is quoting another of Kelly's unpublished manuscripts, "Aporrheton No. 1, To the New Witch," March 1973, p. 1.

39.   May Swenson, "Orbiter 5 Shows How Earth Looks from the Moon," in Robert Vas Dias, ed., *Inside Outer Space: New Poems of the Space Age* (Garden City: Doubleday Anchor Books, 1970), p. 319. A "type-shaped" version of this poem is currently available in Swenson, *New & Selected Things Taking Place* (Boston: Little, Brown and Company, 1954-1978), p. 94.

Chapter 7.   FROM OUTER SPACE TO SERENDIP

1.   Cf. Leslie A. Fiedler, ed., *In Dreams Awake* (New York: Dell, 1975); Robert Scholes, *Structural Fabulation* (Notre Dame: University of Notre Dame Press, 1975); Scholes and Eric S. Rabkin, *Science Fiction* (Oxford: Oxford University Press, 1977); and Pamela Sargent, ed., *Women of Wonder* (New York: Vintage Books, 1975).

2.   In particular her classic, *The Left Hand of Darkness* (New York: Ace Books, 1969), plus *The Dispossessed* (New York: Avon Books, 1974) and *Orsinian Tales* (New York: Harper & Row, 1976).

3.   Aside from the two works I shall be discussing in detail—*The Fountains of Paradise* and *Glide Path*—the most effective examples of Clarke's fiction for me were the novels *Childhood's End* (London: Pan Books, 1956), *Rendezvous With Rama* (New York: Ballantine Books, 1973), and *Imperial Earth* (New York: Ballantine Books, 1976). I shall also be discussing several of his *non*-fiction books below.

4.   Cf. Clarke, *The Promise of Space* (New York: Harper & Row, 1968), *The View from Serendip* (New York: Ballantine Books, 1978), and Olander and Greenberg, eds., *Arthur C. Clarke* (New York: Taplinger Publishing Company, 1977).

5.   This pioneering essay, "Extraterrestrial Relays," is reprinted and its implications are suggested in Clarke, *Voices From the Sky* (New York: Pocket Books, 1980).

6.   Cf. Clarke, *Interplanetary Flight* (New York: Harper & Brothers, 1950). I am grateful to Herbert Childs for loaning me his autographed copy of this book.

7.   Cf. Clarke, *Prelude to Space* (New York: Harcourt, Brace & World, 1951) and *The Sands of Mars* (New York: Gnome Press, 1951).

8.   Reprinted in Clarke, *The Lost Worlds of 2001* (New York: Signet Books, 1972).

9.   Clarke, *The View from Serendip*, p. 6.

10.   Clarke, "Beyond Apollo," Epilogue to Neil Armstrong, Michael Collins, and Edwin E. Aldrin, Jr., with Gene Farmer and Dora Jane Hamblin, *First on the Moon* (Boston: Little, Brown and Company, 1970), pp. 371-421. (I cannot resist interjecting here that my book can be seen as an attempt to re-write Clarke's epilogue to the Apollo 11 landing, an attempt which wants to do deeper justice to the title he chose.)

11.   Clarke, *The Promise of Space*, p. xix.

12.   Harfst, "Of Myths and Polyominoes," in Olander and Greenberg, eds., *Arthur C. Clarke*, p. 93.

13.   Eliade, *Cosmos and History: The Myth of Eternal Return*, trans. Willard B. Trask (New York: Harper & Row, 1959), p. 161.

14.   Eliade, *No Souvenirs: Journal, 1957-69*, trans. Fred H. Johnson, Jr. (New York: Harper & Row, 1977), p. 118.

15.   Clarke, "Beyond Apollo," p. 419.

16.   James Earl Carter, Jr., "On the Uses of Space," *Michigan Quarterly Review* XVIII, 2 (Spring 1979), 351.

17.   Fiedler, ed., op. cit., p. 15.

18.   Clarke, *The Fountains of Paradise* (New York: Harcourt Brace Jovanovich, 1978), p. xiii. Subsequent page references to this novel will appear in parenthesis in my text.

19.   Eliade, *Myths, Dreams and Mysteries*, trans. Philip Mairet (New York: Harper & Row, 1960), p. 59.

20.   Eliade, *Cosmos and History*, p. 16.

21.   Eliade, *Patterns in Comparative Religion*, trans. Rosemary Sheed (Cleveland: Meridian Books, 1963), p. 432.

22.   Eliade, *Images and Symbols*, trans. Philip Mairet (New York: Sheed & Ward, 1961), p. 11.

23.   Larry E. Shiner, "Sacred Space, Profane Space, Human Space," *Journal of the American Academy of Religion*, XL, 4 (December 1972), 426.

24.   Clarke, *The View from Serendip*, pp. 240, 203.

25.   Ibid., p. 203.

26.   The only reference to Ceylon I could locate in Eliade's scholarly works was to the palace-fortress of Sigiriya built by King Kasyapa "after the model of the celestial city Alakamanda . . 'hard of ascent for human beings'. . ." That is, Eliade confirms the paradisal archetype informing Kasyapa's and Kalidasa's projects, if not Clarke's. Cf. Eliade, *Cosmos and History*, p. 9.

27.   Clarke, *The Promise of Space*, p. 151. The photograph is Plate 32.

28.   Clarke, *The View from Serendip*, pp. 5-6.

29.   Ibid., p. 36. Cf. also Clarke, *The Treasure of the Great Reef* (New York: Ballantine Books, 1974).

30.   Ibid., p. 119.

31.   Ibid., p. 120.

32.   Ibid., pp. 4-5.

33.   Ibid., p. 5.

34.   Ibid., pp. 217-18.

35.   Ibid., p. 218.

36.   Ibid.

Chapter 8.   GROUND CONTROLLED DESCENT AT THE DAWN OF THE SPACE AGE

1.   "The Talk of the Town: Clarke's World," *The New Yorker*, December 13, 1982, pp. 39-40.

2.   Clarke, *Glide Path* (New York: Harcourt Brace Jovanovich, 1963). Subsequent page references to this novel will appear in parenthesis in my text.

3.   Clarke, "Extraterrestrial Relays," in his *Voices From the Sky* (New York: Pocket Books, 1980),p. 231.

4.   Cf. Jeremy Bernstein, "Extrapolators: Arthur C. Clarke," in his *Experiencing Science* (New York: Basic Books, 1978), p. 215.

5.   Cf. Aubrey Burl, *Prehistoric Avebury* (New Haven: Yale University Press, 1979), fig. 24, p. 48.

6.   G. Rachel Levy, *Religious Conceptions of the Stone Age* (New York: Harper Torchbooks, 1963), p. 157.

7.   Geoffrey Russell, "The Secret of the Grail," in Mary Williams, ed., *Glastonbury: A Study in Patterns*(London: Research into Lost Knowledge Organisation, 1969), p. 16.

8.   Christine Downing, *The Goddess: Mythological Images of the Feminine* (New York: Crossroad, 1981), p. 63.

9.   Robert Graves, *The White Goddess: A historical grammar of poetic myth*, amended and enlarged ed. (New York: Farrar, Straus and Giroux, 1966), pp. 488-90.

10.   Ibid., pp. 101-106.

11.   Ibid., p. 112.

Chapter 9.   SERENDIPITY, SYNCHRONICITY, SPONTANEITY

1.   C.G. Jung, *Memories, Dreams, Reflections*, recorded and ed. Aniela Jaffé, trans. Richard and Clara Winston (New York: Vintage Books, 1961), p. 289.

2.   Cf. Jung, "Synchronicity: An Acausal Connecting Principle" and "On Synchronicity," in his *Collected Works*, Vol. 8, Bollingen Series XX, Second Edition, trans. R.F.C. Hull (Princeton: Princeton University Press, 1966), pp. 417-519, 520-31.

3.   Ira Progoff, *Jung, Synchronicity, and Human Destiny* (New York: G.P. Putnam's Sons, 1971), pp. 17-20.

4. Cf. Jaffé, *The Myth of Meaning*, trans. R.F.C. Hull (New York: G.P. Putnam's Sons, 1971), Chap. 13 and *passim*.

5. Ibid., p. 151.

6. Jung, "Synchronicity," p. 427.

7. Cf. Progoff, op. cit., pp. 54-56.

8. Jung, *Memories, Dreams, Reflections*, p. 197.

9. Hanns Reich, *The World From Above* (Hill and Wang, 1966), p. 43.

10. Jaffé, op. cit., p. 151.

11. Ibid., p. 143.

12. Ibid., p. 152.

13. Ibid.

14. Ibid., p. 23.

15. Quoted in ibid.

16. Cf. Progoff, op. cit., p. 108.

17. Ibid., pp. 169-70.

18. Ibid., p. 169.

19. Jung, *Letters*, Vol. 2: 1951-61, Bollingen Series XCV: 2, selected and ed. Gerhard Adler with Aniela Jaffé, trans. R.F.C. Hull (Princeton: Princeton University Press, 1975), p. 499.

20. Ibid., p. 500.

21. Theodore G. Remer, ed., *Serendipity and the Three Princes: From the Peregrinaggio of 1557*, Preface by W.S. Lewis (Norman: University of Oklahoma Press, 1965). Cf. p. 15, n. 1.

22. Ibid., Chap. 1. Also cf. E.F. Bleiler, Introduction to his edition of Walpole, *The Castle of Otranto*, with Beckford's *Vathek* and Polidori's *The Vampyre* (New York: Dover Books, 1966), pp. viii-xi and *passim*.

23. Quoted in Bleiler, op. cit., p. xi.

24. Cf. Remer, op. cit., pp. 16-17.

25. Ibid., pp. 3-6. In addition to Remer's transcribed major excerpt on pp. 3 and 6, a photograph of the entire letter in Walpole's hand is reproduced on pp. 4-5.

26. Ibid., p. 29.

27. Ibid., p. 6.

28. Quoted in ibid., p. 20.

29. Ibid.

30. Ibid., pp. 25-26. The definition of "Sharawadgi" is from Osbert Sitwell's *The Four Continents*, quoted by Remer in p. 25, n. 2.

31.   Ibid., p. 5. Walpole's comment occurs in a part of the longhand letter not transcribed into print or discussed by Remer, although it is easily legible in the photograph of the complete text of the letter.

32.   Ibid., p. 30.

33.   Hillman, "Peaks and Vales: The Soul/Spirit Distinction as Basis for the Differences between Psychotherapy and Spiritual Discipline," Hillman, *et al.*, *Puer Papers* (Dallas: Spring Publications, 1979), pp. 54-74.

34.   Ibid., p. 65.

35.   Ibid., p. 67.

36.   Ibid., p. 68.

37.   Hillman, "Senex and Puer: An Aspect of the Historical and Psychological Present," in *Puer Papers*, p. 30.

38.   Ibid., p. 15.

39.   Quoted in Hillman, "Peaks and Vales," p. 60.

40.   Ibid., p. 61.

41.   Hillman, "Notes on Opportunism," in *Puer Papers*, p. 152.

42.   Ibid., p. 156.

43.   Ibid., p. 158.

44.   Ibid., p. 157.

45.   Hillman, "Peaks and Vales," p. 63-64.

46.   Ibid., p. 63.

47.   Ibid., p. 64.

48.   Cf. Gordon, *Synectics* (New York: Collier Books, 1968), pp. 139, 15-19.

49.   Von Franz, *On Divination and Synchronicity: The Psychology of Meaningful Chance* (Toronto: Inner City Books, 1980), p. 79. Another book which attempts to relate these matters to "the feminine"—while comparing synchronicity to the Chinese idea of the Tao—is Jean Shinoda Bolen's *The Tao of Psychology: Synchronicity and the Self* (San Francisco: Harper & Row, 1979). Bolen's lively account employs the fashionable "split-brain" theory to point toward qualities I had been finding central to my search: "The right hemisphere compares through metaphor rather than measurement. Its style is receptive and reflective, a more 'feminine' mode than that of the left hemisphere" (p. 8). She recommends this mode for experiencing the Tao, but her argument in favor of synchroncity's revealing an underlying oneness which is equivalent to the Tao inclines away from the spontaneity endorsed by Hillman. While she does not deal at all with serendipity, her description of how she became a psychiatrist on her way to training in Jungian analysis and schooling in synchronicity contains this statement: "From my encounter with these six patients, I knew within the first week that, serendipitously, I had found my life work" (p. 12).

Chapter 10.   AERIAL ARCHAEOLOGY AS MODEL

1.   Cf. Warren L. Cook, ed., *"Ancient Vermont": Proceedings of the Castleton Conference, Castleton State College* (Rutland: Academy Books of Rutland, 1978), fig. 73 following p. 172. Ring's conference presentation is transcribed in this volume as "Aerial Evidence of Terrain Disturbances near Vermont's Lithic Sites," pp. 26-27.

2.   Ibid.

3.   Ibid., p. 26.

4.   Leo Deuel, *Flights into Yesterday: The Story of Aerial Archaeology* (New York: St. Martin's Press, 1969), p. xvii.

5.   Ibid., p. 6.

6.   Ibid., p. 7.

7.   Ibid., p. 21.

8.   Cf. ibid., pp. 24-25, 29-30.

9.   Quoted in ibid., p. 46.

10.   Cf. Charles Lindbergh, "A Letter from Lindbergh," *Life*, July 4, 1969, pp. 60A-61.

11.   Deuel, op. cit., p. 190.

12.   Ibid., pp. 187-98.

13.   Ibid., p. 212.

14.   Ibid., p. 289.

15.   Ibid., p. 271.

16.   Ibid., p. 6-7.

17.   Benjamin F. Richason, Jr., statement in publisher's announcement for Richason, Jr., ed., *Introduction to Remote Sensing of the Environment*, Second Edition (Dubuque: Kendall/Hunt Publishing Company, 1983).

18.   Edward Lueders, *The Clam Lake Papers: A Winter in the North Woods* (San Francisco: Harper & Row, 1977), p. 40.

19.   Ibid., p. 47.

20.   Ibid., p. 55.

21.   Ibid.

22.   Susan Sontag, *On Photography* (New York: Delta Books, 1977), p. 93.

23.   Ibid., p. 136.

24.   Ibid., p. 133.

25.   Ibid., p. 137.

26. Lueders, op. cit., p. 136.

27. Sontag, op. cit., p. 206.

28. Ibid.

29. Georg Gerster, *Flights of Discovery: The Earth from Above* (New York: Paddington Press, 1978).

30. Sontag, op. cit., p. 176.

31. Gerster, op. cit., p. 6.

32. Ibid., p. 15.

33. Ibid.

34. Ibid., Plate 6.12. The caption is on p. 125.

35. Deuel, op. cit., p. 44.

36. Gerster, op. cit., Plate 6.13.

Chapter 11.   EARTH ART AS MODEL

1. Cf. Robert Smithson, "The Spiral Jetty," in Gyorgy Kepes, ed., *Arts of the Environment* (New York: George Braziller, 1972), pp. 222-32. Smithson's essay was later collected in Holt, ed., *The Writings of Robert Smithson: Essays with Illustrations* (New York: New York University Press, 1979), pp. 109-116.

2. Smithson, op. cit., in Holt, op. cit., p. 113.

3. Douglas Davis, quoted in Kay Larson, "New Landscapes in Art," *The New York Times Magazine*, May 13, 1979, p. 28.

4. Ibid., p. 30.

5. Philip Leider, "Introduction," in Holt, op. cit., p. 1.

6. Ibid., p. 3.

7. Paul Cummings, "Interview with Robert Smithson for the Archives of American Art/Smithsonian Institute," in Holt, op. cit., p. 147.

8. Ibid., p. 152.

9. Smithson, "Towards the Development of An Air Terminal Site," in Holt, op. cit., pp. 42, 43. The photograph of the SECOR satellite is on p. 45.

10. Smithson, "Aerial Art," in Holt, op. cit., p. 92.

11. Ibid., p. 93.

12. Robert Hobbs, "The Works," in Hobbs, with Lawrence Alloway, John Coplans, and Lucy R. Lippard, *Robert Smithson: Sculpture* (Ithaca: Cornell University Press, 1981), p. 96.

13. Smithson, "Aerial Art," in Holt, op. cit., p. 92.

14.   Smithson, "A Museum of Language in the Vicinity of Art," in Holt, op. cit., p. 76.

15.   Ibid., pp. 77-78.

16.   Cummings, "Interview," in Holt, op. cit., p. 149.

17.   Ibid., p. 150.

18.   Hobbs, "The Works," in Hobbs, et al, op. cit., pp. 96-99.

19.   "Discussions with Heizer, Oppenheim, Smithson," in Holt, op. cit., p. 172.

20.   Smithson, "A Sedimentation of the Mind: Earth Projects," in Holt, op. cit., p. 90.

21.   Smithson, "Aerial Art," in Holt, op. cit., p. 92.

22.   Cummings, "Interview," in Holt, op. cit., p. 156.

23.   Ibid., p. 155.

24.   Smithson, "The Spiral Jetty," in Holt, op. cit., p. 111.

25.   Ibid., p. 112.

26.   Cf. Smithson, "A Museum of Language," in Holt, op. cit., pp. 67ff., 75ff.

27.   Smithson, "The Spiral Jetty," in Holt, op. cit., p. 113.

28.   Ibid.

29.   Ibid., p. 114.

30.   Quoted in Hobbs, "Works," in Hobbs, et al, op. cit., p. 194.

31.   Ibid., p. 195.

32.   Smithson, "The Spiral Jetty," in Holt, op. cit., p. 113.

33.   Gerster, op. cit., pp. 125-26.

34.   Cf. John Coplans, "Robert Smithson, The *Amarillo Ramp*," in Hobbs, et al, op. cit., pp. 50-52.

35.   Ibid., p. 54.

36.   "'. . .The Earth, Subject to Cataclysms, is a Cruel Master': Interview with Gregoire Muller," in Holt, op. cit., p. 182.

37.   Lucy R. Lippard, "Breaking Circles: The Politics of Prehistory," in Hobbs, et al, op. cit., pp. 33, 35.

38.   Ibid., p. 35.

39.   Gerster, op. cit., p. 126. The picture is Plate 6.14.

40.   Cf. John Michell, *The Earth Spirit: Its Ways, Shrines and Mysteries* (New York: Avon Books, 1975), p. 16.

41.   Cf. Vincent Cronin, *The View from Planet Earth: Man Looks at the Cosmos* (New York: Quill Books, 1983), p. 239.

42.   Cf. Smithson, "Towards the Development of An Air Terminal Site," in Holt, op. cit., pp. 40-41.

43.   Cited in Michell, op. cit., p. 16.

44.   C.G. Jung, *Flying Saucers: A Modern Myth of Things Seen in the Skies*, trans. R.F.C. Hull (Princeton: Princeton University Press, 1964/1978), p. 131.

45.   Ibid., p. 19.

46.   Cf. Jean Houston, "Putting the First Man on Earth," *Saturday Review*, February 22, 1975, pp. 28-32, 53. I am grateful to Dr. Robert Masters, who has also used the phrase in his work at the Foundation for Mind Research, for helping me to locate this reference.

47.   Dale McConathy, quoted in Lippard, "Breaking Circles," in Hobbs, et al, op. cit., p. 35.

48.   An example would be the remarkable scene of John Glenn orbiting earth while Australian Aborigines chant around a night fire in the film *The Right Stuff*. Because at least two of the Aborigine actors in this scene, David Gulpilil and Nandjiwarra Amagula, were prominent in Peter Weir's *The Last Wave*, a story of tribal myth and sorcery, the conjunction here of the futuristic/celestial and the archaic/earthly, although brief, was particularly powerful. Mention should also be made of critic Vincent Canby's statement at the end of 1984: "It must be significant that the only halfway decent sci-fi films of the year have been those that never quite lose touch with the manners and mores of earth . . ." This judgment is then extended to a hugely popular film from the previous year when Canby adds that "by far the best of them all, John Carpenter's 'Starman,' . . . is essentially a romantic comedy about a grown up 'E.T.'" Cf. Canby, "Seen in 1984, the Future Looks Bleak," *The New York Times*, December 23, 1984, Section 2, p. 19.

49.   Cf. Michener, *Space* (New York: Random House, 1982), and Clarke, *2010: Odyssey Two* (New York: Ballantine Books, 1982).

50.   Even the most optimistic projections do not predict a lunar landing before 2010. I would have to live longer than either of my parents did to see it then. Cf. Thomas O'Toole, "NASA's Master Plan," *Omni*, December 1984, pp. 70-72, 148, 150.

51.   Kurtz, "Conversation with Robert Smithson on April 22nd 1972," in Holt, op. cit., pp. 203-204.

52.   Cf. Richard P. Hallion, "The Apollo Program: A Chronology," in Hallion and Tom D. Crouch, eds., *Apollo: Ten Years Since Tranquillity Base* (Washington: National Air and Space Museum/Smithsonian Institution, 1979), p. 152.

53.   Michener, op. cit., p. 602.

54.   Cf. Szent-Gyorgyi, "Dionysians and Apollonians," *Science*, June 2, 1972, p. 966.

55.   Cf. William J. Broad, "Metaphor Getting Its Due As a Wellspring of Science," *The New York Times*, July 31, 1983, Section 4, p. 8E.

56.   Cf. Jones, *Physics as Metaphor* (New York: Meridian Books, 1982).

57.   Imaginal connections between the Space Age as epochal "opening" and the central Christian notion of *kairos*, or "fulfilled time," are evocatively implied in David L. Miller, *Christs: Meditations on Archetypal Images in Christian Theology* (New York: The Seabury Press, 1981), Chapters 18 and 27.

58.   Another point about closure suggests itself here. At this writing the projected timetable for the book's publication coincides with the arrival, in late 1985, of Halley's comet. When I found out about this final conjunction I was reminded of Loren Eiseley's 1970 vision of the comet's return as a metaphor for the conscious and caring re-entry he felt technological culture needed to make into the green world, the "sunflower forest," of natural processes. While he wrote primarily as a naturalist concerned with the ecological crisis, I came to see during the years after 1970 that his recommendation paralleled my own call for a mythology of terrestrial reconnection. Eiseley also expressed his hope actually to see Halley's comet again—he had been shown it as a small boy by his father in 1910—but he died almost a decade too soon. Had he lived and read about my search I like to think he would have looked with favor on the coincidence between the appearance of his comet and the appearance of this book. Cf. Eiseley, *The Invisible Pyramid* (New York: Charles Scribner's Sons, 1970), pp. 7-9, 150-55, and *passim*.

EPILOGUE

1.   Lucy R. Lippard, *Overlay: Contemporary Art and the Art of Prehistory* (New York: Pantheon Books, 1983). One of the dedicatees of *Overlay* is "Ashwell Farm itself, and the land surrounding it, where I walked daily—the real ground on which this book is built."

2.   Ibid., p. 45.

3.   Ibid., p. 244, n. 6.

4.   Smithson, quoted in ibid., p. 229.

5.   Ibid., pp. 146-49. The Knossos coin is shown as fig. 21C on p. 147; the caption is on p. 146.

6.   Ibid., p. 149.

7.   Starhawk, *The Spiral Dance: A Rebirth of the Ancient Religion of the Great Goddess* (San Francisco: Harper & Row, 1979), p. 3.

8.   Ibid., p. 5.

9.   Lippard, op. cit., p. 187.

10.   Ibid.

11.   Ibid., p. 188, fig. 26.

BIBLIOGRAPHY

Adler, Margot. *Drawing Down the Moon: Witches, Druids, Goddess-Worshippers, and Other Pagans in America Today*. New York: Viking Press, 1979.

Agel, Jerome, ed. *The Making of Kubrick's 2001*. New York: Signet Books, 1970.

American Academy of Religion: 1977 Annual Meeting Program. Missoula: University of Montana Printing Department, 1977.

Argüelles, José and Miriam. *Mandala*. Berkeley: Shambhala, 1972.

Aziz, Barbara Nimri. "Maps and Mind." *Human Nature*, August 1978, pp. 50-59.

Barfield, Owen. *Poetic Diction: A Study in Meaning*. New York: McGraw-Hill, 1964.

Barrett, William. *Time of Need: Forms of Imagination in the Twentieth Century*. New York: Harper Torchbooks, 1973.

de Beauvoir, Simone. *The Second Sex*. Trans. and edited by H.M. Parshley. New York: Bantam Books, 1970.

Bernstein, Jeremy. "Extrapolators: Arthur C. Clarke." In his *Experiencing Science*, Chapter 6, pp. 205-233. New York: Basic Books, 1978.

Berry, Patricia. *Echo's Subtle Body: Contributions to an Archetypal Psychology*. Dallas: Spring Publications, 1982.

_____. "What's the Matter with Mother?" Lecture No. 190. London: Guild of Pastoral Psychology, 1978.

Berry, Thomas. "Spirituality of the Earth." *Anima*, 6, 1 (Fall 1979), 11-20.

Bertine, Eleanor. *Jung's Contribution to Our Time*. New York: G.P. Putnam's Sons, 1967.

Bice, Christopher, compiler. *Names for the Cornish: Three Hundred Cornish Christian Names*. Padstow, Cornwall: Lodenek Press, 1970.

Bleiler, E.F. Introduction to his edition of Walpole, *The Castle of Otranto*, Beckford, *Vathek*, and Polidori, *The Vampyre*. New York: Dover Books, 1966.

Bolen, Jean Shinoda. *The Tao of Psychology: Synchronicity and the Self*. San Francisco: Harper & Row, 1979.

Bord, Janet and Colin. *Mysterious Britain*. London: Garnstone Press, 1972.

Bottrell, William. *Traditions and Hearthside Stories of West Cornwall*. Newcastle upon Tyne: Frank Graham, 1970 reprint.

Briggs, Katharine. *British Folktales*. New York: Pantheon Books, 1977.

_____. *The Vanishing People: Fairy Lore and Legends*. New York: Pantheon Books, 1978.

Broad, William J. "Metaphor Getting Its Due As a Wellspring of Science." *The New York Times*, July 31, 1983, Section 4, p. 8E.

Bubar, Peg. "Tikal: The First Skyscrapers." *The New York Times*, July 17, 1977, Section XX, p. 7.

Burl, Aubrey. *Prehistoric Avebury*. New Haven: Yale University Press, 1979.

Burnshaw, Stanley. *The Seamless Web*. New York: George Braziller, 1970.

Campbell, Joseph. *The Mythic Image*. Princeton: Princeton University Press, 1974.

_____. *Myths to Live By*. New York: Bantam Books, 1973.

Canby, Vincent. "'Close Encounters' Has Now Become A Classic." *The New York Times*, August 30, 1980, Section 2, pp. 10, 17.

_____. "Seen in 1984, the Future Looks Bleak." *The New York Times*, December 23, 1984, Section 2, pp. 19-20.

229

Carter, James Earl, Jr. "On the Uses of Space." *Michigan Quarterly Review* XVIII, 2 (Spring 1979), 350-54.

Christ, Carol P. *Diving Deep and Surfacing: Women Writers on Spiritual Quest.* Boston: Beacon Press, 1980.

_____. "Margaret Atwood: The Surfacing of Women's Spiritual Quest and Vision." *Signs*, 2, 2 (Winter 1976), 316-30.

_____, and Judith Plaskow, eds. *Womanspirit Rising: A Feminist Reader in Religion.* San Francisco: Harper & Row, 1979.

Clarke, Arthur C. "Beyond Apollo." Epilogue to Neil Armstrong, Michael Collins, and Edwin E. Aldrin, Jr., with Gene Farmer and Dora Jane Hamblin, *First on the Moon*, pp. 371-421. Boston: Little, Brown and Company, 1970.

_____. *Childhood's End.* London: Pan Books, 1956.

_____. *The Fountains of Paradise.* New York: Harcourt Brace Jovanovich, 1978.

_____. *Glide Path.* New York: Harcourt Brace Jovanovich, 1963.

_____. *Imperial Earth.* New York: Ballantine Books, 1976.

_____. *Interplanetary Flight.* New York: Harper & Brothers, 1950.

_____. *The Lost Worlds of 2001.* New York: Signet Books, 1972.

_____. *Prelude to Space.* New York: Harcourt, Brace & World, 1951.

_____. *The Promise of Space.* New York: Harper & Row, 1968.

_____. *Rendezvous With Rama.* New York: Ballantine Books, 1973.

_____. *The Sands of Mars.* New York: Gnome Press, 1951.

_____. *The Treasure of the Great Reef.* New York: Ballantine Books, 1974.

_____. *2001: A Space Odyssey.* New York: Signet Books, 1968.

_____. *2010: Odyssey Two.* New York: Ballantine Books, 1982.

_____. *The View from Serendip.* New York: Ballantine Books, 1978.

_____. *Voices from the Sky.* New York: Pocket Books, 1980.

Cook, Warren L. *"Ancient Vermont": Proceedings of the Castleton Conference, Castleton State College.* Rutland: Academy Books of Rutland, 1978.

Cornish Charms and Witchcraft. Truro, Cornwall: Tor Mark Press, n.d.

Critchlow, Keith. *Time Stands Still: New Light on Megalithic Science.* Colour Photographs by Rod Bull. London: Gordon Fraser, 1979.

Cronin, Vincent. *The View from Planet Earth: Man Looks at the Cosmos.* New York: Quill Books, 1983.

Daniel, Glyn. "Pop Goes Archaeology," *The New York Times Book Review*, March 13, 1977, pp. 8, 12-13.

von Däniken, Erich. *Chariots of the Gods? Unsolved Mysteries of the Past.* Trans. Michael Heron. New York: G.P. Putnam's Sons, 1970.

_____. *Gods From Outer Space: Return to the Stars or Evidence for the Impossible.* Trans. Michael Heron. New York: G.P. Putnam's Sons, 1971.

Davis, Elizabeth Gould. *The First Sex.* Baltimore: Penguin Books, 1972.

Deuel, Leo. *Flights into Yesterday: The Story of Aerial Archaeology.* New York: St. Martin's Press, 1969.

Devereux, Paul. "Operation Merlin." *The Ley Hunter*, No. 88 (Spring 1980), 16-19.

Donaldson, Mara. Review of Margot Adler, *Drawing Down the Moon. Journal of the American Academy of Religion*, L, 2 (June 1982), 304.

Doty, William G. *Mythography: The Study of Myths and Rituals.* University, Ala.: University of Alabama Press, 1986.

_____. "Mythophiles' Dyscrasia: A Comprehensive Definition of Myth."

Journal of the American Academy of Religion, XLVIII, 4 (December 1980), 531-62.

Downing, Christine. *The Goddess: Mythological Images of the Feminine.* New York: Crossroad, 1981.

_____. "A Poetics of the Psyche." *The American Poetry Review*, July 1976, pp. 34-35.

Eiseley, Loren. *The Invisible Pyramid.* New York: Charles Scribner's Sons, 1970.

Eliade, Mircea. *Cosmos and History: The Myth of Eternal Return.* Trans. Willard B. Trask. New York: Harper & Row, 1959.

_____. *Images and Symbols.* Trans. Philip Mairet. New York: Sheed & Ward, 1961.

_____. *Myths, Dreams and Mysteries.* Trans. Philip Mairet. New York: Harper & Row, 1960.

_____. *No Souvenirs: Journal, 1957-69.* Trans. Fred H. Johnson, Jr. New York: Harper & Row, 1977.

_____. *Patterns in Comparative Religion.* Trans. Rosemary Sheed. Cleveland: Meridian Books, 1963.

Fell, Barry. *America B.C.: Ancient Settlers in the New World.* New York: Quadrangle/New York Times Book Co., 1976.

Fiedler, Leslie A., ed. *In Dreams Awake.* New York: Dell, 1975.

Fordham, Michael, ed. *Contact with Jung.* Philadelphia: J.B. Lippincott Company, 1963.

von Franz, Marie-Louise. *On Divination and Synchronicity: The Psychology of Meaningful Chance.* Toronto: Inner City Books, 1980.

Fuller, R. Buckminster. *Operating Manual for Spaceship Earth.* New York: Simon and Schuster Clarion Books, 1969.

Gerster, Georg. *Flights of Discovery: The Earth from Above.* New York: Paddington Press, 1978.

Goethals, Gregor T. *The TV Ritual: Worship at the Video Altar.* Boston: Beacon Press, 1981.

Goldenberg, Naomi R. *Changing of the Gods: Feminism and the End of Traditional Religions.* Boston: Beacon Press, 1979.

Golding, William. *The Inheritors.* New York: Harcourt, Brace & World, 1963.

Gordon, William J.J. *Synectics: The Development of Creative Capacity.* New York: Collier Books, 1961.

Graves, Robert. *The White Goddess: A historical grammar of poetic myth.* Amended and enlarged edition. New York: Farrar, Straus and Giroux, 1966.

Griffin, Susan. *Woman and Nature: The Roaring Inside Her.* New York: Harper Colophon Books, 1978.

Hallion, Richard P., and Tom D. Crouch, eds. *Apollo: Ten Years Since Tranquillity Base.* Washington: National Air and Space Museum/Smithsonian Institution, 1979.

Hannah, Barbara. *Jung: His Life and Work.* New York: G.P. Putnam's Sons, 1976.

Harding, M. Esther. *Woman's Mysteries: Ancient and Modern.* New York: Bantam Books, 1973.

Hillman, James. *The Dream and the Underworld.* New York: Harper & Row, 1979.

_____. *The Myth of Analysis: Three Essays in Archetypal Psychology.* Evanston: Northwestern University Press, 1972.

_____. "Notes on Opportunism." In Hillman, et al, *Puer Papers*, pp. 152-65. Dallas: Spring Publications, 1979.

_____. "Peaks and Vales: The Soul/Saint Distinction as Basis for the Differences between Psychotherapy and Spiritual Discipline." In Hillman, *et al.*, *Puer Papers*, pp. 54-74. Dallas: Spring Publications, 1979.

_____. *Re-Visioning Psychology*. New York: Harper & Row, 1975.

_____. "Senex and Puer: An Aspect of the Historical and Psychological Present." In Hillman, et al, *Puer Papers*, pp. 3-53. Dallas: Spring Publications, 1979.

Hitching, Francis. *Earth Magic*. New York: William Morrow, 1977.

Hobbs, Robert, with Lawrence Alloway, John Coplans, and Lucy R. Lippard. *Robert Smithson: Sculpture*. Ithaca: Cornell University Press, 1981.

Holt, Nancy, ed. *The Writings of Robert Smithson: Essays with Illustrations*. New York: New York University Press, 1979.

Houston, Jean. "Putting the First Man on Earth." *Saturday Review*, February 22, 1975, pp. 28-32, 53.

Hunt, Robert. *Cornish Customs and Superstitions*. Truro, Cornwall: Tor Mark Press, n.d.

Jaffé, Aniela. *The Myth of Meaning*. Trans. R.F.C. Hull. New York: G.P. Putnam's Sons, 1971.

Jones, Roger S. *Physics as Metaphor*. New York: Meridian Books, 1982.

Jung, C.G. *Flying Saucers: A Modern Myth of Things Seen in the Skies*. Trans. R.F.C. Hull. Princeton: Princeton University Press, 1969/1978.

_____. *Letters*. Vol. 2: 1951-61. Bollingen Series XCV: 2. Selected and edited by Gerhard Adler with Aniela Jaffé. Trans. R.F.C. Hull. Princeton: Princeton University Press, 1975.

_____, ed. *Man and his Symbols*. New York: Dell Books, 1968.

_____. *Mandala Sysmbolism*. Trans. R.F.C. Hull. Princeton: Princeton University Press, 1972.

_____. *Memories, Dreams, Reflections*. Recorded and edited by Aniela Jaffé. Trans. Richard and Clara Winston. New York: Vintage Books, 1961.

_____. "On Synchronicity." In his *CollectedWorks*. Vol. 8, Bollingen Series XX, Second Edition, pp. 520-31. Trans. R.F.C. Hull. Princeton: Princeton University Press, 1966.

_____. "Synchronicity: An Acausal Connecting Principle." In his *Collected Works*. Vol. 8, Bollingen Series XX, Second Edition, pp. 417-519. Trans. R.F.C. Hull. Princeton: Princeton University Press, 1966.

Katz, Michael, William P. Marsh, and Gail Gordon Thompson, eds. *Earth's Answer: Explorations of Planetary Culture at the Lindisfarne Conferences*. New York: Lindisfarne Books/Harper & Row, 1977.

Kepes, Gyorgy, ed. *Arts of the Environment*. New York: George Braziller, 1972.

Larson, Kay. "New Landscapes in Art." *The New York Times Magazine*, May 13, 1979, pp. 20-23, 28, 30, 33-34, 36, 38.

Layard, John. *The Virgin Archetype: Two Papers*. Dunquin Series 5. Zurich: Spring Publications, 1972.

LeGuin, Ursula K. *The Dispossessed*. New York: Avon Books, 1974.

_____. *The Left Hand of Darkness*. New York: Ace Books, 1969.

_____. *Orsinian Tales*. New York: Harper & Row, 1976.

Lerman, Rhoda. *The Book of the Night*. New York: Holt, Rinehart and Winston. 1984.

_____. *Call Me Ishtar*. New York: Holt, Rinehart and Winston, 1973.

_____. "In Memorium: Elizabeth Gould Davis." *Ms.*, December 1974, pp. 74-75, 95.

Levy, G. Rachel. *Religious Conceptions of the Stone Age*. New York: Harper Torchbooks, 1963.

Lindbergh, Charles. "A Letter from Lindbergh." *Life*, July 4, 1969, pp. 60A-61.

Lippard, Lucy R. *Overlay: Contemporary Art and the Art of Prehistory*. New York: Pantheon Books, 1983.

Lovelock, James, and Sidney Epton. "The Quest for Gaia." *The New Scientist*, February 6, 1975, pp. 304-306.

Lueders, Edward. *The Clam Lake Papers: A Winter in the North Woods*. San Francisco: Harper & Row, 1977.

Mailer, Norman. *Of a Fire on the Moon*. Boston: Little, Brown and Company, 1969.

Marc, Olivier. *Psychology of the House*. Trans. Jessie Wood. London: Thames and Hudson, 1977.

Michell, John. *The Earth Spirit: Its Ways, Shrines and Mysteries*. New York: Avon Books, 1975.

_____. *The View Over Atlantis*. New York: Ballantine Books, 1969.

Michener, James A. *Space*. New York: Random House, 1982.

Michigan Quarterly Review. Special Issue on "The Moon Landing and its Aftermath." XVIII, 3 (Spring 1979).

Miller, David L. *Christs: Meditations on Archetypal Images in Christian Theology*. New York: The Seabury Press, 1981.

_____. *The New Polytheism*. New York: Harper & Row, 1974.

Mitroff, Ian I. "Science's Apollonic Moon: A Study in the Psychodynamics of Modern Science." *Spring: An Annual of Archetypal Psychology and Jungian Thought* (1974), 102-112.

Neudorfer, Giovanna. "Vermont's Stone Chambers: Their Myth and Their History." *Vermont History*, 47, 2 (Spring 1974), 79-146.

Olander, Joseph D., and Martin Harry Greenberg, eds. *Arthur C. Clarke*. New York: Taplinger Publishing Company, 1977.

Ortner, Sherry B. "Is Female to Male as Nature Is to Culture?" In Michelle Z. Rosaldo and Louise Lamphere, eds., *Woman, Culture, and Society*, pp. 67-87. Stanford: Stanford University Press, 1974.

O'Toole, Thomas. "NASA's Master Plan." *Omni*, December 1984, pp. 70-72, 148, 150.

Passeron, René. *René Magritte*. Chicago: J. Philip O'Hara, Inc., 1972.

Poe, Edgar Allan. *The Works of Edgar Allan Poe*. The Cameo Edition. Volume Seven. New York: Funk & Wagnalls, 1904.

Progoff, Ira. *Jung, Synchronicity, and Human Destiny*. New York: Delta Books, 1973.

Read, Herbert. *Icon and Idea: The Function of Art in the Development of Human Consciousness*. New York: Schocken Books, 1965.

Reich, Hanns. *The World From Above*. New York: Hill and Wang, 1966.

Remer, Theodore, ed. *Serendipity and the Three Princes: From the Peregrinaggio of 1557*. Preface by W.S. Lewis. Norman: University of Oklahoma Press, 1965.

Rich, Adrienne. *Of Woman Born: Motherhood as Experience and Institution*. New York: W.W. Norton, 1976.

Richason, Benjamin F., Jr., ed. *Introduction to Remote Sensing of the Environment*. Second Edition. Dubuque: Kendall/Hunt Publishing Company, 1983.

Ring, Noel. "Aerial Evidence of Terrain Disturbances near Vermont's Lithic Sites." In Warren L. Cook, ed., *"Ancient Vermont"*, pp. 26-27. Rutland: Academy Books of Rutland, 1978.

Roberts, Anthony, ed. *Glastonbury: Ancient Avalon, New Jerusalem*. London: Rider and Company, 1978.

_____. *Sowers of Thunder: Giants in Myth and History*. London: Rider and Company, 1978.

Russell, Geoffrey. "The Secret of the Grail." In Mary Williams, ed., *Glastonbury: A Study in Patterns*, pp. 16-19. London: Research into Lost Knowledge Organisation, 1969.

Sargent, Pamela, ed. *Women of Wonder*. New York: Vintage Books, 1975.

Scholes, Robert. *Structural Fabulation*. Notre Dame: University of Notre Dame Press, 1975.

_____, and Eric S. Rabkin. *Science Fiction*. Oxford: Oxford University Press, 1977.

Shepard, Paul. *Man in the Landscape: A Historic View of the Esthetics of Nature*. New York: Alfred A. Knopf, 1967.

Shiner, Larry E. "Sacred Space, Profane Space, Human Space." *Journal of the American Academy of Religion*, XL, 4 (December 1972), 425-36.

Snell, Bruno. *The Discovery of the Mind: The Greek Origins of European Thought*. Trans. T.G. Rosenmeyer. New York: Harper Torchbooks, 1960.

Sontag, Susan. *On Photography*. New York: Delta Books, 1977.

Starhawk. *The Spiral Dance: A Rebirth of the Ancient Religion of the Great Goddess*. San Francisco: Harper & Row, 1979.

Story, Ronald. *The Space-Gods Revealed: A Close Look at the Theories of Erich von Däniken*. New York: Harper & Row, 1976.

Swenson, May. "Orbiter 5 Shows How Earth Looks from the Moon." In her *New & Selected Things Taking Place*, p. 94. Boston: Little, Brown and Company, 1954-1978.

Sylvester, David. *Magritte*. New York: Frederick Praeger, 1969.

Szent-Gyorgyi, Albert. "Dionysians and Apollonians." *Science*, June 2, 1972, p. 966.

"The Talk of the Town: Clarke's World." *The New Yorker*, December 13, 1982, pp. 38-40.

Thomas, Lewis. *The Lives of a Cell: Notes of A Biology Watcher*. New York: The Viking Press, 1974.

Vas Dias, Robert, ed. *Inside Outer Space: New Poems of the Space Age*. Garden City: Doubleday Anchor Books, 1970.

Watkins, Alfred. *The Old Straight Track*. New York: Ballantine Books, 1973.

Wheelwright, Philip. *Metaphor and Reality*. Bloomington: Indiana University Press, 1962.

Wicker, Brian. *The Story-Shaped World*. Notre Dame: University of Notre Dame Press, 1975.

Woodcock, John. "The Garden in the Machine: Variations on Spaceship Earth." *Michigan Quarterly Review*, XVIII, 2 (Spring 1979), 308-317.